Glamour Addiction

Glamour Addiction

Inside the American
Ballroom Dance Industry

❖

JULIET MCMAINS

Wesleyan University Press | Middletown, Connecticut

Wesleyan University Press
Middletown, Connecticut 06459
www.wesleyan.edu/wespress

Cataloging-in-Publication Data is available
from the Library of Congress

ISBN 0-8195-6774-4

Thanks to Ellen Kaisse, Divisional Dean of Arts
& Humanities, University of Washington,
for additional funding.

Contents

Illustrations

Acknowledgments

Many people supported me both in writing and dancing my way through this Glamour Addiction.

I thank my editor, Suzanna Tamminen, the staff at Wesleyan University Press, and especially the anonymous readers for their detailed feedback and advice.

I am grateful to all the photographers who shared their work for this book, particularly Jonathan Marion, who graciously made his impressive collection available to me with swift and expert use of modern technology.

I extend deep gratitude to my graduate advisor, Susan Foster, whose depth of insight and acuity of critical attention shaped my scholarly voice and inspired the scope of my vision. Her patience was unrelenting, and she balanced encouragement and critique with remarkable sensitivity.

I feel particularly lucky to have been pursuing this project alongside scholars whose shared passion for dance and diversity of interest enriched my depth of focus. Students and faculty at the University of California, Riverside, read and discussed sections of my work with thoughtful and generous interest. I thank faculty members Celeste Frazer Delgado, Jacqueline Shea Murphy, Sally Ness, Susan Rose, Marta Savigliano, Anna Scott, Linda Tomko, and Traise Yamamoto, in addition to classmates Patrick Alcedo, Colleen Dunagan, Jeff Friedman, Yatin Lin, Janet O'Shea, and Tom Young. I am especially indebted to Danielle Robinson and Roxane Fenton, who sustained me with their guidance, love, and humor.

I would also like to thank my colleagues at Florida State University, in particular Lynda Davis, John Perpener, Sally Sommer, and Tricia Henry Young, for being supportive of my dual identity as dancer and scholar and for fostering a community in which I could live it. I am exceptionally grateful to Adam Jolles, who offered me not only expert editorial counseling, but much emotional support in the final stages of manuscript preparation.

I am grateful to the dance partners with whom I have shared thousands of hours on studio and competition floors, most of whom were remarkably tolerant of my predilection for analysis when they might have preferred I just shut up and dance. I thank Rick Elliott, Russell Jackson, Radim Láník, Youriy Pavlov, Christian Perry, Sonny Perry, Alex Samuel, Mark Sheldon, and Yuri Tschinkel. I would like to thank the many social dance partners I have danced with into

State University; and the University of Central Florida. Learning was never just one-sided, and I thank you for the Glamour lessons you taught me.

❖

A shorter version of chapter 3 was published as "Brownface: Representations of Latin-ness in DanceSport," *Dance Research Journal* 33.2 (2001): 54–71. Sections of this chapter also appear in my article "Dancing Latin/Latin Dancing: Salsa and DanceSport," in *The Social and Popular Dance Reader*, edited by Julie Malnig (University of Illinois Press, forthcoming).

CONFESSIONS OF A GLAMOUR ADDICT

I am a Glamour addict, struggling to stay clean. Everyone needs a hobby, maybe even a passion. Mine is competitive ballroom dancing. How quaint, people say, how romantic, how Glamorous! After the recent flurry of television shows featuring ballroom dance, most people have a vague, if incomplete, image of what competitive dance entails—faces in too much makeup atop sleek, athletic bodies twisting their limbs and faces into caricatures of human sensuality. I confess that I am in love with the flow of energy between two people, fixated on physical mastery, attracted to the spotlight, and driven by competition. But it was Glamour that pinned me to the wall, that kept me hooked long after commitment and dedication had hardened into obsession and compulsion. Despite all well-intentioned advice against it, I turned my college extracurricular into my career. I knew I would not be satiated with merely physical practice, so I simultaneously began my schooling in dance scholarship. My research has centered on Glamour, a term I use to describe the specific means through which the ballroom dance industry lures its followers and keeps them captivated long after they have uncovered the seedy underbelly of its fairy-tale exterior.

Like most victims of Glamour, my early experiences with ballroom dance appeared innocuous. I was required to take ballroom as part of the Dance Teacher's Club of Boston Teacher's Training Course when I was in high school. The sum total of fifteen hours over three years didn't really amount to much training, especially since none of the other students seemed to take ballroom dancing seriously in a class of just girls. When the seventy-year-old teacher picked a girl out of the class to demonstrate with, I was mystified by her ability to do the steps without any verbal cues to direct her. He didn't go into detail about techniques for leading and following, given the large size of the class, so I remained baffled. I kept hoping to be selected for the demonstration to find out if the magic would work on me. But I never was. It was not until our graduation the third year that I saw a professional ballroom dance exhibition. There must have been a man in the partnership, but I only remember the woman. She was unbearably sexy and sophisticated, and I made up my mind right then and there to become the heroine I imagined her to be.

In college, I discovered a fledgling ballroom dance club at registration. "I'm really interested and I learn really fast," I declared. "How fast can you learn?" came their reply. I was performing in an International Style tango formation the next weekend at Mosley's on the Charles, an old-style ballroom outside of Boston. Finally, I caught a glimpse of the enchanted world I had only seen in my head during those ballroom dance classes in a room full of girls in leotards. It was even better than my imagination. I suspect that dancers of almost any genre are addicted to their practice at least partially because the intense physical activity, combined with the emotional provocations of music and the creative outlet of artistic expression, produces a powerful stress release. Certainly this was the case for me even prior to my exposure to partner dancing. But that respite had always seemed so obviously temporary, so explicitly constructed outside ordinary life. As sheltered as we might have been, my high school dance buddies and I knew that the world comprised more than mirrored walls, lacquered floors, and toothpick-thin teenage girls in spandex and leg warmers. What tricked me that first night at Mosley's was the simulacrum of daily life interwoven into its fantasyland. Here were women *and* men, all ages and sizes, wearing clothes one might see on the street, engaged in the ordinary acts of eating, drinking, and socializing between dances. This was an escape that was so much more compelling than any I had known as the Sugar Plum Fairy or a Jazz Hot Diva because it was so easy to convince myself that it could be substituted for the entirety of life outside dance. This was a dance lifestyle that could sustain and extend an alternate reality, promising that its adherents need never leave for want of food or love. I suspect that my addiction was sealed that night. There was no escape for me. I would spend every minute and dollar I could squirrel away in pursuit of that world, in hopes that I could exist eternally spinning under the disco ball in that ballroom.

Although I participated in social and exhibition ballroom dancing during this initiation event, it was competitive ballroom dance, DanceSport, that became the focal point of my life for the next twelve years. I am certain that the distinction between these three branches of ballroom dance—social, exhibition, and competition—was barely visible to me at the time. Their relative ranking in circles of serious ballroom dancers was, in contrast, immediately evident. DanceSport was the emperor of the ballroom. Social dancing, and to a lesser extent performance in exhibitions, were just means through which to practice and perfect the technique that would be judged in competition. My transition from ballet to competitive ballroom, rather than social dance, was logical given the familiar terrain of disciplining the body into straight lines, right angles, and soft curves. This competition chauvinism, shared by most college ballroom dancers in the Northeast at the time, was the lens through which I learned waltz, rumba, and swing. Not until six years later, after I started social dancing in salsa and swing clubs in Los Angeles, did I begin to question this hierarchy.

Witnessing my first professional ballroom dance competition was an otherworldly experience. I was lost in the costumes. They were arresting in their brightness, similar in color to the neon bracelets I had as a child, but in quantities I had never imagined. Yards of brilliant fabric, with matching feather boa trim, billowed out for several feet around each girl's legs. The delicate chiffon softened the harsh colors, gaudy and gauche turning to Glamorous under the ballroom lights, which reflected rainbows of colors off thousands of rhinestones decorating each dress. These were so far removed from my reference point of $40 recital costumes ordered from a Wolf Fording catalog that I hadn't even been able to envision their existence. I was mesmerized by the rush of colors, more vivid than I thought earthly tones could be, and the power of bodies moving with alacrity and dexterity not normally expected of humans.

I rationalize that I enjoy partner dancing even more than solo forms I have studied because it is more interesting and challenging to coordinate two bodies than one. The kinds of movements enabled by the sharing of weight and momentum are not possible in solo dance forms. But I suppose that my initial fascination with ballroom dance sprang largely from the romance it portrayed, its impossible promise of happiness and acceptance, the assurance that every woman would be accessorized with an adoring male partner, the clothes that signified such elegance and classiness, the inflated importance of each motion of an arm or an eyebrow—in short, the Glamour of it all.

Most of the ballroom classes I took my first year were group lessons. But after three months of study, I decided to pay for my first private lesson, $40 for a whole hour of personal instruction with Julius Kaiser. I was biking across the river to Allston when I passed my dance partner, walking there from the Massachusetts Institute of Technology. "Run, run," I screamed at him as I raced by on my bicycle, furious that he was going to be late when the clock was running on our dollar. It seemed, at the time, an exorbitant rate to pay for a dance lesson. Little did I know that I would soon spend three times that sum for a one-hour class and that my yearly expenditures for dance would outweigh those for housing.

The next year, I started private lessons with Suzanne Hamby, who was still competing and was regularly on television when PBS aired reruns of Championship Ballroom Dancing. Under her tutelage, my partner and I quickly worked our way through bronze, silver, and gold level Standard. We competed in collegiate competitions all over the Northeast, winning a case full of blue ribbons. My joy was not in these small victories, but in the assurance that each stride moved me up the ladder, closer to the "open" level, which, I could clearly see, was where the *real* dancing was happening. To be taken seriously, my partner would have to get a dance tailsuit that didn't bulge at the shoulders like that ordinary tuxedo he had purchased used at Keezer's. And I would have to get one of those dresses. Where would I get even $1,000 for a used dress? I began to fantasize just as passionately about feather-drenched gowns in carnation pink as I did about learning oversways and scatter chasses.

After graduation, I landed a partner who was much more experienced than I, and we jumped right into the highest level of amateur competition—Championship Standard. For two years I biked every day after my job as a research assistant at Radcliffe to practice waltz, foxtrot, quickstep, tango, and Viennese waltz in the third-floor hallway of Building 34 at MIT. Studio space was a pricey commodity we could rarely secure. Instead, my partner selected this corridor for its unusually large size and relatively light foot traffic. I was not discouraged by the noticeable lack of Glamour in that dusty tile hallway, where we had to dodge a crotchety professor who routinely stormed out of his classroom to complain that our barely audible recording of Ol' Blue Eyes was compromising his lecture on thermodynamics. The fact that no one who walked through our practice on their way to study multivariate algebra gave us more than a passing glance did not dampen my enthusiasm either.

But eventually that partner and I split too, and I began the first of several partner searches that involved months of try-outs, travel, and negotiations about relocating. I finally decided on moving to Los Angeles to dance with another amateur partner. But three days before I left, I got a call to try out with a dancer from Iceland who had decided to teach at the Fred Astaire in Boston. He wanted to compete as my partner in professional ten-dance, which encompasses both Standard and Latin. I had always wanted to dance Latin, but I had gotten locked into Standard by default, by choice of the partners I had. So I decided to stay in Boston and teach at Fred Astaire. After a month of practice together, he realized he was too homesick, that he could not stay in America, and vanished on the next flight back to Iceland. By then I had already found a new apartment and resigned myself to making the virtually irreversible leap from amateur to professional dancer. So I stayed at Fred Astaire and entered the world of professional ballroom dancing.

No one advised me to turn pro. In fact, people specifically counseled me to stay amateur, but I refused to listen. I thought they meant I was not good enough, did not have the talent or the discipline to make it as a professional dancer, and I was hell-bent on proving all of them wrong. I didn't realize they were more concerned with my ability to survive the humiliation and isolation they suspected would ensue if I used my Harvard education to pursue a working-class profession. Throughout that first year working at Fred Astaire, I confronted my own class privilege and the practical differences with which it marked me in daily battles of pride and pain. After all of my study of "diversity" in cultural studies classes, I had understood little about its real-life consequences. The only American working at the studio and one of three to have attended college, I was in a very different environment than I had been prepared for by my previous experiences. My new colleagues had very different codes of morality and behavior than my college-educated friends. Whereas I had always gotten ahead in life by doing exactly what was expected of me and following the rules, most of them had been able to improve their social or economic situations only through bending the truth, dodging the system, or manipulating other people. My ethics got me nowhere as an employee in a dance franchise because the entire system built on duping and manipulating the clients. The most successful teacher (measured by income generated for the studio) was a compulsive liar, virtually unable to tell the difference between reality and the truth he invented to suit his momentary purposes. He gave unauthorized discounts and free lessons as incentives to his students, a strategy headquarters had not confronted him with because he generated such high sales figures. But he gave more than discounts, going so far as to have sex with his students in the stairwell during lessons. His case was extreme, but not unremarkable. Behavior that would be labeled sexual harassment in other workplaces is standard at most American ballroom dance schools. You are expected to use the sexually charged environment to sell dance lessons. It is part of the job.

I had to learn to reconstruct my body for sale in the economy of Glamour. My mother didn't wear a bra, and her idea of makeup application was rolling on orange Wet 'n' Wild lipstick purchased at Woolworth's. I was not ugly, but I was a geek, and a feminist one at that. I wore no makeup, did not shave my legs, and wore my clothes three sizes too big. The studio owner's girlfriend (who came from a wealthy Los Angeles family where Glamour was part of the landscape) assumed the role of my personal style counselor. She took me shopping for spandex business suits in bold colors to replace my baggy schoolgirl shirts, ditched my cotton briefs for silk thongs, and told her hairdresser to shape my stringy blunt cut. She convinced me that a little powder on my face was not the cause of global female oppression, and then she took a razor to my legs. Her success in reforming my taste in fashion was remarkable, although I did have several other grooming mentors in later years from whom I learned multiple techniques for eye shadow contouring, hair color highlighting, and acrylic nail maintenance.

Though I soon realized that the life of a dance teacher did not feel anything like its Glamorous image suggested, I was still tempted by the promise of stardom as a dancer. Certainly success as a professional DanceSport competitor would insulate me against the gnawing feelings of helplessness, compromised morality, and inadequacy continually racking my belly. When I left Boston for graduate school in California, I did not for a moment intend to give up my quest to become a DanceSport star. I had barely begun to develop my skills and had not yet realized my talent. Over the four years I was there, I achieved local success as a DanceSport competitor, became friends with many of the country's top dancers, and learned how to hustle for my own business so that I didn't need to take out any more school loans. Outside of the metropolitan New York area (which bleeds heavily into New Jersey), southern California has the highest concentration of professional competitive ballroom dancers, many of them simultaneously chasing dreams in Hollywood. When I first arrived, I was mesmerized to see the dancers I knew from television practicing in the very same studio in which I worked.

But the deeper I delved into this world, the more time and money I invested and the more skill I acquired, the more snobbish I became and the less pleasure I found. Or at least the pleasure was less frequent. There were more bad partners to tolerate and more unpleasant dances to endure; there was less to master and less to desire. I was always scrimping and saving, hoping I would have enough money for more lessons and a new dress. The excitement was in the anticipation of what was to come. How would I feel if I had one of those dresses, if I were one of those perfect people? I think I enjoyed it more when I was desiring, hoping, and dreaming, before I became one of those hypercritical perfect people.

In June of 2001 I left California to pursue a new dance partnership with a Czech immigrant living in Orlando. I quit the job I loved teaching salsa at California Polytechnic Institute and abandoned the gig with Wayne Foster Entertainment where I got paid to do inverted overhead splits to adoring audiences in Beverly Hills and Las Vegas. I left the independent students I had painstakingly built up, the friends I cherished, the new apartment I had just furnished, and the graduate program in which I had invested four years. I gave up all this because the coach I trusted had found me a dance partner for International Style Latin, a partner with whom I could really *go somewhere*. It was much like an arranged marriage: I packed up and moved across the country after only three meetings. Although we were indeed physically compatible, our work styles turned out to be nearly irreconcilable, a strain we grudgingly endured because finding a partner with a complementary body type and skill level is so rare (not to mention that fact that I had already moved three thousand miles). I spent nearly all my savings moving across the country and trying to establish a new business, enduring loneliness and isolation so that I could dance. My story is not unusual. Ballroom dancers will sacrifice almost everything in pursuit of their dreams.

That first year in Florida, I had twelve of those amazing dresses handmade just for me. One had powder-pink fabric drawn together at five points along the back so that it draped over my derriere like a curtain valance in a palace. I had another dress made of a snakeskin print with tango-red Lycra draped over one breast and gold coins dangling from my skirt. One of my favorite dresses was white lace, heavy with pearls and rhinestones, slit all the way up to my butt cheeks in the back. We named another my "Victoria's Secret negligee." It was a sheer red slip with a single red feather shooting up at my shoulder. I had emerald-studded flowers pinned to one breast of a barely-there top that matched the Hawaiian-inspired skirt slung low over one hip. I had rich burgundy velour, elegant and sleek with tassels at the base, completely cut out down my left side.

I adored the tiny black skirt covered in dangling beads and coins, black feathers hanging to my knees. I wore it with a simple black bra, covered in feathers and emerald stones, only a strand of lace and rhinestones criss-crossing at my belly. I was spoiled, my coach said, by a dance partner who was also a fashion designer and who made me new dresses for almost every competition. His back was in knots from the repetitive motion of sewing and gluing, endlessly attaching tiny beads, coins, stones, and feathers to dress after dress. I never appreciated those dresses enough. It was never as much fun being in the dress as it was imagining being in the dress, touching it from afar. The dress was a symbol of Glamour, but it was not Glamour itself. Glamour cannot be caught inside a dress. It is elusive, always slipping away just when it seems within grasp.

My Czech partner and I had a few glorious moments of satisfaction dancing together when our bodies seamlessly stretched and flowed into each succeeding movement. But I remember the pain more clearly, the continual pressure to strive for something we would never achieve, the carrot dangled in front of us. "You should win the National Rising Star Championships this year. You have talent, the look, everything it takes," our coach assured us. But our competition results rarely fulfilled the prophecy, and the discord between what we were promised and what we actually accomplished started to wear on us more and more. Why could we not make it happen? Scarcely more than one year after I moved to Florida, my partner quit dancing entirely. And I was left on my own to reevaluate my Glamour addiction.

The author and her partner Radim Láník in one of the many dresses he created for her during their partnership. Sarasota Spectacular, Sarasota, Florida, September 2001. Photo © 2001 by Alliance Consulting, Gary Stephans, photographer.

Introduction

Competitive ballroom dancing, renamed DanceSport in the 1980s to facilitate an international campaign to win Olympic status, is both familiar and strange to the general public.[1] Although most Americans can envision a basic foxtrot or cha cha, few are versed in the complex rules that govern the competitive iteration of DanceSport. Despite a brief publicity boost when it was granted official recognition as an Olympic sport in 1997, increased visibility in television broadcasts and reality shows, and a general resurgence of interest in partner dancing nationwide, DanceSport is hardly a common American pastime.[2] The raptures and repulsions of competitive ballroom dance are virtually unknown outside a tight-knit community of devotees; prohibitive pricing for spectator tickets ensures that attendees at competitions are primarily other DanceSport practitioners themselves. Although ballroom dancers are notorious proselytizers, continuously preaching the benefits of dance to friends and strangers alike, few are as eager to relate the caustic effects of their passion. In this text, I delve into the splendors and monstrosities of DanceSport, exploring how the practice is produced by and reproduces the economic, social, and historical systems in which it is embedded.

DanceSport is produced through a "machine" I will call Glamour.[3] This machine is made up of the entire network of businesses, traditions, images, and people that maintain American DanceSport. The businesses include competitions and studios as well as dressmakers, shoe manufacturers, magazine publishers, and music distributors, among many others. Though I refer to Glamour as the overarching mechanism that drives the system, I also use the term (with a capital G to distinguish my use in this context) to name its objects of production when they take on value symbolic of the entire system. Goods, services, people, and events at times become the focal point of Glamorous desire, although no single individual or place could hold such power if it were not an agent of the much larger Glamour Machine. Thus, Glamour is both the machine that powers American DanceSport and the industry's primary commodity. Owing in part to the relatively large disposable income of the American population, free-market capitalist enterprise, and immigration patterns, American DanceSport differs drastically from DanceSport abroad, for it is in the American system that Glamour emerges in its most heightened form. And although its American expression is certainly intertwined with DanceSport practice in other countries, relying on importation of bodies and mythology from outside the United States, my project focuses specifically on American DanceSport practices.

The word glamour evokes ideals of beauty, fashion, grace, theatricality, magic, mystery, luxury, impossible perfection, sex appeal, celebrity, and wealth. My own use of the term, which draws on this rich array of popular associations, follows that of scholars who have investigated how it came into general usage in the nineteenth and early twentieth centuries. Both Peter Bailey, in his study of the Victorian barmaid, and Linda Mizejewski, in her work on the Ziegfeld Girl, suggest that the concept emerged to describe women who forged a new identity between that of the lower and upper classes. In the nineteenth century, there was an idealized division of private and public space such that "respectable" women were expected to be secluded in the home and any woman visible in the public sphere was assumed to be a prostitute. However, by the early twentieth century the dichotomy of mother versus whore as defined by private versus public life was compromised by the emergence of new public spaces—department stores, movie theatres, parks—that tempted and drew middle-class women into public visibility. Anxiety over this transition and uncertainty about how to classify women who broke the disintegrating taboos led to the designation "glamorous" for women who could now be identified with both ends of the social spectrum. A glamorous female had the sexual charge of a "naughty girl" but also the decency of a well-bred lady. Bailey writes of the Victorian barmaid in 1890s London: "She was respectable, yes; she was the girl whom a chap might just marry, by jove; she was also the girl who just might . . . without one having to marry her" (ellipsis in original).[4] Likewise, the all-American beauties who became the defining feature of the Ziegfeld Follies revues running on Broadway from 1907 to 1931 were at once naughty and nice. The careful balance between exposing and obscuring their bodies through translucent fabrics certainly marketed their sexuality. But the emphasis on their marriageability, as exemplified by the mythologized conclusion to Ziegfeld Girls' careers in respectable matrimony, underlined their wholesomeness.

Glamorous DanceSport women (and men) are similarly poised between virgin and vamp. I will demonstrate how Glamour enables people to negotiate sexual dichotomies of virtue and vulgarity, as well as distinctions of class or race. DanceSport Glamour enables a third space between binaries of sexual release and restraint. Whereas both Bailey and Mizejewski examine glamorous women in public space in eras when their presence outside the home was still transgressive, I am looking at Glamour in late capitalist American culture, long after even upper-class white women have crossed over into public life. Although Glamour is often gendered female, male bodies are just as central to its production in DanceSport as female bodies. I am not suggesting that the equal visibility of male and female bodies as objects of desire in this economy signals gender equality, but that gender is no longer the dividing line between object and subject of desire.

It is significant to note that use of the word glamour to mediate anxiety about women in public space coincided with the first appearance of public dance halls. Whereas social dancing by the middle and upper classes had previously been confined to private homes, early twentieth-century public dance halls and cabarets brought women's bodies (and their sexuality) into the public sphere in unprecedented numbers. Dozens of antidance treatises, which specifically warned that dancing would compromise the moral honor of any "respectable" woman, published in the late nineteenth and early twentieth centuries attest to the central role of social dance in debates about women's new role in the social order.[5] Many dance historians have already drawn attention to the significance of public dance halls as a space in which women redefined their identity in the public sphere.[6] Several scholars have also theorized that the term glamour emerged to mediate social class binaries during the same transition for women entering public life.[7] I bring the two discourses together to suggest that the modern use of glamour and modern ballroom dancing arose out of the same impulse to forge new class positions in a society that had not yet come to terms with the public presence of women.

Glamour production involves, according to Mizejewski, the "public visibility of a desirable object, its management or control, and its resulting value as class marker or commodity."[8] Glamour, in other words, depends upon an object's being simultaneously visible and inaccessible, a conflict that produces desire. For example, Ziegfeld Girls were both visible and inaccessible to the common audience member. Although the spectacle they produced was visually accessible, the ideal of femininity they represented was not attainable for the general public, and the sexual availability they implied was likewise out of reach for most audience members. DanceSport Glamour is also defined by measured regulation of visibility and inaccessibility of its objects of desire, the calculated tension between intimacy and distance, resulting in increased status for Glamorous objects and icons.

The proximity of the various agents and consumers of Glamour in Dance-Sport produces a unique, arguably more intense tension between accessibility and inaccessibility. Linda Mizejewski bases her analysis on distancing techniques that allow visual access but prohibit physical touch. Such mechanisms include a department store window display, a film screen, or a fashion magazine. The DanceSport industry, as I will illustrate in chapter 1, relies on the continual presence of very personal, intimate, and sensual kinds of touch as well as sight. The DanceSport competition, for example, has no backstage, virtually no separation between performers and audience. Competitors emerge from the ranks of the audience and then meld back into it once their round is over. The offstage area is fully lit, creating the illusion that the mechanisms for producing this spectacle are in full view—the judges standing on the edges of the dance floor with their serious faces and guarded clipboards, the competitors scurrying into the ballroom with fuzzy pink slippers peeking out from underneath their exquisitely decorated gowns, the millionaire sponsors sitting in their VIP seats, the disc jockey in the corner producing endless cuts of strict-tempo music, and the wide-eyed newcomers gawking in their chairs.

Not only are all participants and spectators close enough that they *could* reach out and touch these elements, *actual* touch is crucial to the industry. Dance lessons are its primary commodities—sessions in which consumers touch, caress, and hold the DanceSport superstars. Touch is the hook that makes the desire produced by DanceSport Glamour so powerful. The physical proximity of desired objects (including people, costumes, money, and dance skill) and that which they symbolize (fame, power, recognition, and intimacy) intensifies the promise of eventual accessibility.

Glamour production relies not only on the public visibility of objects of desire but also on their use as class markers. Ziegfeld Girls were associated with wealth. The authenticity of the ornate fabrics (real silks) and jewels in which the Girls were draped was stressed in publicity materials, such opulence and excess in costuming rubbing off on their reputations as well. Ziegfeld Girls became markers of high class in part because they were surrounded by wealth but also because of the upward class mobility they achieved through new social alliances that supposedly led to marriage. They were more respectable than risqué, their class status derived through their higher position in the patriarchal sex trade, potential wives rather than prostitutes. Ziegfeld Girls were classy not only because they exhibited upper-class tastes in fashion and manners, but also because they became fashionable commodities, either as idols of female emulation or as objects of male sexual desire.

DanceSport Glamour is likewise classy partially by virtue of the expensive and elite fashion exhibited by its participants, but the relationship of DanceSport to systems of social class is about more than clothes. Class stratification, the system by which individuals in society are grouped and ranked, is determined by (and to a certain extent determines) family ties, education, occupation, income, wealth, and taste (the ability to differentiate and appreciate culturally significant classifications of preference). I will borrow from the influential French sociologist Pierre Bourdieu the labels "economic capital" (income and wealth), "social capital" (familial background), "educational capital," and "cultural capital" (the capacity to make distinctions of good taste) to describe the components that establish and reveal social class status.[9] Bourdieu's theory has limitations, particularly in its failure to adequately theorize class mobility and instability, but his concept of cultural capital is particularly useful to my analysis of Glamour.[10] In his much-quoted declaration "Taste classifies, and it classifies the classifier,"[11] Bourdieu points out not only that consumer choices mark where the consumer fits in established class hierarchies, but also that cultural consumption is a site at which class divisions are contested and redrawn. Upward class mobility, for example, is secured as much through acquiring cultural capital as through formal education, increase of material wealth, or marriage into an influential family. Measuring economic, educational, and social capital is, with some major exceptions, relatively straightforward (i.e., count the cash and assets, rank the degrees and the institutions, determine the income and occupation of one's parents). However, who determines and who recognizes the relative value of cultural capital (the judgment that a taste for Stravinsky or vichyssoise is superior to a taste for Sting or french fries) has been a topic of heavy debate. In fact, demonstrating that people use, interpret, and appropriate culture for various and contestatory means and ends has been a major focus in the field of cultural studies.[12] Glamour, as a cultural commodity, both represents and contributes to defining social classification. How Glamour classifies its producers and consumers, to what class Glamour belongs, and to whom this status is evident all remain flexible and polysemic.

The division between amateur and professional dancers in America (glossing over several exceptions) often breaks down along class lines when measured by economic and educational capital.[13] According to the United States Amateur Ballroom Dancers Association rulebook, "a 'Professional' is an individual who uses his or her dance skills in order to receive monetary gain as a full or part-time occupation, and/or one who is registered with a member organization of the WD&DSC [World Dance & Dance Sport Council] as a Professional Member."[14] Unlike those professional sports wherein an elite group has been invited to join the professional ranks by virtue of demonstrated excellence in amateur competition, anyone can become a professional ballroom dancer by accepting money for dance services or by entering a professional competition. Thus, skill level and experience differ drastically among professional ballroom dancers. DanceSport professionals are much more similar to one another, however, in class background—few have education beyond high school, experience in work outside the entertainment business, or financial stability. In contrast, amateur ballroom dancers usually have college degrees, prestigious careers in fields other than dance, and substantial disposable incomes with which to support their expensive hobby. Since DanceSport does not draw major television coverage or backing from big business, there is no significant prize money for either amateur or professional competitors: a winning purse of $1,000 barely covers travel expenses.

The class distinction between amateur and professional dancer is particular to the American DanceSport industry. In contrast, both amateur and professional ballroom dancers in England are commonly considered upper working class.[15] In many of the former communist countries of Eastern Europe, DanceSport is still taught in large government-funded classes that attract children from many different backgrounds. Although American ballroom dancers have implemented youth outreach programs as an investment in an Olympic future, U.S. amateur DanceSport athletes must have substantial financial backing from their parents in order to pay for lessons, costumes, and travel.[16] Aspiring dancers without economic resources are either barred from the sport entirely or can enter only as novice professionals—employees in someone else's school. Arthur Murray and Fred Astaire studios bring most new American professionals into the business, offering training programs for prospective teachers in basic ballroom technique. Once hired, new teachers are paid modestly per hour of enrolled dance instruction and are continually pressured to generate higher sales. Free training, although often very poor in quality, and the lure of a better life promised by Glamour keeps many of these new converts in exploitative working conditions long enough to become studio managers or to break out on their own as independent ballroom teachers.

The mapping of amateur or professional dancer to a particular social class position is not, however, a static assignment. Bourdieu's theory does not assume that taste is merely learned but rather that it is a product of what he calls "habitus." Habitus refers to one's view of the world as conditioned by circumstances. For Bourdieu, individuals of the same social class will have similar experiences that determine their understanding of society and dictate the choices they make to negotiate their way through it. Thus, people of similar class standing will have similar tastes because their preferences are to a certain extent predetermined by habitus. Significant for me is Bourdieu's insistence that habitus is an embodied belief system:

> It follows that the body is the most indisputable materialization of class
> taste. . . . [It is through] the seemingly most natural features of the body,
> the dimensions (volume, height weight) and shapes (round or square, stiff or
> supple, straight or curved) . . . and also, of course, through the uses of the
> body in work and leisure . . . that the class distribution of bodily properties is
> determined.[17]

Although Bourdieu's concept of habitus seems to preclude the possibility of change through new life experiences and thus does not adequately explain class mobility (particularly in the contemporary American context), the notion that embodied taste is central to determining and revealing class position helps to explain the potency of DanceSport Glamour.

If, as Bourdieu suggests, cultural capital is not easily faked because the body will reveal its true habitus, ballroom dancing offers participants a means through which to transform their physical habits. The dance historian Julie Malnig has suggested that early-twentieth-century ballroom dancing provided the opportunity for individuals to perform and perhaps even to improve their social class position.[18] Likewise, twenty-first-century DanceSport does not simply teach technique for movement on the dance floor—successful indoctrination will dictate how an individual moves, dresses, and socializes even off the dance floor as well. Thus, DanceSport Glamour is an embodied ideology that just might enable consumers (such as the nouveau riche, whose pedigrees might not be as impressive as their bank accounts) to convert economic capital into cultural capital. And Glamour capital, once sufficiently embodied, can be converted into economic capital through sale of dance lessons or as a dance partner. At least this is the myth the Glamour Machine perpetuates. So although amateur and professional DanceSport competitors may enter the system from opposing positions on a class grid, DanceSport appears to offer both some degree of class mobility through capital conversion, ensuring some degree of ambiguity about their relative class status within the ballroom.

Adding to the illusion that transformation is possible is the fact that DanceSport is, as a sport, also a game. Games are about order and hierarchy (there are winners, losers, runners up, semifinalists, etc.), but they are also about the potential reordering of hierarchy. There is always the possibility of a previous loser becoming a winner. The sociologist John MacAloon explains this view by summarizing Pierre de Coubertin's arguments for resurrecting the Olympic Games in 1892: "games model egalitarian systems. Where the rules are known and accepted, they are equally binding on all, and a person's status or wealth has no direct bearing on the outcome of the game."[19] In reality, of course, status and wealth have a direct bearing on the outcome of most games, DanceSport in particular. The frame of the competition as a game, however, suggests that there is a blank slate each time one begins and the possibility of finishing the game with a new status in the hierarchy. Thus, DanceSport's competition format further enables the illusion that honing the techniques required for winning (flawless rumba walks and feather steps) directly maps to more generalized elevated social class position.

Consumers of Glamour are partially drawn in by the promise of class ascendance (or the validation of high-class status), but equally compelling are fantasies of personal transformation along lines of race, gender, sexuality, ethnic assimilation, and nationality. I have begun with a theoretical discussion of class not because it is the only or even the most important social issue to be implicated in the Glamour Machine, but because it is the most visible. My analysis will reveal how perceived escape from the limitations created along one axis of identity necessarily relies on the invocation of another category of difference, allowing for only temporary shifts and ultimately thwarting significant change in cultural systems of identity. I will demonstrate how DanceSport convenes participants from divergent class, racial, sexual, educational, social, and national backgrounds, binding them together through mutual fascination with each other's differences and the fantasy of transcending their hierarchies. Rarely, however, is a radical shift of social status enabled by DanceSport. Glamour sustains its power by sustaining social inequalities. Erasure of significant difference would render the fantasy of transformation inconsequential. The power of Glamour is located in its ability to suspend consumers in a state of perpetual longing, intensifying their desire by dangling symbols of its fulfillment within sight while simultaneously preventing its ultimate satisfaction. Furthermore, the actual fantasies and desires that compel a Glamour addiction are often obscured by their projection onto the visceral, often sexual pleasures of participatory dance culture.

Because ballroom dancing is ostensibly a form of courtship, the confusion of sexual desire with other kinds of desire invoked through Glamour is one of its most powerful tools. Such layering of sexual and class transgression was illustrated in the 1987 feature film *Dirty Dancing*. The film establishes clear class differences at the outset between the working-class professional dancers and the upper- and middle-class families vacationing at the swank Catskills resort. Though the entertainment staff may embody and teach a perfected performance of courtship in their dance routines, they are explicitly forbidden from actually courting patrons. In contrast, the waiters, college boys on summer break from Princeton and Harvard, are encouraged to date the young women, their education putting them on a social par with the clients. The film's heroine, Baby (Jennifer Grey), the daughter of a successful Jewish doctor, ventures across the class divide, lured by the intoxicating social dancing she discovers at an off-hours entertainment staff party where ballroom dance partnering techniques are applied to playful and often explicitly sexual improvisation.[20]

It is unclear to what degree the ingénue's fascination has to do with the sexual nature of the dancing and its connection to her own sexual awakening, the excitement of entering forbidden class territory, or the physical exhilaration of improvisational dance independent of its sexual content. The conflation of these factors intensifies their poignancy both in this film and in the case of Dance-Sport Glamour. On the one hand, the inseparability of sexual and class transgression intensifies both. Baby's access to the working-class world of the dancers is enabled partially through her sexual relationship with the lead dancer, Johnny Castle (Patrick Swayze). This physical experience allows her direct access to his body's knowledge, and her parents' discovery of the relationship causes familial rejection that mimics the ghettoization experienced by the dancers. Class difference makes their sexual activity more objectionable, and the sexual nature of the class transgression strengthens its potency to disrupt class boundaries. The possibility of pregnancy and marriage signifies an immediate means of class mobility (either upward or downward) for both parties.

On the other hand, sex and class each serve to diffuse the disruptive potential of the other through distraction. The excitement of sexual transgression overshadows the fact that its exhilaration is created partially by class transgression, and vice versa. Representation of both class and sexual tension through dance furthers the confusion. The dangers and excitement of transgression are represented in and by dancing, an intense desire for dance being the main effect of this film on its viewers. So, although audiences that emerged from theaters aching to find a secret dance community may have been aware that their appetite for dance was tinged with sexual desire, many had forgotten the class tension on which it was built, obscured by the whirling, sweating, pulsing bodies.

DanceSport initiates are similarly caught up in a tripartite swirl of desire that prevents their separating sexual passion from fascination with class difference and elation produced by physical movement. I am not suggesting that the pleasures of the body that dancers adore and crave are not real or satisfying in and of themselves. To the contrary, I believe that the exhilaration of movement and the experiences of freedom, release, presence, connection, and euphoria that dance generates are its most sincere gifts. However, the sheer joy of dancing often drives people to ignore the multiple social structures and histories in which a dance practice is embedded, and the politics and cultural models it nourishes and repeats. It is to these broader social issues that I turn my analytical lens.

Throughout the book, I use examples from fictional dance films such as *Dirty Dancing* to illustrate how the Glamour Machine functions. I invoke media images for two reasons. First, they are a convenient reference point for my readers, who are more likely to have seen film and television representations of ballroom dance than a live competition. More important, I introduce cinematic images of ballroom dancing because Hollywood is the mother of all Glamour Machines. No promise of radical personal transformation is more mythologized than that of the silver-screen star. The dream of being "discovered," launching one on a rapid ascent to the height of fame and fortune, motivates not only aspiring actors. The symbol of film as fulfillment of fantasy mediates almost every moviegoer's experiences. Hollywood films have come to represent, for their creators and consumers alike, transportation away from, if not complete transformation of, ordinary life. Wider in its scope (American media images reaching nearly every corner of the globe) and deeper in its corruption (the multi-billion-dollar industry inspiring colossal greed and deception), Hollywood's Glamour Machine dwarfs that of DanceSport. Though I do not purport to describe here the mechanisms by which Hollywood's Glamour Machine sustains its power, I would like to point out how DanceSport feeds off of associations with Hollywood Glamour.

Because representations of ballroom dance are widely circulated through film and television, the transformative power of ballroom dance is conflated with the transformative promise of media celebrity. Although my introduction of fiction as *illustration* should not be confused with ethnographic *evidence,* the data upon which I base my analysis, these films do shape common perceptions and fantasies shared by the general public and ballroom dancers alike. The delusions of metamorphosis DanceSport Glamour engenders are reinforced by their representation in Hollywood. For example, *Saturday Night Fever*, which ushered in the return to "touch" dancing in 1977, portrayed a narrative of upward class mobility enabled through disco dancing that fed into and buttressed similar assumptions about the power of social dance to change social class that have been part of the American imagination for over a century. The increasing visibility of ballroom dance not only in film, but also on television, bolsters the common misconception that success in DanceSport will lead to generalized fame and riches. Although several American ballroom dancers are enjoying high-profile media exposure on shows such as *Dancing with the Stars,* the "stars" referred to in its title are not the ballroom dancers. Even when they appear on network TV, professional ballroom dancers cannot seem to escape their role as service industry workers who, although clearly benefiting from the close association with their celebrity students, are never themselves the subjects of the program.

In the following pages, I undertake a cultural analysis of the contemporary American DanceSport industry, tracing its production and consumption of Glamour. My project departs from that of Mizejewski and other scholarly investigations of theatrical excess such as Robert Allen's monumental work on burlesque by placing the subjective experiences of the Glamorous icons at the center. Whereas these scholars have interrogated the effects of glamour on cultural identity for the general public, I focus more narrowly on the effects of Glamour for the individuals whose bodies produce it. I build on the small body of literature examining the social dance industry as it took shape at the beginning of the twentieth century (see Julie Malnig, Danielle Robinson, and Linda Tomko) to demonstrate how its early impulses to regulate the changing boundaries of race, class, and gender intensified as the century progressed. I am grateful to scholars who pioneered cultural studies of dance, including Sally Banes, Ann Daly, Jane Desmond, Susan Foster, Mark Franko, Brenda Dixon Gottschild, Susan Manning, Randy Martin, Sally Ness, and Cynthia Novack, all of whom provided me models for unraveling the ways in which social, cultural, political, and personal meaning is created through dance practice. They demonstrated that dance not only reflects the values, practices, and relationships of the people who practice and consume it, but also produces, influences, and changes society. Dance reflects trends in society, and society is shaped by its dances.

Following their lead, I consider multiple ways in which DanceSport is influenced by and in turn defines its social environment. For example, I do not assume that gender roles in DanceSport are merely a mirror or a model for gendered behavior off the dance floor; rather, I question how they construct and map each individual's relationship to the historically and culturally produced concept called gender. The ways in which gender is defined, performed, and challenged in DanceSport become the means through which participants negotiate a more generalized gendered identity. I am also influenced by the work of Ann Cooper Albright, who in her book *Choreographing Difference* examines how cultural values and identities are produced through particular dance performances. Dance, she argues, foregrounds the unstable process of identity formation because it is both representation and materiality at once: "Dancing bodies produce and are produced by their own dancing."[21] This double articulation exposes the instability of identity and suggests to Albright possibilities for intervening into that unstable process for its reconstitution. Although DanceSport's representation of identity may not model the heterogeneous and inclusive world Albright envisions, DanceSport participants may still use it to construct and reconstruct personal identity as it relates to larger racial, class, national, and sexual group identities.

The means by which individual and social identity is formed through Dance-Sport is only one aspect of my project. I also interrogate the DanceSport industry as a network of power relations based on historical and continued participation in larger imperialist and capitalist structures. In this endeavor, I am most indebted to the path-breaking work of Marta Savigliano, whose book *Tango and the Political Economy of Passion* provides a model for theorizing how a dance form interlocks with larger political economies. Adding to the commonly circulated economic theories of traffic in material and labor, Savigliano suggests that emotional capital is likewise extracted from the third world for sale in the first. She argues that this emotional capital of Passion takes the form of exoticism. People, objects, and cultural practices from the third world with high emotional capital are reframed as exotic for sale and trade in the West.[22] Savigliano draws parallels between the economy of Passion and the general economic system of goods and labor created through imperialist conquest of non-Western cultures, which relies on their continued subjugation to Western power. The economy of Passion is likewise dependent on and implicit in an unequal relationship between the West and its exotic Others. By historicizing and deconstructing the process by which culture is exoticized, Savigliano hopes to denaturalize the "exotic," "primitive," and "uncivilized" stereotypes that continue to define colonized peoples in their relationship to the West.

Savigliano proposes that an international trafficking in the emotional capital of Passion is brokered through the tango. She follows tango's international journeys—its reconstitution in foreign and local contexts as tango practice and representation are appropriated by Europeans and reappropriated by Argentineans—tracing the process by which dances originating in the third world are "whitened" and "cleaned up" for consumption in the first world. Similarly, I analyze analogous routes traversed by Latin dances that eventually landed in DanceSport competition. Each Latin dance adapted by the ballroom industry underwent a process of colonization that depended on and reproduced the traffic in exotic culture exposed by Savigliano.

Exoticism and its economy of Passion share much in common with the economy of Glamour upon which the DanceSport industry is built. Both depend on and sustain difference, desire, exploitation, and social inequality. Exoticism arises out of gross economic and political inequity between the first and third worlds. Savigliano explains that even though the economy of Passion may appear on the surface to validate and perhaps even glorify non-Western culture, it actually relies on the continued marking of hierarchical difference:

> Thus, "exotic" objects have been constituted by applying a homogenizing practice of exoticization, a system of exotic representation that commoditized the colonials in order to suit imperial consumption. In other words, peripheral-"exotic" Passion is molded in the shape of the world's core unfulfillable Desire. The colonizer constitutes his own "progressive" identity—Civilized, Enlightened, Democratic, Postmodern—on the basis of this confrontation with exotic, colonized (neo- and post- as well) Others.[23]

"Exotic" is a meaningful signifier because of its distance from Western culture, a difference dependent on a perpetuation of the very discourses which enabled Western global domination.

Savigliano interrogates traffic in Passion as a fundamentally global, international phenomenon. The economy of Glamour I expose emerges out of the same history of imperialism and global capitalism, albeit operating in a more narrowly circumscribed geographic locale. Although linked to global economies, the economy of Glamour I scrutinize is specific to the United States. Such divergence in scope reveals a dissimilar axis of difference through which each capital is produced. Exoticism is primarily created through national or cultural difference, whereas Glamour is principally generated via class difference. Neither, however, is exclusively about cultural or class disparity. Savigliano points out that exoticism can also be created through class difference and describes how nineteenth-century European opera houses produced exotic spectacles by borrowing from the social practices of the poor (or foreign) and cleaning them up for consumption by the elite. Conversely, Glamour, which is primarily produced through such class appropriation, can also be created through national or cultural distance. National difference, for example, can increase the value of an immigrant dancer's Glamour capital. Both exoticism and Glamour emerge out of fascination with and fear of difference, a simultaneous desire to understand and to own the Other.

Like exoticism, Glamour has a power that is imbued with gross inequalities. Unlike exoticism, which Savigliano suggests is fashioned in the interests of the West, DanceSport Glamour actually feeds on desire from both ends of the social ladder. Exoticism and Glamour do, however, share a predilection for sustaining the inequalities upon which the fascination and desire that create them are based. Thus, Glamour and Exoticism both contribute to maintaining discourses of power. The specific case of tango as a mediator of exotic culture also runs parallel to the use of ballroom dancing as an agent of Glamour. Savigliano theorizes that tango was sexualized in order to universalize and disguise the class and racial tensions out of which it was born.[24] Likewise, the class and racial tensions on which the American ballroom dance industry is constructed are often obscured by its sexualization, as illustrated in the example of *Dirty Dancing.*

Despite the commonalities in theoretical framework, the scope and methodology of Savigliano's project differ significantly from those I employ. She examines not only the global circulation of dance practice, but also disparate images and representations of tango in photographs, film, music, and popular discourse. Savigliano asks not primarily what tango means to those who have committed their lives to its propagation, but what the dissemination of such representations of tango has done to promote and define exoticism. In contrast, I look only tangentially at representations of DanceSport in popular iconography and focus instead on the community that practices DanceSport. As an in-depth analysis of a community that convenes around a dance practice, my project has much in common with ethnographic studies of dance, such as Cynthia Novack's research on contact improvisation or Sally Ness's work on *sinulog* in the Philippines.[25] Both these authors use extensive research as participant observers to examine the relationship between the aesthetic values of a dance practice and the cultural values of its practitioners, situating both in changing historical contexts. And because my research is rooted deeply in participant observation, my analysis entails descriptions of movement, of competitions, of studio structure, and of the individuals who are lured by a life of Glamour. Though I do not attempt a simple mapping of the aesthetic values articulated in a DanceSport performance onto the moral or political values of its proponents, I do suggest that dance is deeply intertwined with larger discourses of power. The social practice and the system of representation interact to build, reinforce, and at times counter ideologies circulating in American society.

The community I describe is not defined by particular geographic boundaries; rather, its constituents identify themselves through common participation in an activity practiced at disparate locations—studios, ballrooms, and competitions—throughout the United States. Although large groups do convene regularly at competitions that bring practitioners from distinct geographical regions together, the community is created by replication of common circumstances rather than by actual shared experience of the entire group.[26] My ethnographic data is drawn from twelve years as a critical observer and participant in the DanceSport community between 1991 and 2003, bolstered by significant research in social practices of salsa and West Coast swing. I have traveled extensively throughout the United States, attending over one hundred competitions nationwide, and during my research process have lived in three metropolitan areas: Boston, Southern California, and Orlando. I cannot deny that there are minor regional differences in these cities, which are more pronounced in the social dance practices than in competitive or studio dancing; yet, the structure of the American ballroom dance industry is national, and the circumstances I describe are relatively consistent across the country.

I was a member of this community before I began conscious analysis of it and will likely remain a member of it after I have declared my research concluded. My position has advantages and disadvantages. Since I was simultaneously pursuing my own career as a DanceSport competitor, there were risks I was not willing to take, conversations I was afraid to have for fear of damaging my own reputation. At times, it has also been difficult for me to gain the "critical distance" often cited as necessary for analysis. I could not always untangle my priorities as researcher from my interests as competitor, teacher, student, and friend. These drawbacks notwithstanding, I believe the insights I gained through my dual position were enormous. This is an industry that relies on creating and maintaining illusion for its economic survival. Secrets are well guarded, not lightly revealed to interlopers. It was only after I had crossed the chasm that separates amateur and professional ballroom dancers in America and worked several years as a DanceSport professional that I began to unravel many of the mechanisms by which DanceSport seduces its devotees. I have occupied many positions at opposite ends of the spectrum, including amateur and professional, franchise employee and independent instructor, pro-am student and pro-am teacher, newcomer college competitor and professional champion. There are also several positions in the system I have never personally experienced, such as that of judge or wealthy patron. But the range of my experiences and that of my informants is vast, giving unparalleled depth to my research into the rarely interrogated community of competitive ballroom dancers.

Although my analysis focuses on the for-profit American ballroom dance industry, there are several peripheral communities of DanceSport practitioners whose relationship to Glamour may differ significantly from the models presented here. Competition ballroom dancing is taught in several high school and university dance programs that are relatively inexpensive for students and that foster relationships among peers rather than across the vast gulfs of difference invoked by Glamour. DanceSport is also practiced in a variety of communities that coalesce around cultural or religious identity. There are, for example, several studios that primarily cater to Chinese, Filipino, Vietnamese, Russian, or Polish immigrants. DanceSport is very popular in Utah, where the overwhelming majority of residents are members of the Church of Latter-day Saints, which endorses DanceSport as a healthy activity for its youth.[27]

Although each of these communities is implicated in the Glamour Machine (their participants revere DanceSport superstars as their idols), each uses DanceSport as a vehicle through which to mobilize a more homogenous community. Glamour functions differently if major class differences (in these local school-based programs) or cultural differences (in the case of ethnic studios) are eliminated. For example, by maintaining language, music, and values specific to each national group during DanceSport classes, studios offer participants a way to negotiate entry into American culture that does not deny their own cultural heritage. Similarly, DanceSport provides Mormons a connection to those outside the church, a bond forged through a common passion for ballroom dancing. I do not examine these specific communities and their unique involvement in DanceSport Glamour in this project, but their presence suggests sites for further investigation at points where interruptions of the system I describe may already be brewing.

At its most narrow, my project will explain and expose the political economy of Glamour in the American DanceSport industry. My work also offers a significant contribution to the field of dance scholarship through analysis of a dance form nearly untouched by scholars. I continue to expand the scope of legitimate subject matter for dance scholarship, which until recently focused on concert dance or ethnographic study of non-Western dance, to include social and popular dance forms in the United States. Dance scholars have developed tools for analyzing the aesthetic qualities and representational meaning of dance performance, but the experiences of dancers have too frequently dropped out of scholarship not based on a classic ethnographic model. I hope that my combination of methodologies developed by anthropologists, historians, linguists, sociologists, and philosophers will expose the critical political and social issues embedded in a dance practice without denying the pleasures and vitality of its lived experience.

In chapter 1 I reveal how Glamour functions in the DanceSport industry. I illustrate the production of Glamour by describing the people who participate in its creation and consumption as well as by detailing the structure of competitions and ballroom dance studio businesses. The people are represented by eight characters (fictional composites of actual individuals I met during fieldwork) representing Glamour agents and addicts from various social positions. I also scrutinize the production and consumption of Glamour at competitions and in studios, linking DanceSport to other discourses of desire, image, and consumption. The chapter integrates theoretical analysis of the Glamour Machine with tantalizing description of its pleasures.

In chapter 2 I examine the relationship between social dance and competitive dance in the history of the American ballroom industry, revealing how crucial the conflation of these two forms is to the production of Glamour. This genealogy also exposes the continual projection of distinctions of race onto those of class and vice versa, an elision that likewise aided in the development of a distinctly white and upwardly mobile dance practice. I am particularly attentive to the continual erasure, elimination, control, and reappearance of improvisation in the standardization process. Primarily through oral histories and archival work, I begin to fill in egregious gaps in the history of American ballroom dancing, picking up from its relatively well documented emergence in the 1910s and tracing changes as the industry evolved into one that is focused on the sale of Glamour and DanceSport competition.

Chapter 3 examines representations of Latinness in DanceSport, looking specifically at the development of the Latin dances, the practice of brownface, and concurrent practices of salsa. I invoke comparison of the tanning creams used for Latin DanceSport competition to blackface used in minstrelsy in order to reflect on the racial and potentially racist consequences of discourses enacted by DanceSport. Although the majority of this chapter focuses on the Latin category of DanceSport competition, I also look at salsa, a contemporary practice of Latin dance outside the ballroom industry, in order to consider how alternative discourses of Latinness are being forged by a competing dance industry in which ethnic Latinos wield a majority influence.

Chapter 4 revisits many of the problems created by the Glamour Machine, exploring moments of resistance and alternative structures that challenge its hegemony. Much of this section focuses on attempts to bring DanceSport to concert stages. I do not argue that DanceSport competition should be replaced by theatrical ballroom dance on stages (certainly they can be concurrent practices); however, the creation of alternative venues for ballroom dance performance would help to destabilize Glamour's power. I also describe two ballroom dance programs that diverge from the studio model upon which the Glamour Machine depends, each one pointing toward an alternate structure for teaching ballroom dancing. If the current competition system were not the organizing force for the ballroom dance industry, patterns of obsessive and compulsive behavior might be reoriented, and the positive social benefits DanceSport fanatics croon about might actually outweigh some of its more detrimental effects.

Glamour promises transcendence of particular stereotypes and limitations of personal identity—most obviously those of class, but also those produced by race, nationality, gender, and sexuality, as well as the less politicized aspects of social identity attributed to popularity, attractiveness, social ease, and desirability. In the following pages I will explore particular mechanisms of Glamour production and consumption to reveal how they are dependent on cultural ideals of and confusion about class, class mobility, and classiness; social constraints on gender, heterosexuality, homosexuality, and romance; and common anxieties and assumptions about racial assimilation and ethnic difference. By analyzing how this process works in the very specific case of the contemporary American DanceSport industry, I hope to suggest how similar processes are at work throughout American consumer culture.

one

The Glamour Machine

I like the way the ballroom is classy. I like the way people hold themselves up in the ballroom. I love the fact that it is larger than life, comic book over-the-top. You know, it's powerful to be one of those perfect people. I like the way the women are perfectly put together from the eyelashes down to the shoes, it's just right. It's sort of like that Clark Kent–into–Superman transformation. Like when he goes into the phone booth. When you go into the dressing room and put on the makeup and the costume, and you come out and you're ready to fight evil in the world. Now I'm not saying it's exactly like that, but it's sort of like that metamorphosis. I can be anything I want to be. And when I get out there on that competition floor, I am going to feel like I have really made it, like I have arrived.

Professional ballroom dancer
anticipating his first competition

Identity in the ballroom is a double performance. Every body in this system is marked at least twice, once by the identity he or she performs in the ballroom and again by the identity by which his or her body is marked offstage. In making this claim, I borrow from Judith Butler the theory that identities come into existence through performative acts in daily life. Butler argues that gender (or any sociopolitical aspect of group identity) does not exist prior to its articulation in culture. There is no "I" before speaking, no sex before gender, no self before the performance of identity. We are always performing ourselves, a series of repetitive iterations of identity which when taken together begin to seem natural, biological, predetermined, and real.[1] If identity, as Butler suggests, is already constructed through performative acts in ordinary life, then the ballroom dancer's performance in competition doubles the layers of construction. It is at the intersection of these identities, the on- and offstage personas and the fantasy of their convergence, that the power of DanceSport Glamour can be located.

DanceSport competitors perform gendered or racial identity in their daily lives, but they have the chance to perform distinctly different identities through their performance on ballroom stages. It is through this second performance opportunity that transformation of the first identity seems possible. Whatever they are seeking escape from—class background, racial stigmas, immigration status, prescriptive gender roles, aging bodies, sexual identity, or any other outsider social position—DanceSport's champions offer evidence that anyone can be transformed through mastery of Glamorous bodily codes. The fantasy of ducking into the symbolic phone booth and emerging prepared to dispel adversity, if only for one waltz, offers many participants tremendous personal comfort and strength. This temporary respite does not, however, usually empower individuals to fight evil or injustice outside the ballroom. More often than not, it enmeshes them in destructive cycles of desire and consumption within it. Much like their comic-book counterparts, DanceSport idols prove powerful only in the fantasy world out of which they emerge, offering their followers distraction and momentary escape from the realities of life without. This chapter exposes the inner workings of DanceSport's Glamour Machine—the people captivated by it, the competitions at its center, and the studio system that fuels it—in order to explain why its promise of radical transformation is so seductive.

STAGING GLAMOUR: THE CHARACTERS

The airport shuttle bus has just pulled up at the front lobby of the Grove Park Inn, a posh resort in the Blue Ridge Mountains of North Carolina. As the driver unloads garment bags and makeup cases, an unusual assortment of passengers emerges from the bus. A Russian immigrant in his mid-twenties steps down before offering his hand to a heavy-set woman in her mid-forties whose broad smile draws attention away from a large nose set on her puffy, pockmarked face. Next, a bright-eyed Asian American girl in her early twenties descends, appearing a bit timid in present company. A slim teenage boy in designer shoes and leather coat slips off the bus, accompanied by an adolescent girl. They appear to be a couple, although the usual aura of teenage romance gushing with expectancy and uncertainty is absent. Instead, they act like a middle-aged society couple, maintaining their marriage only for public appearances. Behind them emerges a bleached blonde, looking much younger than her twenty-nine years and trying to hold herself taller than her five-foot-two-inch build. Finally a Latino man hops off, short in stature but broad in his effervescent gesturing and cooing declarations of "fabulous" every fourth word. All look freshly tanned, as if they had just stepped off a Caribbean cruise. Upon gathering up their bags, the dancers scatter to their rooms in preparation for the competition already underway.

I introduce this typical cross-section of participants at a competition in order to illustrate the range of people attracted to, necessary for, and reproduced by the Glamour Machine. Each one is a composite of two or more individuals I have known over the past twelve years of my research project, fictional representations based on the actual lives of DanceSport competitors. Though I have altered the characters and some details of their lives to protect their identities, the actual experiences recounted are not exaggerated or fabricated. I use these characters to demonstrate how each is hooked into the Glamour Machine from a different angle. By suggesting that these characters are representative of people in comparable positions who share analogous experiences with Glamour, I do not wish to suggest that individual identity can be stripped down to a stereotyped caricature. On the contrary, I theorize these identity positions through the experiences of individuals to highlight the specificity of their lives, the complexity of which it is impossible to reproduce in any theoretical framework.

In the interest of saying something that is meaningful beyond the scope of one individual life, I do make generalizations about groups and the behavior of their constituents (e.g., gay men, straight women, professional dancers, immigrants, etc.). However, I have situated each of these fictional characters along at least two axes of identity. Igor is representative of an Eastern European immigrant who is a professional straight male dancer, locating him at the nexus of several lines of identity. Beatrice's perspective is similar to that of other middle-aged female competitors who compete in pro-am partnerships. Karen is symbolic of the young college-educated devotee and is also a second-generation Asian immigrant. Victor and Isabella characterize Eastern European immigrant teen dancers who compete in amateur divisions. Misty epitomizes the American-born female DanceSport professional, although she confronts issues tied to her class, gender, and national position. And Carlos shares experiences similar to those of many gay male professional dancers and also of other Latinos. Each one is promised a different kind of transformation by the Glamour Machine, but their interdependence is crucial to the entire system.

The Heritage Classic is one of the five largest DanceSport competitions sanctioned by the National Dance Council of America (NDCA). It lasts for five days and draws approximately fifteen hundred people over the course of the weekend. Most people know each other, at least by face if not by name, since they see each other at similar events throughout the year. Some attend only a handful of select competitions, while steadfast competitors may travel several times a month. A DanceSport competition usually lasts three or four days, with events running from 8:00 A.M. until 1:00 A.M. the next day. Competition in each of the four major styles of DanceSport competition—International Standard (waltz, tango, Viennese waltz, foxtrot, and quickstep), American Smooth (waltz, tango, foxtrot, and Viennese waltz), International Latin (cha cha, samba, rumba, paso doble, and jive) and American Rhythm (cha cha, rumba, swing, bolero, and mambo)—are offered at numerous age and proficiency levels ranging from pre-teen through octogenarian and newcomer through professional. Separate events are run for amateur, professional, and pro-am partnerships. "Pro-am" is the term for competitions in which amateur dancers (am) hire professional dancers (pro) to compete as their partners.

Recent upscaling has moved competitions from seedier hotels to ballrooms of four-star resorts. Most of the participants stay in the host hotel for the duration of the event, forcing a perpetual performance by the actors as they continue to interact far beyond the duration of the ostensible "competition." At most theatrical events, the cast does not spend the whole weekend with the audience and critics. They are able to step out of character when the show is over. But there is no offstage at a DanceSport competition. The performance lasts the entire seventy-two-hour duration of the event. Members from each category of participant—neophyte competitor, experienced amateur, insecure professional, professional champion, novice judge, senior adjudicator—perform their position in this hierarchy through self-conscious carriage of the body and its wardrobe, calculation in gesture and facial expression, and association with DanceSport celebrities. No one is ever satisfied with where he or she fits on the grids of hierarchy, always evaluating himself or herself against the other participants. Anxiety about status, classification, and categorization produces strained social performances throughout the industry, culminating in its most extreme manifestation at DanceSport competitions.

Igor escorts Beatrice upstairs before going down to the ballroom to check the time of their first heat. As he leaves her door, his body relaxes slightly and his breathing becomes less labored. He had been on duty the entire flight from New York, accompanying his most important client to the competition. Beatrice takes three hours of lessons every day from Igor and travels to all the major competitions. Her competition fees include Igor's airfare and hotel, which is how he is able to work the circuit with his own professional partner. The salary he gets from teaching Beatrice goes a good way toward paying the $180 per hour Igor scrapes together to pay for his own lessons. Every ballroom dance teacher has one student like Beatrice: a student both know he can't afford to lose. It is her awareness of this situation that leads her to constantly push the boundaries of her privileges. Because she pays thousands of dollars every week to his studio, she expects special treatment in return. As a competing pro-am student, she pays for his time during dance lessons and for his company during competitions—both as a partner on the dance floor and as an escort throughout the weekend. Should this fee give her the right to know where he is every minute of the competition or to expect his help with intimate tasks such as applying tanning cream to her back? Igor and Beatrice are continually negotiating these boundaries. It is awareness of his own dependency that leads Igor to constantly thwart her attempts to control him. His rebellions are small—making her wait for him longer than necessary, hiding from her in the bar, telling white lies to escape her grip. Each insurgency helps him to feel for a moment that she doesn't own him—that he is engaged in a business relationship, not indentured service. However, for a ballroom dancer like Igor, a recent emigrant from Eastern Europe, his life is virtually that.

Throughout much of the history of the American ballroom dance industry, American studios had a very high turnover rate of undertrained dance teachers. Usually, new teachers were trained for a few weeks or months before being booked for high-priced private lessons (ranging from $70 to $120 per lesson in the late 1990s). New teachers usually take home between $7 and $15 per hour, the rest of the money supporting studio expenses and owners. Becoming a studio trainee and new teacher has traditionally been the only entry point into the business for American-born dancers. Once they gained sufficient skills, many of them quit studio jobs and began teaching independently, causing bitter battles and even lawsuits over the clients they lured away from former places of employment. After the fall of the Soviet Union, studio owners discovered a flood of highly trained ballroom dancers from Eastern Europe eager to make their fortune in America. Because Europeans had, until recently, been so much more successful than American dancers in international DanceSport competition, it was relatively easy for studios to secure working visas for these immigrants with "special skills." Immigrants were promised a new life in America in exchange for a three- to five-year teaching contract in an American studio. Even on the meager salary they make while under contract to the studios, many of these immigrants find economic opportunities far greater than those available in their home countries.

Igor makes $18 for every lesson he teaches, but he must be in the studio from 1:00 P.M. to 10:00 P.M. Monday through Friday regardless of whether he has a lesson booked. On a good week, he teaches twenty-five hours. When Igor signed the contract, he thought he would be rich in weeks. Compared to the opportunities available to him back home, Igor's economic situation is very good. But his expenses are high. As a competing professional, he has to pay for coaching, travel to competitions, and costumes. Igor pays his coach $180 for each forty-five-minute lesson and helps his partner pay for her dresses, which cost $1,000 to $3,000 each. In order to maintain the image of Glamour icon, Igor has amassed substantial credit-card debt buying designer street clothes. Igor practices every day from 10:00 A.M. to 1:00 P.M., so the only time he has to earn extra money is on weekends when he is not competing. He uses these free weekends to supplement his income by teaching secretly at a Chinese studio in Queens. Sometimes these students pay him to escort them to their dance parties. Occasionally he will cancel one of these outings, since he gets paid only $40 an hour to escort five women at once, their hunger for dancing not allowing him rest for even one song. By exercising his right to refuse such work, even if only on rare occasions, Igor feels agency. He is not a slave, because he can say no. But if they paid him $100 an hour, he confesses, he would not refuse.

After leaving his student Beatrice at her hotel room, Igor rushes into the main ballroom to pick up a schedule for the competition. The pro-am solos, as opposed to the pro-am group competitions where all the couples dance at the same time, have been going all morning. Once the mainstay of American ballroom competition before the English system of competition was introduced in the 1960s, these events are now relegated to the early hours of competition before most people have arrived. One by one pro-am couples take the floor for three-minute choreographed routines to the music of their choice. Rules are minimal in this category. As Igor enters, a seventy-eight-year-old Chinese woman of ninety pounds is spinning upside-down in a one-handed, overhead lift. The sparse audience is clapping at this physical feat, seemingly at ease with the image of a gay man in his thirties dancing an acrobatic duet of romantic love with a woman old enough to be his grandmother. She's been able to afford three face lifts, why not a full body lift as well, if it makes her happy? This is the rhetoric used to normalize such an incongruous practice. Igor breezes by the dress designers displaying their latest bodices adorned with twenty-gross Swarovski rhinestones and runs upstairs to tell Beatrice she is dancing her first heat at 7:38 this evening.

It's been two years since Karen graduated from Yale, where she was very successful on the university ballroom dance team. Ballroom dancing had been her main activity in college, the haven where she found like-minded friends who would rather spend their Saturday nights dancing foxtrots and cha chas in an old ballroom than guzzling beer at a dorm party. Since graduation, she has been working at a small marketing firm in Manhattan and has grown progressively more obsessed with DanceSport competition. She spends all her disposable income on lessons, and most of her free time as well. If she's not practicing ballroom, she's taking class in ballet or flamenco. Her Korean immigrant parents don't understand her interest in dance and are unsure of its value in the American social system. They didn't pay for their daughter to go to Yale and become a dancer. She has been studying ballroom for only five years, and she recognizes her disadvantage compared to the Russian kids who started when they were five years old. Karen believes she could be just as good as they if only she had a partner, which is why she is here. Karen hopes that by dancing the pro-am scholarship, the highest level of pro-am competition and the only one in which amateurs can win money (which can only be used for additional dance lessons because the check is written out to the student's teacher), she will increase her visibility in the industry, improving her chances of landing an amateur partner. Despite its roots in social dance, DanceSport is not practiced informally in social settings. To participate, one must be in a partnership—an agreement to train and compete together negotiated after several try-outs. Competitors do not dance casually or indiscriminately with friends or acquaintances—partners dance only with each other. There is no DanceSport practice session where one can drop in alone expecting to dance with whoever is available. In between partnerships, amateurs can only continue their training if they take pro-am lessons. Professionals have even fewer choices and between partnerships are likely to dance only with their students. Partnership searches may constitute a significant portion of a competitor's career.

Karen doesn't quite fit into either the group of amateur dancers who started as children or those who began as adults. Each of these groups has its own social and competitive ladder, one's accession on the former being contingent on the latter. Most of the adult competitors aspire to rank highly either in pro-am competition or in senior (over thirty-five) amateur competitions. Others are the best dancers in their own studios or at small regional competitions and enjoy being admired and recognized in local spheres. However, it is the amateur dancers who began training as children whose competitive presence is recognized at national and international levels. Karen began dancing at age nineteen, and she has worked diligently to improve her skills. She was one of the best dancers in college, but in the New York amateur scene where Russian child prodigies dominate, she is barely on the radar. Karen is able to compete because she can afford to take pro-am lessons and pay her teacher to dance with her at a few pro-am competitions each year. But pro-am dancing, where she has to pay for every hour of practice, is not Karen's goal. She has her sights set on serious amateur competition. Karen wonders how invested her teacher really is in finding her a partner, since he makes a considerable income off of her lessons. If she found a partner, he might lose her as a student, or at least as such a profitable one. Karen knows it would be easier to find a partner if she were Russian because they help their own. And the Korean dance community is of little help. Ballroom dancing is very popular within several Asian communities in major U.S. metropolitan areas, but the studios there are geared toward the older adult amateurs. And even though Karen started dancing at the same age as the majority of American-born professional DanceSport female competitors, both the professional-amateur divide and her elite education separate her from this group as well. Not challenged enough by the older amateur community of dancers, but not quite good enough to compete with the amateur youth, Karen hovers on the edge.

Karen has learned that rising on this scale of Glamour is about transforming the body through knowledge not only of ballroom technique, but also about how to buy the most fashionable clothes on a modest income, how often to go to the tanning salon, which kind of acrylic nails will endure five rounds of cha cha, the brand of hairspray that creates a neat but natural look when you're sweating under the lights, and the trick of using spirit gum under the earrings to hold them on even during the jive. Creation and maintenance of the Glamorous body is not a natural affair; it is expensive and time-consuming. To the amateur dancers at her studio, Karen is the epitome of Glamour, but to the higher-ranked dancers at a large competition such as this, she is just an unremarkable amateur dancer. Not rich enough to stir too much cloying attention from the professionals, not good enough to be noticed by the highly ranked dancers, Karen longs to be recognized for her dedication and skill. She starts browsing through the new Latin CDs and jealously eyes the young couple briskly walking by to the practice room.

Victor and Isabella sit coolly on the side of the room as they put on their shoes. They do not speak, already jaded at age sixteen from too many hours by each other's side. They have been dancing together for four years, every day, two hours after school and then again in the evenings on group practice nights. Their hard work has paid off. They are national youth ten-dance champions and fourth in the country in youth Latin. Victor's family came to New York from the Ukraine when he was eleven, and his parents enrolled him in a dance school within a month. His teachers back home had said he showed great promise, so his mother started working at the studio's front office to help pay for lessons. Since most of the other kids at the studio are Russian, his mother doesn't really have to learn English. She knows her son will take care of her. Every trophy he has ever won is in the living room of their tiny apartment, symbolizing the investment and pressure his family has put on him to pull them out of poverty. His family anticipates that he will be on TV soon, just like another Russian boy who trained at Victor's school. And certainly then he could buy the family a DVD player, maybe he could buy one every day if he wanted to.

Victor's participation in DanceSport both connects him to his cultural heritage and helps him assimilate into American life. Dance has long been valued in Russian culture, and DanceSport in particular has become increasingly popular among Russian youth. So even though it is not a specifically Russian dance form, DanceSport is a link to Victor's ethnic and national heritage: it is something that he did before he left home, that his parents understand and support, and that he can do in a community of other Russian immigrants. But Victor's current participation in DanceSport is peculiarly American. In Russia he would not have had access to the kinds of teachers he has here, nor would he have had the kind of financial support he gets as one of the most promising youth dancers in America. Victor and Isabella are sponsored by a costume designer, so they don't have to pay for new dresses every few months. They are often paid to perform in shows at the numerous Russian nightclubs in Brooklyn, and the United States Amateur Ballroom Dancers Associations pays for their trips to the world championships.[2] With such limited financial resources and so many kids dancing, such stardom would never have been possible in Russia. Dancing is not exactly an accepted pastime for teenage boys in America, but Victor's success earns him a bit of prestige at his public high school. Victor is especially proud of the red, white, and blue jacket he is going to wear at the world championships when he represents America, signaling his triumph as an American

Training in DanceSport Glamour begins early. Armen Petrosyan and Nicole Pyatetsky. Yankee Classic, Boston, Massachusetts, June 2005. Photo © 2004 by Jonathan S. Marion.

athlete. It is unlikely that Victor will go to college; he is too completely absorbed in his dancing career to take time out at such a crucial age for university. If he's lucky, Victor's success as a DanceSport athlete may lead to social connections and financial opportunities that will bring him success in a world larger than DanceSport.

By 6:45 P.M. Misty is knocking on the door of room 313. A balding gentleman in his early fifties decked out in a pinstriped vest and matching trousers answers the door. He smiles to see his dance teacher dressed in an elegant lavender gown that drapes low over her shoulders. Purple satin pumps wedged under her arm and makeup case in hand, she asks rather matter-of-factly if he is ready to go downstairs. But Morgan tries to stretch out the time she is in his hotel room as long as possible. "You look stunning, my dear," he exclaims, lingering too long with his lips on her cheek. Misty does not mask her momentary discomfort. She draws his attention to the competition number lying on his bed and asks if he needs helping pinning it on. He nods and she easily relaxes into the ritual task of pinning a paper number onto her partner's back.

Misty has been teaching ballroom dance since she was sixteen, although she had to lie and pretend she was eighteen to get the job. After three years of teaching at a chain studio, she was able to get herself a job in a bigger city, moving away from her family and small-town life. Eventually she moved to California after she was offered a job working on staff at an independent studio. After a year she left that studio too. Now she works for herself, renting space and hustling for students. Misty is typical of the American-born white female Dance-Sport professional. She comes from a rural working-class background and has used DanceSport as a means of improving her social status. Like so many of the American dancers, Misty answered an ad for new dance teachers at a local ballroom dance franchise studio. When she arrived at the studio to inquire about the job, Misty asked to speak to Fred Astaire himself—she was so far removed from the world his image symbolizes that she was completely unaware that Fred Astaire was a national icon, not the local studio owner. Her early dance training was minimal compared to her training in sales and psychology. After two weeks of dance training, she was teaching foxtrot and rumba to new students, selling $1,500 contracts her second week on the job. Like many chain studios where higher emphasis is placed on social services (friendly atmosphere and parties) than on dance skill, Misty's first studio owner discouraged the students and the staff from exploring ballroom dancing outside the dominion of the franchise. It was eight months before Misty accidentally stumbled into a National Dance Council of America competition and began to realize that DanceSport extended beyond the dominion of Fred Astaire Studios.[3]

Misty competes professionally in the American Rhythm division. Of the four main styles of DanceSport practiced in the United States, American Rhythm is considered the least serious, and its practitioners are often stigmatized as less skilled dancers than those in the more competitive field of International Latin. American Rhythm is based on the American Style Latin social dances taught at American dance studios. Although the social versions of these dances are significantly different from their International counterparts, the competitive versions have generally failed to develop a style that is distinct from International Latin. One of the main differences people claim between the American and International Styles is the continual motion of the body in American Style, the body rhythm taking precedence over the clean and readable lines of International Latin.[4] Therefore dancers who are short or stocky are encouraged to dance American Rhythm rather than the International Latin, which privileges long and lanky bodies that can make the elongated lines, which are adapted from ballet. However, lacking significant differences in choreography or technique, American Rhythm is often assumed to be a lesser version of International Latin, its practitioners more needy of validation because their chosen form is the least respected. Misty never had the opportunity to study International Latin since most of the American chain studios don't teach it (or didn't until they started importing European teachers), and she is acutely aware of her inferior status. Even though she has spent her entire adult career as a dancer, she does not think of herself as a dancer—not like the International competitors, who have had so much more professional training. Misty could hardly consider the majority of her training formal, crediting her experience dancing in topless bars with how she learned to dance seductively. But Misty is often accused of looking too strong on the floor and overpowering her partner. There is nothing about her life that is meek or submissive, and it is difficult for her to hide this on the competition floor.

Misty and Morgan enter the ballroom, linked arm in arm. "Hi, how's it *going*," Carlos cries upon seeing his friends. "Isn't the hotel *amaaazing?*" he declares, stretching out his last word so long that it takes on absurd significance. Misty and Carlos teach out of the same studio in California, so they see each other on a daily basis. He hugs them with theatrical fervor, his gestures appearing over-the-top and slightly disingenuous. "Did you see the new boy from Idaho?" Carlos whispers to Misty. "He's got eyes to die for." Here under the ballroom lights, where all movement is exaggerated, colors are intensified, and even eyelashes are worn at three times the normal length, Carlos's mannerisms blend right in. Gay masculinity as expressed through flamboyance, though not necessarily displayed by all gay ballroom dancers, finds like company in and is fundamental for producing the ostentatiousness of DanceSport Glamour. Gay men constitute nearly half of the population of male ballroom dancers, most drawn to the Latin division, where physical melodrama is the essence of the sport. Though they are not so open as to hold hands with a male lover at a ballroom dance competition, gay men hardly need to be secretive about their sexual preferences to be successful in DanceSport. Top world and national champions are openly gay, their sexual orientation commonly known to the entire dance community.

Carlos will eagerly discuss his most recent male love interest, and his everyday body language marks him as gay in most contexts. But he is obsessed with looking straight on the dance floor. "I want everyone to think I am having a passionate love affair with my partner," he explains. Though he does not have to pass as straight off the dance floor as many gay men do in their places of work, he does use the competition performance to prove that he can. In rehearsal for a recent dance show in which he and Misty performed, Carlos complained that one of the moves the entire cast was required to execute, a twist of one leg, looked "too gay." He insisted that changing the angle of the knee rectified the objectionable situation. He accepted the rest of the routine, including flicking white-gloved outstretched fingers at the end of downturned wrists, without incident. Having chosen careers in dance, an activity considered effeminate and unmanly by most American standards, male ballroom dancers often need to redraw distinctions between masculine and unmasculine movement. By defining their own boundaries of effeminacy, gay and straight men can be assured that even though they move their bodies with a grace and agility usually attributed to women, they are still men.

Participation in a sport where they portray heterosexual romance does not seem ironic or unusual to the gay men who do it. To most it becomes a way to be accepted as men on heterosexual terms, without denying their homosexual identity. It is a space in which heterosexual and homosexual masculinity can be united. Gay men can be lauded for knowing how to treat women on the dance floor, for knowing their place in the heterosexual couple as protector of and backdrop for female beauty, and still be cruising for a male sexual encounter in the same ballroom later that night. In DanceSport, Carlos has found a community of other gay men with similar interests and experiences. Several of the gay men from Eastern Europe Carlos has befriended have discussed how much easier it is for them to explore their gay identity in America. Most were forced to keep their sexual identity secret at home because the common sentiment amongst their friends was "If I ever met a gay man, I'd kill him." Like many other artistic spaces, DanceSport offers a haven for many gay men to find community and professional recognition without disguising their sexual orientation.

Carlos makes a respectable living working as a dance teacher. He has a strong work ethic and is a very skilled dancer, but his success is largely due to his ability to respond to the emotional needs of each one of his students. His main focus in teaching is not on increasing the skill of his students but rather on making them feel as if they are beautiful, sexy, important, unique, elegant, and loved. The husbands of his married clients feel safe leaving their wives in Carlos's care, confident that he will provide protection, companionship, and excitement without sexual threat. His marked difference as a gay man adds to his Glamour value. His exaggerated mannerisms are different enough from the men most of his clients know to be charming and alluring, but not so different to be threatening. Carlos has another advantage that straight teachers do not. His lovers are unlikely to get jealous of his students or partners, a continual negotiation and source of stress for straight men and women working in the industry.

Although he does not feel discriminated against as a homosexual in DanceSport, Carlos does believe he faces racism as a Latino. His short, stocky body does not conform to the aesthetics of International Latin, which favors the long, thin bodies of European heritage. Many people suggest that Carlos enter the American Rhythm division, but he only wants to compete in International Latin since it is regarded as the more difficult form. Judges and coaches assume that because he is ethnically Latino what he does as a dancer is "natural," not the result of hard work and analysis. But Carlos insists that he can explain in detail how he produces each body action, that it is the result of education and discipline, not untamed talent. He knows his technique must be twice as precise as that of non-Latino dancers in order to prove that his skill comes from more than just inborn rhythm.

All of these characters—Igor, Beatrice, Karen, Victor, Misty, and Carlos—desire and experience escape from the limits of their own lives and transformation at multiple levels, often along one or more axis of sociopolitical identity. Victor and Igor are anticipating transfiguration of both their class status and their position as immigrants. For Igor, the promise of transcendence is more directly about class and economic status, driven by an overwhelming need to prove his financial success to his family back home. Victor, who does not feel monetary pressures to nearly the same degree while still under the roof of his parents, is more concerned with fitting into American society and securing a higher position in a very capricious teenage social stratum. Though the American-born dancers do not fantasize about national assimilation, they are all likewise motivated by fantasies of class ascendance. Misty's dream to escape the social position of her birth is similar to Igor's, her proximity to such opulence and wealth perhaps equally incomprehensible to her family. Karen and Beatrice do not necessarily seek upward class mobility, but both long for excitement that they see or imagine is experienced by those outside their own class. So even though they may not strive to shift their own social classification, they do covet something that they can only acquire through class transgression.

Each of the women negotiates her gendered identity through participation in DanceSport. Despite the relatively narrow representation of femininity on the dance floor, many women find that DanceSport offers them an access point through which to validate their own relationship to the feminine, particularly if the complexity of their own lives seems to exceed the boundaries of its traditional representation. DanceSport assures each female competitor affirmation of her femininity and sexual desirability without denying her recognition for hard work, physical strength, and achievement. Misty can be independent, business-savvy, and assertive without forfeiting her position as a sexy, desirable female. Beatrice, who has never been beautiful by Western standards but has achieved considerable success in the male-dominated world of finance, becomes a princess in her satin gown, dancing in Igor's arms. Like the women, Carlos (as well as, to a lesser extent, Igor) negotiates his gender and sexual identity through alignment of qualities that are often portrayed as mutually exclusive in most other areas of cultural representation. He can be simultaneously masculine (as defined by its corollary relationship to femininity) and homosexual (or heterosexual with an interest in aesthetics).

Although the realignment of sexual orientation and gender with qualities to which they are not traditionally ascribed offers these individuals partial resolution of anxiety on a personal level, it does little to broaden the scope of gender roles in the larger cultural system in which they are embedded. Persistence of gender inequality even within the industry suggests that redress at the personal level may actually perpetuate structural inequalities because tension is relieved rather than channeled into political struggle. In comparison to male counterparts, female ballroom dancers earn less money, have less political power, sustain greater expenses, experience more difficulty in finding dance partners, are required to study harder to be able to translate their skills as dancers into skills as teachers, and are more likely to experience sexual harassment. Certainly many of these conditions are no different from sexism women experience in other industries. However, they are often more acute in the ballroom dance industry, partly due to the disparate gender roles required by the form.

The male leader initiates movement and the female follower reacts, mirroring and recreating the active-passive binary traditionally associated with male and female behaviors. When faced with such accusations of sexism, many dancers are quick to point out that the leader is dependent on a receptive follower in order to adequately execute his part, implying that mutual dependence is the same as equality. Although I agree that both roles are equally important and may be equally difficult, they are not the same. Each role requires and cultivates a unique skill set. There are many aspects of the follower's role that empower her (i.e., she is the center of visual attention), and she is never as passive as the rhetoric implies, but the leader's role is ultimately a more powerful position. Because the man or leader makes all the decisions about when and where to move on the dance floor, he has much greater control. He chooses the steps and their order, avoids or collides with other dancers, establishes and maintains a relationship to the music, and determines the strength and tone of their physical connection. Though a follower may influence any of his selections, choice is primarily his domain. There are many frameworks through which one could argue that the leader-follower dichotomy does not perpetuate gender inequality, but my extensive experience as a professional follower has convinced me that rampant gender inequality stems directly from this distinction.[5]

Race, while perhaps most visibly at issue for Carlos, underlies every identity story.[6] Karen's drive to perform "passion" on the dance floor is partially based on her need to counter stereotypes that Asians are emotionally stoic. The white dancers as well are shaped by their own racial backgrounds. Unable to accept public performance of sexual desire as their own, white dancers project it onto another racial group when dancing in the Latin category. In addition to racial identity shaping each dancer's view of himself or herself, race also plays into other aspects of identity. Class, immigration status, sexual orientation, and gender are always dependent on racial assumptions and histories, and each emerges as significant through some aspect of racial identity. For example, DanceSport Glamour rewards particularly white definitions of class, gender, and sexuality. So even though racial assumptions in the ballroom may at times be obscured, I will demonstrate in chapters 2 and 3 how absolutely crucial they are to its construction.

These prototypical characters and their real-life counterparts will continue to negotiate their fantasies of transformation as the competition unfolds over the next several days.

STAGING GLAMOUR: THE COMPETITION

Evening sessions at competitions are the weekend's main attraction. Professionals and advanced amateurs compete for championship titles during these long nights, which are somewhat like a cross between a hockey game and an opera. There is plenty of milling about and screaming for one's favorite dancers, but no one shouts insults to the other teams (although plenty may be whispered in haughty judgment). Depending on the size of the competition, events might have upward of fifty couples entered. In large fields, couples will dance three or even four qualifying rounds, usually in heats of twelve to twenty-four couples, before the final choice is whittled down to six couples. There are typically five to ten separate competitions scheduled for one evening, so rounds of the Professional Latin Championships will alternate with Youth Amateur Standard, for example. Each championship category has five dances that are danced with only a fifteen-second break in between, so stamina, especially by the final round, becomes part of the contest.

The syntax and style of DanceSport choreography are ruled by the conventions of competition format. Each dance lasts a maximum of two minutes and is performed in the round amidst dozens of other competitors. Competitors must be able to adapt their choreography to any music within an expected style and tempo range, because dancers do not know the melody for any round of competition until the first few notes float through the ballroom. The choreography must enable couples to travel and turn frequently enough to be seen by each judge and member of the audience. Sudden changes of speed and dynamics are effective at catching attention, as are moves that appear particularly difficult or unusual or that command excessive space. Choreographic strategies commonly employed by concert dancers such as repetition or theme and variation are not useful in DanceSport because viewers do not watch a single couple from beginning to end. Thematic developments must be condensed into a few seconds if they are to register with an audience whose attention is constantly shifting. Instead, couples perform basic moves and innovative stunts at relatively consistent intervals so that they can prove their competence and versatility to any eye that rests on them for only a few seconds. There is no narrative arc in competition choreography, no climax or denouement. The dance must awe from first step to last. By the time the finalists for each event are announced, the spectators have had a chance to carefully scrutinize each dancer, comparing strengths and weaknesses. It is not only the judges who are evaluating competitors. Everyone has a personal favorite by the time the results are announced.

Judges and the audience members take into consideration a variety of factors when making their assessments, including footwork, frame, body line, partnering, musicality, athleticism, artistry, and grooming. Foot placement is clearly prescribed for each step, as is the part of the foot to be used—inside or outside edge, ball, heel, or whole foot. A good dance frame requires strong vertical posture and arms that remain locked in position with one's partner, even when dancers are moving at high speeds. Dancers create pictures with their bodies similar to those seen in ballet—limbs fully extended into classical geometric shapes (clean diagonals, circles, and lines). Partnering skills are measured by how efficiently energy is transferred from one person to the other. Hand or body connections should appear seamless, neither individual appearing to be pulled off balance or to be overpowered by the other. Dancers are expected not only to stay in time with the music, but to display a sense of musical phrasing through syncopations and of originality through use of rhythmical accents. Because the most aerobic dances are last in each heat, judges can watch for those competitors who start to look tired or weak under the physical strain, making their overall level of physical fitness decisive. In addition to being superior athletes, winning competitors must also display artistry through convincing characterization and emotional expression. And though it is not expressly part of the competition, every judge will agree that grooming matters. Poorly designed costuming or a disheveled hairstyle detracts from a performance and negatively affects the results. Finally, judges consider basic skills expected of any dancer, including balance, control, strength, flexibility, speed, and ease of movement.

Although there are many published rules by which competitors must abide, there are no clear, written standards for judging in handbooks or manuals. Judges, who are by requisite prior champions themselves, come to share a simi-

Standard competitors showing off a perfect frame even as they fly high off the ground in the athletic quickstep. United States Ballroom Dance Championships, Miami, FL. Photo by David Mark.

lar set of criteria primarily through their own experiences as competitors, their success in the system attesting to their comprehension of its values. In making their evaluation, judges take all the aforementioned factors into consideration, although each individual judge decides the relative weight each criterion bears on the final outcome. The structure of DanceSport competition necessitates that judges resort to the use of one additional criterion—the reputation of the couple. Most judges are loath to admit that a couple's reputation—including their established competition record, perceived moral character, and suitability as ambassadors for DanceSport—affects judging because it makes an already subjective system seem even more biased and subject to favoritism, if not actual fraud.[7] Time pressures tend to strengthen judges' tendencies to base their marks on preconceptions. Unlike ice dancing competitions, in which couples execute routines one at a time, DanceSport requires all couples to perform simultaneously. This structure enables competitors to be compared side by side and forces them to deal with unknown elements (such as traffic and changing spatial openings) so that their improvisational skills are tested. The disadvantage of this system is that judges have very little time to focus on any single couple. Judges have 105 seconds to assess all couples, and most do it within the first 60 so as not to be left standing without a final decision. In earlier rounds, when many couples are on the floor, only a few seconds are spent evaluating each couple. In the final round, when there are only six couples on the floor, each couple may draw 10 seconds of each judge's attention. Numerous campaigns to revise DanceSport judging have been considered, but no superior system has yet been agreed upon.

At precisely 9:38 P.M. the semifinal round of the professional International Standard Championships begins. Number 217's stride is both stoic in its strength and soft in its agility as he glides down the side of the ballroom before suspending his movement at the top of a phrase, the tails of his jacket swinging ever so slightly as he hovers to the swelling music. It is the consistency of his poise, stretched but not brittle amidst this flurry of action, that is seductive. His partner follows him so effortlessly that they look almost like some two-headed creature. But underneath her layers of georgette, petite feet in satin pumps etch out the mirror image of his steps, perfect synchrony below supporting the blissful calm above. They have stopped inches from the audience, teasing them as he allows her to stretch so far over his arm that the beautiful arch threatens to break her back in two. But he swoops her up before the ecstasy turns sour, and they dart toward the next corner. The hem of her dress sweeps the faces of two spectators who scream in delight as the entire cluster of onlookers joins them in cheers.

Two other couples are engaged in a battle for control over the cluttered northwest side of the dance floor. One pair has nearly backed into the other, but the second dancers have such a mesmerizing arsenal of weaves and pivots that

Undefeated U.S. Amateur Latin Champions Eugene Katsevman & Maria Manusova. Embassy Ball, Irvine, CA, September 2005. Photo © 2005 by Jonathan S. Marion.

they are able to change course without dropping even one beat of synchronicity. They appear unperturbed by this incident, their tranquility of expression and smoothness of movement evoking another cry of support from nearby viewers. The music fades after exactly one minute and forty-five seconds, and the twelve gentlemen, in nearly identical white tie and tails, finally release from their holds twelve ladies, who spin out for demure bows. As the announcer thanks the couples for their waltz, one competitor adjusts his bow tie, another wipes the sweat off his brow, and a third flicks off a rhinestone that is wedged into the bottom of her shoe. They shuffle positions in the hybrid walk-strut of the dancer-athlete, awaiting the first bar of tango music before resuming their embrace.

Some spectators barely notice the performance on the dance floor; they are more interested in the choreography of the audience members as they continually rearrange themselves into new clusters like guests at a cocktail party. This is where crucial alliances are formed, political ties forged, and careers made or broken. People gather around the bar, near the vendors, at select tables, or outside in the smoking area for moments of guarded small talk mediated by wandering eyes keeping track of shifting social formations. Just like the keen competitor, whose strategy requires maintaining a constant awareness of all other dancers' positions on the floor, the audience members are likewise tracking each other's locations and social interactions. Fashion worn at the tables around the dance

U.S. Open Amateur Standard Championships. United States DanceSport Championships, Holly-wood, Florida, September 2004. Photo © 2004 by Jonathan S. Marion.

floor is just as carefully selected as that exhibited by the competitors. Double-breasted suits, French cuffs, pointed lapels, and cowled dresses offer an updated complement to the slightly old-fashioned references to high fashion worn in competition.

Even those who are not highly skilled competitors themselves can mark themselves as members of the expert community by flaunting their insider knowledge. Internet discussion boards dedicated to DanceSport are beset by amateur dancers debating ad infinitum the results of recent dance competitions, arguing about the merits of one couple's dancing over another's, criticizing with authority a missed connection, drooping top line, or unsteady ankle. In face-to-face social interaction, dancers will assert their position on the Glamour knowledge scale by casually reciting the world rankings, speaking easily in DanceSport jargon with reference to "rule 11" to insinuate intimate knowledge of scrutineering rules, bandying about first names of champions as if they were personal friends, or flawlessly rolling a long string of foreign surnames off their tongues.[8]

As if the public performances of audience members in their personal tête-à-têtes were not enough distraction from the main events on the dance floor, competitors and audience members continually exchange places, further blurring the dubious distinction between observer and observed. Latin competitors warm up on the sides of the ballroom, spinning to their own internal music as the foxtrot competition continues in the center of the room. As they are called to line up, they drop their warm-up suits to reveal coordinated outfits, sleek and bold. The Standard competitors file off the dance floor, dropping their poise and their partners as they step onto the carpeted area that designates "offstage" to dash for water.

The evening continues to unfold with round after round of competition, conversation, rattled nerves, and tense exchanges. Competitors nod to each other politely from within their pre-competition bubbles, maintaining focus and isolation in the crowded room. Energetic explosions of force and speed staged center floor are scrutinized and evaluated over and over again. Audience members continually meander to the bar and the bathroom just to look around and see what is happening elsewhere in the resort, to ensure that they don't miss any of the action transpiring off the dance floor. Only newcomers are impressed by the skill of the dancers; everyone else is more absorbed in criticizing and posing than in enjoying a good show. Because participants from radically different social positions are converging in the same space, even those in the "audience" are performing for each other. Those in a higher social class (as measured by rankings in the ballroom or by more general markers of class status) must reinforce their status, ensuring everyone of their superior ranking through their dress, movement, and speech. And those aspiring to improve their social position can both perform an upwardly mobile identity and attempt to forge alliances with those who can actually help them improve their position.[9]

The competition is over by 12:30 A.M., all the results announced and expectations sustained or dashed. In the suite reserved for the after-hours pro party, competitors are still on display. Though food, drink, and jokes provide some release from the tension of the day, it is hardly a relaxed environment. Behavior in this space can mean as much for a career as that on the dance floor. Champions must be good ambassadors for ballroom dance, and their suitability to the task is often measured at such social gatherings. Political and sexual liaisons are fostered at these late-night functions, their overlap sometimes so blatant that, like everything else in DanceSport, it seems too overdone to be serious. One of the gay judges whispers his room number into the ear of a handsome young male dancer. "You want to be a star, don't you?" the judge says with a wink. An evening of sexual indiscretion with a judge never hurt any competitor's marks. Other competitors make a show of performing the stability of their relationship, a happily married couple always regarded as a good ambassador for the sport. The dancers gradually retire to their rooms, alone or with a conquest, to prepare for the next day of competition.

The ballroom is usually open all night, although much of the Glamour Machine has been put to sleep. Tablecloths are spread over the displays of glistening necklaces and patent leather shoes, revealing a broken earring under a chair or a loose piece of chartreuse feather as the brightest object remaining in what now appears to be a very unassuming room. Several couples are usually practicing in the ballroom until 3:00 or 4:00 A.M., performing a ritual of dedication and intimidation. These midnight sessions are usually the only chance competitors have to rehearse while they are traveling because the ballroom floor is occupied at all other hours by the competition itself. Tense bodies clad in carefully chosen practice outfits (simpler versions of competition fashion) prance about, "feeling the floor," blocking out routines, working out (and working up) last-minute nerves, and challenging each other in a subtle game of chicken. The competitors strain to appear focused on their routines, pretending not to notice who else is in the room, acting as if they do not care what kind of an impression they make, as if this performance were of no consequence. But it is in this stripped-down setting, with no lights, costumes, or spectators, that the true quality of one's dancing is most visible. Nerves are always on edge at these sessions, and those couples who can make it through one of these rehearsals without snapping at each other gloat in this rare victory. When the anxiety of a pre-competition midnight practice leads to curt exchanges and exasperated accusation, dancers are tortured by their own inability to live up to the perfection their public personas falsely project. By the time the last sore body straggles out of the ballroom, the next day's competitors are already at their dressing tables setting their hair and eyelashes into place. The interdependency of Glamour's euphoria and monstrosity becomes transparent as the evening's final activities melt into the first heats of morning competition.

PRO-AM: THE GLAMOROUS AND THE GROTESQUE

Under the warm stage lights flooding the morning ballroom, dozens of "senior" (i.e., older) women are strutting and gyrating in the arms of their much younger male partners to the sounds of Jennifer Lopez's hit "Let's Get Loud." Unlike the wild flailing typical at most American social dance gatherings, this is highly organized and codified movement, arms and feet thrust into precise locations. Their dresses—bright, ornate, sparkling, and skimpy—look like a cross between those seen on the catwalk and those seen on the boardwalk. References to both class and trash abound. Dozens of tanned and glittered bodies dart past with the intensity and enthusiasm usually only expressed by their grandchildren. Directly in the center of the floor is a woman of well over three hundred pounds whose round and rolling flesh is adorned in traffic-officer orange, trimmed with rhinestones the size of quarters. Her partner, who is dwarfed by her, attempts to match the magnitude of her girth with expansive presentation of his arms and slender body. Beside them dances a woman well into her sixties, her fuchsia fringe dress whipping the chest of her twenty-year-old partner as she distorts her face into exaggerated caricatures of sensual delight. Another couple flanks them, deadly serious in their execution of an advanced sequence of turns and checks. He pauses to steady her as she wobbles ever so slightly in her three-inch jeweled heels, her knobby knees and spindly legs struggling to support her. Her disorientation is palpable, but he strikes the floor again with determination as intense as her canary yellow dress, carrying her resistant body with apparent ease. She smiles as they turn to face the audience. Given the media's tendency to represent female sexual desire as exclusively the domain of the young and thin, such public celebration of sexuality by mature women may initially shock viewers. But the delight with which each woman moves is infectious, and many on the sidelines are soon admiring the pride they take in "getting loud."

The particular American practice of pro-am DanceSport competition, in which amateur dancers pay professional teachers to perform with them in competition, produces these moments of disjunctive juxtaposition. Age, body shape, physical attractiveness, and skill level are often severely mismatched in these displays of heterosexual courtship. Separate categories are offered for both male and female pro-am dancers (the moniker "pro-am dancer" referring to the amateur member of the partnership), although the number of women willing to pay a professional partner to fulfill what for many has been a lifelong dream—to become a dancing star—is more than triple that of men. Daytime at competitions is reserved for pro-am, where categories determined by the student's age and experience level and the couple's dance style are so profuse that a single teacher may enter up to two hundred events with the five to ten students he or she has competing that weekend. But not all teachers are such good salespeople, and some may have only twenty entries. Often an event (i.e., gentlemen, aged forty-five to fifty-five, intermediate bronze waltz) that has only a single entrant will be run simultaneously with other events so that students feel as if they are dancing against the other twelve competitors on the floor.

The pro-am relationship benefits both professionals and amateurs. It offers amateur dancers the opportunity to compete when they cannot find an amateur partner. Particularly for older women who are single or widowed or whose husbands don't dance, pro-am offers a forum in which to practice DanceSport that would not be possible under a system that required a partner of similar age and skill level. Savvy to their own position as the financial backbone of the industry, pro-am students have recently demanded more serious consideration as athletes. Their efforts have resulted in increased coverage for pro-am competition in *Dance Beat,* the national DanceSport newspaper, and the development of competitions in which pro-am is the central event to which amateur and professional heats are appended as minor attractions. The centrality of pro-am competition in the United States enables any well-mannered, well-dressed dance teacher with even mediocre dance training to make a living selling its Glamour. Thus, European dancers flock to the United States in search of a better life in the land where DanceSport is more than merely an art or a sport—it is a business. Though teachers may experience pleasure dancing with students and pride in their progress, the benefits they gain from the relationship are primarily financial. Some pro-am teachers are able to foster an atmosphere in which their students are more focused on a relationship with dancing than with their teacher, while others end up in relationships that feel more like escort services. Pro-am students fill up the majority of teachers' schedules (and consequently pay their salaries), and their entry fees bankroll the competition itself. Cultivating many active pro-am students is a wise political move for a professional. Drawing so much cash to the competition increases a teacher's standing in the industry and can potentially influence judges' opinions even in professional events, since most judges are also competition organizers.

The pro-am system is one that is so profitable for the teacher and so addictive for the student (it's a whole lot easier to pay for a partner who is already a great dancer than to negotiate a partnership with another novice) that it remains the driving force of the American DanceSport industry.[10] Pro-am competition was, in fact, chosen for the format of two reality television programs in 2005. In ABC TV's *Dancing with the Stars,* celebrities are paired up with DanceSport champions, and TLC's *Ballroom Bootcamp* features "average Joes and Janes" (people with no dance training or celebrity status) partnered by professional dancers. Although neither show accurately reproduces the ordinary studio pro-am relationship (since it is the network and not the amateur student paying the professional's salary), these hit television shows demonstrate how central pro-am DanceSport competition is to the Glamour Machine as it mobilizes to conquer an expanding public market.

Pro-am is not unique to DanceSport. Both tennis and golf have well-established pro-am traditions in which high-profile professionals are paired with amateurs willing to pay hefty fees (commonly several thousand dollars) for the privilege of holding their own racquets and clubs next to those of the stars. As in DanceSport, these pro-am relationships are often built on inequality and difference. Amateurs are generally successful businessmen with connections that could lead to profitable deals or sponsorship for the pros, while the professionals have the physical prowess and fame that amateurs covet. The sports writer John Feinstein, describing how pro-am golf can benefit the professionals financially when they cultivate friendships with the amateur players, concedes that nonetheless, "under any circumstances, pro-ams are work for the pros. For the money they pay, amateurs rightfully expect the pros to be friendly and attentive."[11] DanceSport professionals are likewise expected to be cheerful and supportive in the presence of their amateur students, but DanceSport pros face additional burdens. Pro-am DanceSport partnerships are long-term relationships in which the professional coaches the amateur for months and often years before the competition, rather than the single-shot pairing common in golf or tennis. Secondly, whereas golf or tennis pro-ams are generally all-male events, DanceSport pro-ams are mixed-sex partnerships that require intimate physical contact. The ongoing strain of such sexually charged business relationships results in a much greater drain on DanceSport professionals than pros in other sports experience.

I am not suggesting that those who participate in pro-am competition are innocent dupes. On the contrary, people who choose to use this system for temporary satisfaction of their needs have actually figured out how to make the perverse system work for their benefit. In her chilling analysis of the relationship between cultural representation of corporeality and the material experiences of specific individual and collective bodies in American society, Susan Bordo describes how what may appear to be grotesque behavior is a logical response to an illogical system. Bordo argues that the prevalence of unrealistically thin, taut, white, and beautiful female body images in American society results in women's obsession with body-altering practices such as dieting, plastic surgery, and hair straightening. Instead of viewing these women as unenlightened victims of the system, she maintains that they have, in fact, interpreted quite accurately the rules by which women are rewarded in society. She suggests that those who wish to broaden the range of culturally acceptable body types for women should turn their focus away from the women, who are simply playing out a logical conclusion to conflicting messages about women's bodies, and turn their critical attention instead to the cultural system itself.[12]

Bordo's most extreme example, that of women who so internalize conflicting cultural codes about female corporeality that they become anorexic, provides the most compelling illustration of this point. It is not merely the cultural prescription to be thin that these women internalize, but a conflicting cultural message that women who want to enter public space must adopt codes of masculinity without losing their femininity. Bordo points out that masculinity and femininity have been historically defined as mutually exclusive. The anorexic has figured out how to unite these two polarities on one body. Through analysis of social codes and images, Bordo identifies the social construct of "femininity" as a complete repression of female hunger (both literally and figuratively), a denial of one's own needs in the service of others. She likewise ascertains that "masculinity" has traditionally been defined as active self-control. Anorexics, she suggests, are able to exercise complete control over their bodies and thus enter the masculine sphere without violating the codes of femininity, which require women to deny their own needs. These women are not the ones whose behavior is illogical. They are actually embodying the logical conclusion to an illogical cultural system.[13]

Likewise, women who purchase Glamour in the DanceSport industry are able to display certain qualities traditionally associated with masculinity—athleticism, physical strength, public display of skill—without giving up white American conceptions of beauty and femininity. Many independent, smart, and assertive women are drawn to ballroom dancing not, according to Bordo's logic, because they are being duped by the system, nor because they think their performance of femininity in this realm is inconsequential. It is precisely because they know how much it matters that they inhabit a "feminine" body in order to be rewarded in this culture. Furthermore, DanceSport offers lessons in a physical technique that promises closer and closer mastery of "femininity" and, by extension, the feminine ideal circulated in popular iconography. Bodily preparations for a DanceSport competition are equivalent to those other women undertake for their prom or their wedding. These once-in-a-lifetime public performances of exaggerated femininity promise transformation through public display of physical mastery over bodily codes of gendered identity. In her ethnographic study of the cultural significance of proms, Amy Best points out that the prom is represented as "a privileged space in which bodies are magically reworked and identities completely refashioned."[14] Although these one-time events acquire such importance precisely because they take place only once, the DanceSport competition's power to transform is in repetition. The competition replays itself over and over again every week, each iteration providing an opportunity for the woman to revise her last performance, improving upon the hair, the dress, the nails, the skin, the jewelry, the smile, the gestures, and the dancing.

Although Glamour depends on a fantasy of transcending all that is ugly and grotesque, it actually relies on a union of opposites—ugliness and beauty, lower class and upper class, tawdry and classy. The pro-am relationship offers one of the most poignant examples of the intertwining of the Glamorous and the grotesque in DanceSport. When I describe the female pro-am ballroom dancer as grotesque, I do not intend this as insult. Following Mary Russo in her book *The Female Grotesque* and the dance scholar Ann Cooper Albright in *Choreographing Difference,* I recover the term as one of progressive feminist energy. Russo and Albright's theories of the female grotesque build on two major bodies of scholarship—one associated with Bakhtin's carnivalesque and the other with psychoanalytic writing on the uncanny.[15] Though they differ in their focus on the social versus the psychological, both approaches to the grotesque center on the body as a site of transgression. The grotesque body exceeds normative expectations, bulging, protruding, and excreting beyond its own limits. Scholars of the grotesque commonly find joyful generative power in the ambivalent, unfinished state of the grotesque. In other words, the impossibility of containing or even completely knowing the bounds of grotesque excess leave it open to positive as well as negative exaggeration and proliferation. The grotesque can be an agent of individual and social change. Russo's specific analysis of the female grotesque attempts to expand social expectations for women in the public sphere by celebrating those bodies that have been labeled "mutant" or "freak." In reclaiming grotesque as a positive, progressive, female identity, Russo proposes to expose how gender and identity are commonly constructed and to imagine new possibilities for their reconstruction. Albright likewise invokes the grotesque in her scholarship on disabled dancers. By refusing to read dancers who are bound to wheelchairs against the aesthetic standards established for the "classical" body, she suggests that the grotesque disabled dancing body may actually expand how all of us understand and accept bodily difference. In a similar spirit, I hope that by calling attention to the ways in which the female pro-am dancer is typecast as grotesque, I can diffuse the negative power of this interpretation.

Many pro-am women, who are considered by most American standards too old, too fat, or too ugly to be drawing the kind of attention to their bodies that their costumes and movements demand, might be considered grotesque from many frames of reference. They might be condemned for, in the words of Mary Russo, "making a spectacle" out of themselves. Russo explains that such an accusation implies that they "had done something wrong, had stepped, as it were, into the limelight out of turn—too young or too old, too early or too late—and yet anyone, any *woman,* could make a spectacle out of herself if she was not careful."[16] Once inside the ballroom, however, such excess is no longer grotesque. All women, no matter their age or shape, have equal right to center stage in DanceSport. While there is a willing suspension of "normal" standards in order to increase profits (pro-am women pay to be treated as beautiful and sexy), there is simultaneously a validation of older women's right to the spotlight. Where else in American society do women have the option of only competing against those in their own age category for recognition of their beauty and sexual desirability? Dressing older women in costumes intended to showcase the physical attributes of twenty-year-olds can be read as a reflection of a culture in which beauty and sex appeal are overvalued for women, but the older women who participate in this system are not merely its victims. Recognizing that they live in such a culture, they choose to enter into a space in which their physical beauty is validated.

By turning the critique onto the cultural system that creates the grotesque spectacle, I hope to reveal that the pro-am women are hardly the only aberrant, freakish, or monstrous elements in DanceSport. In fact, the grotesqueness of the pro-am student is so closely linked to the Glamour of the professional dancer that the two quickly become conflated. Russo writes, "The proximity of female grotesques to their attractive counterparts has a long history in the typology of Western art and theatre, especially comedy, in which the whorish matron, the crone, the ugly stepsisters, and the nurse are brought onstage for comparison and then dismissed."[17] Likewise, it is the female pro-am presence at a competition that enables, in economic terms, the Glamorous professional female partner to appear later in the evening session. The professional female dancer seems to be everything the amateur woman is not: young, thin, beautiful, and sexy. Nevertheless, the pro-am woman also represents that which the younger woman is not—financially independent. It is not just the physical comparison that enables the professional women to be Glamorous; it is the desire of the pro-am woman to become what her professional counterpart represents and vice versa that enables either to be at all. The grotesque and the Glamorous are dependent upon each other for survival. Beyond mutual dependence, the pro-am and professional dancers flip-flop their grotesque and Glamorous roles. The pro-am woman puts on her costume and makeup under the ballroom lights and becomes Glamorous. The professional woman sells her body for competition with a pro-am man and she becomes part of the grotesque spectacle. Each is actually a constituent part of the other—the grotesque is embedded within the Glamorous, and the Glamorous is necessary for the grotesque.

Russo writes specifically about the female grotesque, fleshing out specifics of gender glossed over by other theorists. I have used female pro-am dancers in this example because they greatly outnumber male pro-am students, but also because the analysis does not work quite the same way for men. The man's job in the dancing is not to draw attention to himself but rather to showcase his partner. Even the older male pro-am dancer is making a grotesque spectacle not so much of himself as of his partner. So although men are complicit in the performance of grotesque, a male body never becomes the site of its condensation. Such an inequity offers yet another illustration of how DanceSport reflects and magnifies the very gender disparities its participants may wish to escape.

The duality of Glamorous and grotesque is only one example of how the Glamour Machine relies on the symbiosis of opposites. Applying Bahktin's theories on carnival and the grotesque to a variety of social phenomena, Peter Stallybrass and Allon White demonstrate that high and low culture are constitutive of each other, the high always invoking and defining the low in order to establish its own superiority. Thus, the high already contains the low within it, a disenfranchised part of itself that, because sublimated, is particularly prone to reappearance. Application of their theory to DanceSport further reveals how the Glamour Machine draws together such disparate elements from both high and low culture. The classiness (and whiteness) projected by DanceSport defines and contains lower-class (and nonwhite) cultural references. No longer is upper-class courtship constrained by the subtle and refined movement that has traditionally defined it, nor is lower-class revelry as exemplified by wild physical antics destined to remain tawdry and classless. Augmented by lavish costumes, decadent ballrooms, and chivalrous manners, the activity projects an image of abundant wealth and upper-class status. However, the eclectic images gathered together under the pretense of Glamour (gaudy costumes, ostentatious colors, overstated makeup, movement that is both refined and excessively expressive) actually come from disparate class backgrounds. For example, the white tie and tails worn by men in the standard division is modeled after Western upper-class finery, but the Las Vegas–style excessiveness of the jewels on the dresses with which it is paired is more similar to lower-class tastes. Nodding back to the Ziegfeld Girls of the early twentieth century, who negotiated high- and low-class sexual mores by devising a space in which the two could coexist, Glamour continues to enable the union of elements from both ends of the spectrum, promising transformation for anyone or anything that enters the system.

GLAMOUR FACTORIES

Although competition is its most condensed exhibition, Glamour must first be primed at dance studios, where its manufacture is almost as ritualized and predictable as the competitions themselves. In studios across America, DanceSport professionals spend two to four hours a day rehearsing their competitive choreography and another six to ten hours initiating new converts and re-enrolling established students. On a typical weekday morning at an independent studio in southern California, one of the teachers is walking arm in arm with his student, a seventy-two-year-old great-grandmother.[18] This is the start of their daily three-hour lesson, which she takes just before going to the stables to attend to her horses. A twenty-nine-year-old computer engineer has taken his lunch hour early so that he can come in and practice his cruzado walks alone in front of a mirror. A top-ranked professional couple is bickering in Russian as they stop at every few steps of what to even the most critical eye approaches one of the most stunning foxtrots worldwide.

A young female teacher softens her face as she broadens it into a warm smile to greet her new student walking in the door. She guides him past the commotion on the main dance floor so that they can talk intimately at one of the tables along the side of the room. Hesitantly, he explains that he started dating a girl who is a great dancer and he wants to be able to impress her. With unwavering conviction, she assures him how easy it will be to master the basics before coaxing him to step onto the dance floor. He seems slightly overwhelmed by the activity around him, but she builds an invisible wall around them as she soothes him with her nursery-school-teacher voice and a gentle squeeze of his arm. She gently places her hands on his hips to relax them and guides his palm to her back, quickly breaking down the usual boundaries of personal space. Gradually his limbs start to cooperate, and his body begins to follow hers as they march in time to the rhythm of the music. Her momentary excitement is genuine as he finally masters these basic movements and they gloat together in his first victory. What has always seemed incomprehensible and mysterious to him, the ability to move to the music with another person, has been explained in such simple terms (and with such expert backleading) that for a moment he feels like Fred Astaire. She shares in his euphoria, not only because as his teacher she experiences vicariously the thrill of first discovering dance, but because she knows he will not be able to reproduce this illusion at home and will have to come back again for more of this intoxication.

The power a ballroom dance teacher acquires over his or her students through the intimacy of private lessons can be astounding. All business plans are structured around its potency. Studios operating under the successful model developed by Arthur Murray advertise a free or drastically reduced introductory special, which always includes a private lesson. It is during this first lesson that the foundation for Glamour seduction is set. Students succumb to the pleasure of being gently touched and coaxed by attractive and charming teachers whose appearance and manners are as carefully constructed as the lesson plans. American ballroom teachers rarely use the stereotypical ballet sergeant's strict pedagogical model, at least not on beginning students. Patient repetition and intense personal attention sell dance lessons. No student realizes his or her own ineptitude for dancing in a private lesson, unable to fall behind the other students in a class of one. Single students staring into their teachers' eyes often mistake love of dancing for a nascent love affair, forgetting that their teachers are being paid to treat them with such fondness. Couples taking a joint private lesson are less likely to consciously fantasize about a relationship with the teacher, but they may become equally entranced by new possibilities of romantic interaction within their own relationship, associating their renewed enchantment with their dancing instructor. With a moderator present to thwart any disagreements, gender roles are so simply delineated that most couples are eager to return for more of this fairy-tale romance. Students are not necessarily ignorant of the contestatory realities this romanticized image covers over. But much like the visitor to Disney World, who simultaneously does and doesn't believe in magic, they consent to be fooled by the mechanisms of Glamour in order to enjoy the temporary escapism it offers.

The classic studio model for recruiting new clientele includes an evaluation of each student at the conclusion of the first private lesson and then a dance course recommendation. Prices are revealed only after the student is giddy from his or her first dose of Glamour. Unlike a ballet school audition, in which only the gifted few are selected for admission, these evaluations offer every student the hope of future success. Each potential student is assured of his or her natural ability and promised that apparent deficiencies can be corrected through proper training.[19] Most dance courses include some combination of group classes, private lessons, and studio practice parties. Each of these elements has proven essential for studio success. Parties foster social interaction and build a sense of community and loyalty to the school. Group classes do the same, but, more important, they serve to inflate the number of teaching hours each course includes. Because adding one more student to a group class costs the studio nothing, buffering a course with group classes makes its value appear greater to the student without incurring additional cost for the studio. Private lessons, however, are the core of the ballroom dance business, not just as high-market items, but because they are vital for indoctrinating students into their position in the Glamour Machine.

Any teacher's power over a student can be considerable, but the careful balance between intimacy and distance ballroom dance teachers maintain in private lessons enables them to manipulate students' choices with surprising ease. Students quickly become susceptible to suggestions by their teachers that only a few weeks or months before seemed absurd—buying more expensive dance courses, entering competitions, paying for special choreography or a showcase routine. Tom Chapman, the founder of TC Dance Club International, writes in his irreverent manual/memoir about dance studio management, "If you told a new prospect there was a fifty-fifty chance they would soon invest a thousand dollars or more, they'd laugh at you. If you told them there was also a chance they would spend upwards of five thousand, they'd call the cops. That they haven't already done so is a tribute to our care in presenting programs."[20] I suggest that "care in presenting programs" is a euphemism for skill in emotional manipulation of their consumers. Ballroom dance teachers employed in the American studio system are trained first and foremost in sales; skill in dancing or teaching is sometimes little more than an afterthought. Teachers are specifically trained in seeking out the greatest emotional need for each student. Once identified, each student's program is tailored to meet, or at least to appear to meet, that emotional void. Students who are lonely are showered with warm affection by the staff; students who seek public recognition for achievement are taken to competitions in which they are assured of victory; and students who are looking for love may be persuaded that finesse on the dance floor is the quickest way to amorous conquest.[21]

Once students have been ensnared by this emotional hook, the studio uses a variety of tactics to squeeze their wallets dry. Almost all chain studios require students to sign contracts committing to a specific number of lessons and a payment plan in exchange for the studio's guarantee to teach a certain skill set. For example, a student might sign a bronze contract of one hundred lessons, which stipulates that the student will have mastered the bronze syllabus at its conclusion. Even after laying down several thousand dollars, students may be approached only a few weeks later for another course because their current contract does not include a showcase routine or competition preparation. The studio will argue that if the student diverts from the mutually agreed upon course plan, the studio guarantee that bronze-level competency be achieved by its completion would be void. Thus, students may be pressured into paying for a competition or showcase lessons in addition to their regular classes. These studios usually have a "closer" who goes over the finer points of contracts, keeping the student's relationship with their teacher removed at least one degree from the uncomfortable discussion of money. Such a separation of the economic exchange from the individual whose services are being purchased further intensifies the illusion of intimacy. At other studios, teachers are expected to be financial advisors to their clients. One employee revealed that management actually sent the teachers to seminars in home finance in order to be better prepared to explain how to take out a second home mortgage in order to finance expensive dance courses or trips. Not all studios practice such tactics, and indeed many of the more extreme sales procedures have been curtailed as the result of lawsuits and legislation. Some of the more egregious examples of avarice, such as selling multiple lifetime contracts to octogenarians, have been outlawed by the Federal Trade Commission. However, the uniform format of private lessons continues, empowering teachers with astonishing influence over their students' spending.[22]

Almost all students expect a combination of three elements during a dance class: acquisition of new skills, enjoyment of movement, and social interaction.[23] A successful dance teacher can determine what percentage of each the student expects to receive. If the students are engaged in regular practice with a partner, private lessons are utilized primarily for teaching new skills and affirming those already acquired. One challenge (not specific to ballroom dance teachers) is balancing class time spent on giving out new information and that spent reinforcing and assimilating that knowledge through practice. Too much instruction and the students never get to enjoy the movement itself; too little new information and the students are bored and frustrated with their progress. But the unique job of the ballroom teacher is to balance the kind and amount of social interaction between instructor and student. In group classes, the social interaction can be fostered primarily among students. In private lessons, however, almost all the social interaction is between teacher and student. This interaction varies from casual, friendly, or nurturing to intimate, sensual, or sexual. Beyond their desire for a personal connection, students are invested in a relationship with the teacher as a symbol of Glamour. It is not merely sex or companionship that the students desire, but the cache of being associated with the dance teacher, who functions for them as a source of Glamour.

The personal relationships male teachers develop with their clients tend to be under the guise of "friendship" or mother-son bonds rather than overtly sexual ones. In Florida in particular, where there is a large population of older retired women, dance escorting is big business. One Fred Astaire employee in Boca Raton recounted how he and several other teachers went to Europe for a week, each one escorting an elderly woman who paid $20,000 for the privilege of having a young, well-mannered man by her side. Each teacher earned $1,000 in exchange for being arm in arm with his charge from 7:00 A.M. until 11:00 P.M. for the length of the trip (the rest of the fees split between studio profit and travel expense). Such trips usually include some social dancing, although dance teachers primarily supply companionship off the dance floor rather than guidance on it. While such a trip is hard work for the male dance teacher, who must pretend to be invested in the social relationship he has with his student in order to sustain her fantasy, he rarely has to endure the kind of sexual harassment that is standard for the female dance teacher.

Single adult men attracted to ballroom were often lonely (maybe recently divorced) or socially awkward before their experience with ballroom dancing. Most start dance lessons hoping that they will meet a woman. Unlike the married women whose husbands are willing to pay for their wives' dance lessons as a necessary entertainment expense, very few men who take private singles dance lessons are married. If they are married, they typically take lessons with their wives or extra lessons by themselves in addition to the time they spend dancing with their spouses. Single male students often get hooked by the pleasure of successfully interacting with a woman on such intimate terms. Male students who spend large sums of money for one-on-one time with a young, beautiful woman are rarely content to stay within the realm of fantasy. Many male students fully expect that their investment will pay off and they will date or have sex with their dance teachers. The female dance teacher must more often sustain the fantasy that she will eventually date her student than merely that she is his friend and confidante. Male dance teachers may also have to sustain the fantasy that they too will one day sleep with their students. In fact, some male teachers regularly do sleep with their students, sustaining for each a fantasy that she is his only lover.

Gender differences in courtship, however, lead to very different kinds of burdens for male and female dance teachers. Since men traditionally play a more aggressive role in courtship than women, male dance teachers can control romantic fantasies by the kinds of actions they initiate, allowing them to feel a relatively greater sense of control. If a male dance teacher doesn't make a move on his female student, she might continue her romantic fantasy privately for years without taking any outward actions to consummate it. Female dance teachers, however, are subject to a continual barrage of verbal and physical passes from their male students, which they must neatly ward off without being too discouraging. A male student calls his teacher every day. "Thank you for last night," he coos into the phone, twisting the previous evening's dance lesson into a secret romantic tryst. He stretches out his slobbery wet kiss, the standard greeting of good manners and European taste, into a stolen moment of sexual bliss. Is this or is this not part of her job? She loses track. The strain is the duplicity of the job, knowing that he thinks their relationship is built on mutual friendship and love, not on his financial support of her own Glamour addiction. Her vulnerability is often compounded by her own loneliness. Always teaching nights and weekends, dance teachers have little opportunity to meet potential mates outside the workplace. Many fall into relationships of convenience with other dancers after discovering that nondancers can rarely contain their jealousy of a woman's passion for dance. What man could a dancer expect to wait at home for her while she was out spinning and dipping in lustful heat with other men, knowing that he was not man enough for her on the dance floor?

Female professionals are engaged in continual negotiation with their students and themselves as to how much harassment they will tolerate. Most female teachers have at least once cut off a profitable male client who was too sexually aggressive. They feel brief empowerment in adhering to some (if inconsistent) ethical standards, hoping such actions separate them from prostitutes. The comparison of dance teachers to prostitutes is not a uniquely American phenomenon. A Chinese ballroom dance film, *Dance of a Dream,* features a scene in which a successful female executive hires a male dance teacher to perform with her at a gala. A guest at the banquet comments, "Is she paying him? Isn't that a gigolo?" Her companion replies, "It's different. This one is cheaper."[24] This dialogue exposes the deep investment ballroom dancers have in drawing a clear line between selling one's body for sex and selling it for dancing. The joke is poignant because the fear that pro-am dancing is prostitution is allayed in the definitive assertion that "it's different." The momentary comfort is immediately undermined with the clarification that the difference is only one of price, the dancer's lower price inverting the expected social order. The exchange reveals three points of view that are held in constant tension: ballroom dance teachers are no different from prostitutes; ballroom dancers are categorically different from (i.e., have a higher status than) prostitutes; and ballroom dancers are lower than prostitutes (who at least have the wisdom to charge a high price for their services). Although most ballroom dancers attempt to maintain the position that a comparison of their jobs to those of prostitutes is ungrounded, the tripartite interpretation continues to haunt them.

Touch, one of the primary mechanisms through which the power of Glamour is established, appears to be very intimate, especially the kind of touch practiced between ballroom dance teachers and students.[25] And yet for professional dance teachers, who press their own bodies up against those of their students all day long, such seemingly intimate and personal touch tends to lead to a separation of emotions from the physical gestures to which they are generally attached. A caress becomes merely a mechanized action of the hand rather than an act of personal connection. The practice of teaching often desensitizes professionals to the very pleasures they initially experienced through the intimacy of partner dancing. In the early stages of learning partner dancing, physical pleasure (romantic or otherwise) usually intensifies as skills are perfected. But there is a point after which increased skill does yield increased pleasure. In order to keep its adherents active after they cross this threshold, the Glamour Machine shifts their focus from experiential physical pleasure during dancing to desire for its perfected representation in performance. Since DanceSport is often represented as the superlative expression of social ballroom dance, which is itself a romanticized expression of courtship, the logic implies that one would feel the thrill of intimacy at its most heightened during competition. Therefore, the Glamour Machine substitutes the pleasure people once felt in their own spontaneous social exchanges for a spectacularization of intimacy in competition performance. Dance professionals become the focal point of desire for others' fantasies, and an obsession with perfecting the competition performance becomes the fixation of the professional dancers themselves. Neither representing the pleasure to others nor chasing the idealization of its theatrical representation leads to a recovery of the excitement that initially seduced each Glamour addict.

For the student, however, there may be little separation between the physical intimacy experienced in the dance lesson and a sense of emotional intimacy. The system relies on students' continual misinterpretation of a teacher's touch, imbuing it with an emotional significance that the teacher doesn't intend and generating personal attachment on the part of the student that the teacher rarely reciprocates. Some students may be genuinely confused by the casualness with which touch occurs during lessons and assume that the privilege of touching others extends to social situations as well.

Despite the amount of time he or she spends in physical contact with other bodies, the life of a professional ballroom dancer can be extremely lonely. Real friendships with students are nearly impossible to establish. Chain studios forbid fraternization between students and teachers, fully aware that if students are permitted to spend time with the teachers for free, they are less likely to pay exorbitant rates for their company during lessons, competitions, and studio outings. Even independent teachers know that their value is much greater than the sum of their knowledge in dance technique. As symbols of Glamour to their

Rhythm competitors Tony Dovolani and Inna Ivanenko in a passionate embrace that displays the elegant, long arch of her body. Embassy Ball, Irvine, California, September 2005. Photo © 2005 by Jonathan S. Marion.

students, DanceSport teachers are critically aware of the necessity for disguising the ordinary and onerous in their own lives. As the cultural critic Virginia Postrel so clearly articulated:

> To portray a world without tradeoffs or compromises, glamour may sometimes demand opulence or aesthetic excess, but it always requires meticulous selection and control. The creator must edit out discordant details that could break the spell—blemishes on the skin, spots on the window, electrical wires crossing the façade, piles of bills on the kitchen counter. . . . If all this sounds like selling and manipulation, it is. Glamour is deceptive. It hides the textures of life, and the skill and effort behind its own achievement.[26]

Teachers cannot openly confide in their students through honest conversation because they would undermine their own business by failing to maintain the illusion that Glamour inoculates its inductees from tedium and strife.

Although DanceSport professionals commiserate with other professionals in a candid manner impossible around students, meaningful relationships with other competitors are likewise difficult to sustain owing to the jealousy and backbiting endemic in the industry. Every competitor is fighting to make it to the top of the competition ladder. But spots close to the top are scarce, and one competitor's success depends on another's failure. Given the opportunity to help one's own career at the expense of a friend's, almost any DanceSport competitor will ignore bonds of trust and friendship. Nor can DanceSport competitors be friends with judges or coaches, who are trapped in their own roles in the Glamour web, dependent on maintaining for the professional competitors (who are their clients) a similar illusion of privileged access to the nucleus of Glamour. Furthermore, the judges are expected not to fraternize with competitors at a competition, since such associations could lead to accusations of favoritism in judging. The isolation of the DanceSport competitor often leads beyond simple loneliness to a battered sense of self as he or she struggles to survive in such a competitive environment with virtually no sympathetic support network.

Another powerful tool of the Glamour Machine is denial of the negative through a reconceptualization of every situation in positive terms. The absurdity of this mandate was captured in the film *Strictly Ballroom,* in which the hero's mother is frequently pictured screaming hysterically in the back room of the studio. She then declares she must "put on her happy face" and emerges to teach class, veins popping out of her neck from the strain of her clenched smile. Glamour requires that no problem, pain, or unpleasantness ever be publicly admitted. Participants may not believe such a utopia actually exists, but they find such a strategy of escapism useful. For example, when the air conditioning broke one summer day at a Florida studio, the oppressive heat made the studio almost unbearable for even moderate physical activity. When the students complained, one teacher cheerfully boasted, "I love this temperature, it's a great temperature." "They taught us to say that at Fred Astaire," he added unapologetically. He was proud of his own ability to reframe a situation he could not control. Although the unceasing cheerfulness that characterizes public interactions in the ballroom industry is useful for creating the romantic escapism that attracts new inductees, those who live too long in the world of Glamour may lose their own sense of agency to inspire change.

Such a practice of reinterpreting every negative as a positive can encourage people to deny their own political power, sustaining existing structures of inequality.[27] Creating this fairy-tale world where there is no public pain requires that its workforce cover up and deny evidence contradicting the facade. The magic of DanceSport is similar to that produced by Disney World, where the corporation conceals illness, crime, accidents, and poor working conditions to produce the illusion of the "happiest place on earth."[28] Likewise in DanceSport, Glamorous bodies produce themselves as such by disguising and denying the negative. It is partially out of a need to convince themselves that their lives are not so bad that many DanceSport professionals will avoid discussing the bleakness of their situation. But it is also because they know that appearing to have a highly desirable, Glamorous life is necessary for their economic survival.

THE MAGIC SYSTEM

In many ways, the Glamour Machine functions similarly to the modern advertising industry, which creates associations between consumer products and unrelated human needs. The cultural studies theorist Raymond Williams has described the advertising industry as a "magic system" whereby these false connections between the products and their promised effects obscure the fact that real human needs, those promised by advertising, are still unmet by current social structures. Instead, we continue to be seduced by the illusion that consumerism will succeed where other means of satisfaction have failed:

> If the consumption of individual goods leaves that whole area of human need unsatisfied, the attempt is made, by magic, to associate this consumption with human desires to which it has no real reference. You do not only buy an object: you buy social respect, discrimination, health, beauty, success, power to control your environment. The magic obscures the real sources of general satisfaction because their discovery would involve radical change in the whole common way of life. Of course, when a magical pattern has become established in a society it is capable of some real if limited success. Many people will indeed look twice at you, upgrade you, upmarket you, respond to your displayed signals, if you have made the right purchases within a system of meanings to which you are all trained. Thus the fantasy seems to be validated, at a personal level, but only at the cost of preserving the general unreality

which it obscures: the real failures of the society which however are not easily traced to this pattern.[29]

The ballroom industry, as part of the capitalist economy and consumer culture, is also implicated in the magic system. Glamour is a commodity. The products that are sold as expressions of Glamour include dance lessons, clothing, costumes, shoes, hairstyles, makeup, competitions, social dances, music, videos, dance manuals, and magazines. Each of these items promises to transform the consumer's body into a Glamorous body (through actual DanceSport technique or through codes of grooming and dress associated with it) and/or assures time spent with Glamorous DanceSport celebrities. Through the magic enacted by the Glamour Machine, these commodities are aligned with eternal youth, beauty, sexual desirability, romance, social acceptability, success, wealth, classiness, and passion. Dance lessons and other products of the Glamour Machine appear to solve a multitude of problems, including loneliness, social ineptitude, unattractiveness, and the effects of age. They also promise fame, upward class mobility, and escape from the drudgeries of ordinary life. Williams warns that the magic system works, at least temporarily, if everyone is similarly trained to recognize its referents. Corporeal mastery of ballroom technique does increase one's social position in the ballroom. Students generally feel loved, suave, handsome, and young as long as they stay inside the ballroom industry's social networks. Successful DanceSport competitors become celebrities, the envy of everyone in the industry. These illusions cannot survive outside the dance studio, however, and the students become addicted to the fantasy within it. What is accomplished through the sale of dance lessons is not a solution to the students' problems but an obstruction of them. The Glamour Machine obscures the failure of society to provide, for example, adequate physical and emotional intimacy in an increasingly isolationist culture.

But if DanceSport appears to offer a solution to some of consumer culture's flaws, it has also folded these solutions back into the capitalist system itself, offering intimacy as a form of commodity that only sustains further inequality. The visual studies scholar Stuart Ewen proposes a theory that further elucidates why DanceSport Glamour is a particularly effective capitalist commodity. Style, as Ewen defines it, is the marketing of visual images (in print, television, film, malls, etc.) that, once detached from the materiality of their sources, become symbols for a way of life, usually one that is unattainable for most of its consumers. In his classic work, *All Consuming Images,* Ewen traces the development of style and its conspicuous consumption, demonstrating how the increasing separation between visual images and what they represent has led to the mass production and proliferation of images whose promise of pleasure is a sham, completely divorced from the reality of actual experience. According to Ewen, an image can be marketed as style if it is (a) separable from its source, (b) mass producible, and (c) capable of becoming merchandise.[30] DanceSport Glamour, which is successfully marketed as a lifestyle by a number of conspiring images, fails to meet each of these criteria at certain points. Ironically, it is precisely because of this failure that DanceSport succeeds so powerfully as a commodity.

The style sold in DanceSport is not entirely separable from the bodies that sell it, bodies that are at once the marketed images and their material source. Because style in DanceSport is still largely dependent on the presence of its celebrity bodies—the DanceSport professionals whose bodies must appear on the competition floors and in dance studios across America—DanceSport continually reenacts its own failure at mass marketability and entry into mainstream American culture. Those attempting to drastically increase the number of DanceSport's consumers are thwarted by the limited reproducibility of its primary commodity: one-on-one personal interaction. Simple economic motivation drives most studio owners and teachers to strive to expand their markets. Because finding a suitable dance partner is one of the most persistent sources of aggravation for all ballroom dancers, most practitioners display proselytizing zeal in their recruitment efforts in hopes of increasing the pool of potential partners.

No one in the ballroom industry is exempt from the effects of this magic system, especially the Glamorous professionals who are its sorcerers. Sarah Thornton notes a similar phenomenon with club owners in her analysis of rave culture when she writes that "those in the business of creating the night-time fantasy world often become their own worst victims."[31] DanceSport professionals are often more fully seduced by the promises of Glamour than their students. Knowing how to work this sorcery does not inoculate teachers from its effects. All it takes is a few minutes in the arms of a dancer who is more skilled than they, and ballroom dance teachers themselves will buy lessons they can't afford to sustain their own fantasies of becoming DanceSport superstars. Professional competitors often spend $30,000 a year on coaching, costumes, and travel in hopes of improving their competition ranking and moving up on the Glamour scale. Much like movie stars and pop icons, who do not generally enjoy power commensurate with their wealth, DanceSport celebrities are not actually any closer than their admirers to the power they represent.[32] Unlike celebrities who have amassed enormous financial wealth as a result of their fame, DanceSport celebrities usually have far fewer economic resources than their fans. Although abundant wealth is certainly a part of the image portrayed by DanceSport, its champions are often completely devoid of any material wealth, having spent every penny in pursuit of their titles.

Rewards for the perfect embodiment of Glamorous technique rarely provide professional competitors with a more lasting transformation than that experienced by their students. Many DanceSport professionals are lured into the Glamour Machine by a promise of upward class mobility. On their way up the competition system, professional competitors master marketing and sales strategies that gross substantial profits, putting them in possession of economic capital previously out of their grasp. In turn, DanceSport professionals learn how to spend their new capital in ways that signify expensive taste—designer clothes, luxury cars, gourmet meals—in an attempt to prove their command of cultural capital as well. So although the promise of class transformation lures many professional dancers into the circuit, economic capital is rarely enough to change one's social status. The conspicuous consumption required to sustain the image of class transformation keeps DanceSport competitors from amassing significant economic capital. Although DanceSport professionals may earn impressive incomes compared to their friends or family, they usually spend more money than they earn in order to produce an image of success. Furthermore, DanceSport stardom is hardly the road to an economic windfall. There is no mass consumption of DanceSport, no large economic base from which to support an elite minority as in sports or mass entertainment. Although there may be a handful of competition organizers and coaches who earn over $250,000 a year, a more typical yearly income for a DanceSport professional is $40,000.

After paying for their requisite conspicuous consumption of designer goods, DanceSport professionals reinvest their income back into the Glamour system. In fact, most do without basic safety nets, forgoing health and disability insurance or retirement savings in favor of more coaching lessons. Additional investment in Glamour does not necessarily net one more economic capital. Though it is true that top-ranked competitors can command a higher fee for coaching or for shows and may attract more wealthy pro-am students, the ability to translate competition success into financial rewards is more closely linked to skills in self-promotion than it is to competition placement. Glamour capital does not always lead to economic success, but it does buy respect, admiration, envy, and notoriety within the ballroom dance community. Perhaps because competitors cannot completely transcend their social class status outside the ballroom, or maybe because their total immersion in life inside the ballroom has distracted them from pursuit of a life without it, DanceSport competitors are addicted to pursuing social status as DanceSport celebrities. So even though it does not completely transform a dancer's social class status, Glamour offers the individual an opportunity to transcend his or her class outside the ballroom by promising a new social position within it. Codes of beauty, physical carriage, and style rewarded in DanceSport are similar to those of upper-class Western culture, enabling DanceSport celebrities to experience some degree of awe and respect when entering public gatherings outside of DanceSport. However, this promise fails to build other kinds of capital that will sustain the newfound social position once the body fails to properly display the Glamour capital it has acquired.

Retired DanceSport competitors become judges, coaches, and competition organizers and often occupy all three positions simultaneously. Ostensibly at the top of the Glamour chain, judges and coaches are often its worst victims. Their reputation is primarily based on who they *used to be* as Glamorous stars. Their most significant power is now in determining the next Glamorous star. It is not uncommon for (often male) judges to abuse this power to seduce hopeful male and female rising stars in a linking of sexual liaisons to success that resembles similar practices in film or modeling. New career opportunities arise out of sexual liaisons; it is part of the business. Sexual harassment is hardly a viable concept in an industry based on sale of sexualized physical contact. Amongst themselves, the judges are just as competitive with each other for the limited coaching jobs as are the professional competitors for competition ranking. Thus, competitors are wary even of their own coach's advice, since the coach's income is largely dependent on convincing each client that that coach's method of training is superior to every other, regardless of its suitability for the individual student. Without their own Glamorous bodies on the competition floor, judges and coaches find their positions on the scale are even more tenuous and their methods for hanging onto their reputation, at times more nefarious.

Despite the severity of its shortcomings, DanceSport competition offers many real benefits to its participants. These include improved self-confidence through mastery of one's own body, increased physical and social interaction, a forum for personal expression, public recognition for skills and accomplishments, a form of recreation that is not dependent on drugs or alcohol, a chance to face one's own fears about competition and failure, and experience in highly interactive partnerships. Nearly every neophyte coaxed into competition leaves the dance floor intoxicated with the emotional rush that comes from such an intense condensation of physical and emotional exertion. The combination of colors created by the elaborate costumes and lights, the intensity of the music, the sweat of another person in one's arms, the explosive energy of the other competitors on the floor, and the support from a crowd cheering on the sidelines is so seductive that most competitors return for a second chance in the public spotlight. It is dress-up and make-believe playtime for adults, DanceSport's version of the annual dance school recital in which every student gets the opportunity to shine, regardless of talent or skill. Participants may reap enormous psychological benefits from these experiences. However, these joys are dependent on the illusion of Glamour and the structure of competition, which brings with it another set of drawbacks.

Because the ballroom dance industry offers few alternatives to competition for practicing high-level dancing, its proponents are often addicted to competition long after it has stopped bringing them pleasure. There are some competitors for whom winning is not crucial for their enjoyment of DanceSport, but most are so deeply invested in becoming champions that repeated poor results in competition may cause as much emotional and psychological damage as it healed in that first glorious moment on the dance floor. There are many responses to hitting this wall, including changing partners, seeking new coaching, commissioning new costumes, trying new hairstyles, or quitting competition altogether. A competition is, however, designed to determine winners and losers, and the odds are stacked against the former. So although the competition format is what first produces the intoxicating rush of emotional richness, it is also what ultimately tortures many of its addicts. Much like the capitalist system itself, which relies on an unfulfilled desire to consume, the DanceSport industry relies on a ceaseless desire to master one's body, a desire that likewise can never be satiated. Even winning the world championship does not quell the desire because there is always pressure to maintain this ranking longer than the last champion, to stay ahead of the younger, faster, more supple upstarts threatening to take away the champion's title.

Once used primarily to describe dependence on alcohol and drugs, the word addiction is now commonly used to describe repetitive patterns of behavior. People refer to gambling addictions, eating addictions, sex addictions, even shopping addictions.[33] Though not medically defined as addicts of Glamour, Dance-Sport participants exhibit many of the same behavior patterns that identify other addicts. Medical definitions of addiction include four categories of behavioral patterns: progression, preoccupation, perceived loss of control, and negative long-term consequences.[34] Many DanceSport enthusiasts playfully refer to their own participation in dance as an addiction, qualifying this statement by claiming it is a "healthy addiction." They rationalize that the nourishing combination of physical exercise, social interaction, and musical stimulation keeps participants from turning to drugs or alcohol for entertainment. So although they recognize the progression of their obsession with dance, which often leads to preoccupation that drastically changes their other social or occupational behaviors, most DanceSport proponents deny that their addiction has any negative long-term consequences. An addiction to dance may not be physically or psychologically dangerous, but addiction to the Glamour Machine in which it is embedded may be damaging to one's financial security, self-esteem, and social adjustment.[35]

Glamour addiction is hard to break. The problem was succinctly stated by John Travolta's character in *Saturday Night Fever,* the film that ushered in the return to "touch" dancing, when he declared, "I would like to get that high [from dancing] someplace else in my life." The layering of physical, emotional, and creative exertion, condensed into the focal point of desirous gazes, produces such a powerful rush for the dancer that few other experiences can match its intensity. Over and over again competitors declare their retirement, renouncing the sport only to return to the competition floor five months later. The industry offers virtually no preparation to its champions for life after competition. Many spend the rest of their lives searching to discover who they are when not defined by the judges' marks and the cheers of an audience in whose eyes they can see the reflections of the jewels on their costumes. Many a retired competitor imagines staging a comeback, conjuring images of past victory fading from memory. Even those who have recognized the treadmill nature of their pursuit have difficulty quitting. One competitor was remarkably articulate about the futility of her pursuit. She explained how clearly she had felt, dancing with her most recent partner, that the industry was all about ego inflation. "Before you know it you're thirty, and you're old and ugly from all the makeup and tanning cream, and you have no friends or money because you spent all your time and money on dancing," she said. That day she was not looking for a new partner; she was not interested in competing again. But three months later I saw her practicing for competition with a dancer who had likewise declared retirement. "It just feels so good with him," she said with that starry-eyed sense of hope one could easily mistake for love. The loss of daily practice and the intensity of competition can be almost unbearable without a significant substitution to fill the void. Instead, dancers continually convince themselves that with each new partner it will be different, that they have learned from past mistakes, that they can beat the system, that they can do it for the intrinsic joy of dance and not get caught up in the pursuit of victory at all costs. It is a nearly impossible gamble, but one that is difficult to resist.[36]

The inability of dancers to move on after competitive success or failure is due to more than their reluctance to relinquish the limelight. Success as a DanceSport competitor requires almost total commitment to the field. Because of the training and travel requirements of a competitive career, few dancers invest in college or alternative career preparation. Immigrant competitors are often more deeply entrenched than their American colleagues. Many learn English only after they arrive in the United States, their poor language skills putting them at an even greater disadvantage, far less likely than American-born dancers to pursue another profession that would allow them to maintain a similar standard of living. Independent dance teachers are accustomed to setting their own schedules and earning $50 to $70 an hour. The financial rewards of teaching often continue to seduce after the Glamour has worn off. But to maintain a clientele in the Glamorous DanceSport industry requires that the teacher remain Glamorous. Dancers who manage to get some training in another career gradually wean themselves from dancing, often making sporadic comebacks as they struggle to find meaning elsewhere. Women are sometimes able to detach from competition by having children, refocusing their energy on raising a family. Men, who rarely consider parenting an alternative career option, tend to stay in the business longer.

Although I have suggested that the Glamour Machine extracts outrageous costs from its practitioners, even those addicts most attentive to the insidious mechanisms of its operation are loath to give it up. Despite the high price of Glamour, DanceSport offers individuals enormous benefits. Dance teachers and students alike will attest to the confidence they have gained through their experiences in ballroom dancing, its positive effects on their lives rolling off their tongues with sincere rapture and gratitude. It offers a ready-made social community and a welcome escape from the toils of ordinary life. The fantasies of transformation it feeds are not produced by the DanceSport industry but rather stem from much larger social divisions, including those of class, race, gender, sexual orientation, and age. DanceSport offers people a means of coping with existing patriarchal, Eurocentric, and class structures by negotiating them in a system that celebrates artifice, pretense, and dreams. So powerful is Dance-Sport's simultaneous engagement of physical, emotional, and intellectual faculties in an activity that enables momentary fulfillment of countless fantasies that few are willing to trade in their Glamour addiction. Though DanceSport may sustain some of these inequalities, people living with perpetual hope of escape from them may fare better than those who live with no hope at all.

I suspect that the Glamour Machine can be interrupted only through social change instigated at levels beyond the scope of DanceSport practice. Many theorists of culture have identified the postmodern world in which we now live as one in which surface, appearance, and simulacra dominate the landscape. The proliferation and intensification of media images, audio-visual technology, and consumer culture have led to the separation of both language and images from the objects they represent. In the terms of semiotics, the linguistic study of signs, signifiers can no longer be easily mapped to that which they signify. Life must be negotiated in a complex sociocultural system of signs that relate back only to other signs, no object or concept existing outside its relationship to and construction in a social world.[37]

DanceSport is both an illustration of this phenomenon and a reaction to its inadequacies. DanceSport is a laying bare of the "society of spectacle," the term used by the neo-Marxist Guy Debord to describe contemporary life where appearance is all that is of consequence. The tangible world is replaced by spectacle, Debord argues, which gives people the illusion that there is cohesion and community but in fact just reifies isolation.[38] Whether or not the spectacle of thirty men simultaneously seducing thirty women is connected to the actual experience of seduction between these individuals is irrelevant. How good the dancing feels is of no significance to viewers and judges of a competitive performance; appearance is everything. DanceSport, so up front about its celebration of surfaces, calls attention to the disjuncture between appearance and reality through its failure to cover over the growing chasm. The spectacle of Dance-Sport competition may indeed allow some viewers, particularly those watching from a distance, an ironic commentary on just how far the cult of surfaces has gone. And for some DanceSport aficionados, a postmodern sensibility for pastiche just might explain their enthusiasm. Most DanceSport practitioners, however, are gravely serious about their sport, and few read their own practice as an ironic celebration of the contradictions, fissures, and instability of postmodern life.

Instead, DanceSport offers to its affiliates a forum for manipulating these surface signs while simultaneously experiencing something very "real." DanceSport depends on very real-feeling physical, intimate interaction. Even those individuals who have intellectually conceded the impossibility of access to a reality outside its social construction often act in ways that reveal a need for deep emotional and physical sensations. What feels more real than the personal connections fostered through dance? Apart from verbal language, in the language of dance, participants may strive for exchange outside, beyond, or before their entry into the symbolic. I am not suggesting that DanceSport is the answer to postmodern alienation or that its participants have found the hidden fountain of reality. But DanceSport does call attention to a growing problem in American society. The crisis of consumer culture is not merely that it obscures real needs by replacing them with commodities, but that there is a mounting need for the real. Unless we commit more energy to creating space for real-feeling experiences such as those enabled through the artifice of Glamour, activities such as DanceSport, which extracts enormous costs for its payoff, will continue to thrive.

Standard competitors Victor Fung and Anna Mikhed teasing the audience as they hover inches away from onlookers. Embassy Ball, Irvine, California, September 2005. Photo © 2005 by Jonathan S. Marion.

Smooth competitors Hunter Johnson and Maria Zee Johnson exhibiting a delicate balance of passion and control. Desert Classic, Palm Desert, California, July 2005. Photo © 2005 by Jonathan S. Marion.

U.S. Smooth Champions Nicholas Kosovich and Lena Bahcheva in the midst of dramatic ges-tures typical of American Style tango. United States DanceSport Championships, Hollywood, Florida, September 2005. Photo © 2005 by Jonathan S. Marion.

Latin competitors Valentin Chmerkovskiy and Valeriya Kozharinova in a classic International Style cha cha move called a "New York." Yankee Classic, Boston, Massachusetts June 2005. Photo © 2005 by Jonathan S. Marion.

Modestly covered in costuming typical for their division, 2005 U.S. Amateur Standard Champions Egor Abashkin and Katya Kanevskaja compete in clothes that do not draw attention to their sexuality. Yankee Classic, Boston, Massachusetts, June 2005. Photo © 2005 by Jonathan S. Marion.

Rhythm competitors Jesse DeSoto and Jackie Josephs in a position that illustrates the distance between DanceSport and casual social dancing. Embassy Ball, Irvine, California, September 2005. Photo © 2005 by Jonathan S. Marion.

Latin competitors Maxim Kojevnikov and Eulia Zagorouitchenko embrace each other in a moment that seems almost spontaneous in its intimacy, although the precise composition of her leg line betrays the fact that the move has been carefully choreographed. Emerald Ball, Los Angeles, California, May 2004. Photo © 2004 by Jonathan S. Marion.

The author and her partner Sonny Perry in competition brownface, which has started to run down Sonny's face. Embassy Ball, Irvine, California, September 1999. Photo © 1999 by Dave Head.

two

Representations of Social Dance:
A Genealogy of Improvisation

It was a Saturday evening in late October 2001. Just before midnight, a group of friends scurried into the entryway of a building on West Thirty-fourth Street and headed up to "Club Maricopa." They arrived at a private Manhattan apartment, furniture displaced to accommodate strobe lights and speakers so that the majority of the space was open to the bodies already cluttered inside. The partygoers, numbering over one hundred, were primarily in their twenties, almost half of them Russian immigrant ballroom dancers. Tonight, however, no one was doing any recognizable form of ballroom dance. The scene rivaled any the creators of *Dirty Dancing* could have envisioned. Bodies were grinding, pulsing, thrashing, and rolling against one another, sensuality and wild abandon steaming through the room. Space was limited, so none of the exaggerated gestures or expansive steps practiced in DanceSport were in evidence. Instead, people were adapting the partnering skills they had acquired as DanceSport competitors for physical repartee. People danced in small groups, solo, and in couples, blending in and out of these formations without any formal invitations to dance. Although primarily heterosexual, partnering also occurred between same-sex couples.

  Much of the movement resembled dancing typical at contemporary nightclubs playing techno music, except for the extraordinary partnering skills displayed by this group of individuals. Moments of solo movement merged into dips and turns borrowed from ballroom that blended back into free-form gyrations and rhythmic play. No one danced the cha cha or the hustle, but at moments people used elements from each. One man dipped and rolled the torso of his partner in constant undulations of suspension and release typical of DanceSport rumba, but without any similarities to rumba in footwork or timing. Another couple was engaged in a series of fast swivels and weight changes common to cha cha, interspersed with periods during which they broke away into freestyle hip-hop. A mixed-gender twosome trapped another man between them, forcing him to the ground in a slow hip grind. Half the people in the room were teachers of social ballroom dancing, but no one was teaching his or her students *this*.

The contrast between the kind of dance practiced at this party and that exhibited at most ballroom dances, even those advertised as socials, was stark. This event was rich with ballroom dancers doing *social dancing*, not performing *representations of social dance*. The distinction I draw between these two categories is nuanced and has frequently been overlooked. Nevertheless, I define social dancing as an activity between or among participants.[1] In contrast, performance-oriented representations of social dance—both theatrical and competitive—are primarily performed for an audience that does not include the dancers. There is very little recognition of the distinction between these categories in the ballroom dance industry, a confusion that I will demonstrate is crucial for its financial viability and the production of Glamour.

Although inspired by social dance and dependent upon visual references to it, DanceSport is *not* social dance. Its practitioners are evaluated on their ability to display their finely tuned skills and stamina before judges and an audience. Thus, DanceSport foregrounds the legibility of body lines and rhythms, expansive presentational movement, dynamics, speed, control, dramatic tricks, and visual effect. Social dancing, in contrast, often emphasizes play, musicality, improvisation, subtlety, exchange between partners, leadability of vocabulary, and the feeling of the moves for the dancers themselves. Many of these qualities are common in contemporary nightclub dancing (or private parties such as that at Club Maricopa) and can be found in salsa, swing, and tango, whose practitioners separate themselves physically and ideologically from the ballroom dance industry.

Social iterations of ballroom dance, however, rarely utilize improvisational play typical of other twentieth-century social dance practices. Despite the fact that social ballroom dance is geared for participation and not spectatorship, it looks much more like a performance-based representation of social dance. There is very little in common between social ballroom *dance* and other partnered forms of social *dancing* I have described. It is the present progressive form of the verb "to dance" I wish to stress. Dancing is something that is in progress—active, alive, changing, and growing in the very moment of its execution.[2] It is created and recreated by the practitioners each time they engage in the activity. Social ballroom dance, however, contains little of this progressive energy, in which dancers themselves participate in creation of their own practice. Instead, it has more in common with representations of social dance on theatrical and competition stages, with their emphasis on predetermined steps and precision of body line.

It is my contention that this slippage between social dancing and theatrical and competitive iterations of social dance is necessary for the economic viability of the ballroom dance industry, a strategic marketing tool utilized at least since the 1910s. Furthermore, the codification of social dancing into a saleable product has resulted in the elimination of improvisation from social ballroom dance

Rhythm competitors Lori Putnins and Edgar Osario seducing the audience in an outward-directed pose. Emerald Ball, Los Angeles, California, May 2004. Photo © 2004 by Jonathan S. Marion.

practice, thus linking it more closely with performance forms of dance and separating it from improvisationally based social forms such as salsa or swing. In this chapter, I trace the suppression of improvisation by the U.S. ballroom dance industry, starting in the 1910s when the industry emerged as a viable network of interrelated business enterprises. I then follow its transformation as a result of Arthur Murray's wildly successful franchise and compare the American dance standardization process to concurrent developments in England. I track the importation of the English system of ballroom dancing in the 1960s and the subsequent shift in the U.S. industry to competition dance. Finally, I expose how the contemporary ballroom dance industry structure continues to stifle improvisation through its conflation of social dance and competitive DanceSport. By highlighting improvisational techniques used in salsa and West Coast swing and comparing them to these very absences in social ballroom dance, I hope to suggest how social ballroom dancers might infuse their practice with the very qualities the dance business has repeatedly excised.

At each juncture I illustrate how market forces encouraged confusion between social dance and its representation in staged exhibitions and how that alignment helped to drive improvisation out of social dancing. I also argue that these economic forces were often compelled by racial prejudice disguised in class terms. And I suggest that the legacy of social ballroom dance as a means of performing class and racial status contributes to its role in the production of Glamour.

THE EMERGENCE OF THE BALLROOM DANCE INDUSTRY

Social ballroom dance has enjoyed prominence as an American pastime for several centuries, but the dance boom of the 1910s marked substantial shifts in the basic structure and implicit values of ballroom dancing. Dances popular in the nineteenth century, such as quadrilles, lancers, and English country dances, emphasized group cohesion, order, and harmony. The early-twentieth-century "dance craze," as it was dubbed by the media at the time, brought about a change of focus from group dances, in which a couple's individual choices were subservient to the spatial and temporal design of the entire group, to dances in which individual couples could choose how to construct their paths through the dance anew each time they performed it. The waltz, which was popular in the United States throughout much of the nineteenth century, is an early instance of this shift in focus from group to individual; but the 1910s ushered in a multitude of new dances, including ragtime and "animal dances" (e.g., the turkey trot, the bunny hug, and the grizzly bear) that stressed improvisational choices for individual couples. No longer was skill measured by how well one maintained the order and design within the group choreography. Nineteenth-century social dances required that all members of the group perform their part in the predetermined sequence of steps and trajectory through space. In contrast, the new twentieth-century ballroom dances gave little prescription for a single couple's relationship to the rest of the group. Spatial relationships to other couples on the dance floor were no longer predetermined but emerged rather haphazardly. Dancers—or at least the male leader of each couple—were now allowed to choose the pattern and order of steps. What became important in this new era was *how* individual dancers executed particular steps. Success was defined less by community cohesion than by individual virtuosity.

The shift is clearly illustrated in the differing content of dance manuals from one century to the next. Nineteenth-century dance manuals such as *Ball-room Dancing without a Master* (published by Hurst in 1872) offer very few details about how to execute particular steps and instead diagram each dancer's trajectory through space as it relates to the design of the entire group. By contrast, J. S. Hopkins's *The Tango and Other Up-to-date Dances* and Vernon and Irene Castle's *Modern Dancing,* both published in 1914, describe the movement itself in detail.[3] They emphasize such specifics as which foot begins each step, the timing of each movement, the amount of turn each action takes, and the quality with which it should be executed. Little is included about the dancer's relationship to the group; the emphasis is on how the dancer interacts with his or her partner. Some dance teachers, such as G. Hepburn Wilson, writing in 1914, went so far as to explicitly stress the new focus on individuality: "No more than any two individuals should *dress alike* should they *dance* alike. *Dress must express individuality and so must the dance.* While there necessarily must be some fundamental thing in common in dances as in dress, there still must be a wide latitude for individuality and self-expression" (emphasis in original).[4]

The dance scholar Julie Malnig argues that these changes in dance were part of the broader social revolutions taking place in the United States. Dance practices were not merely becoming a symbol of these social transformations but in some cases actually enabling their progress. Malnig stresses that the flow of influence between dance and larger social trends was reciprocal—dancers changed the fabric of social life as much as new social trends altered the texture of the dances. Malnig points out that although the social-dance revolution did not necessarily instigate these broader social movements, it was bound up with concurrent developments in other arenas. These included the Industrial Revolution, urbanization, an immigration surge, the growth of the middle class, the emergence of consumer culture and the advertising industry, women's rights movements demanding greater social and sexual freedom, technological developments such as railroads and phonographs, and Progressive Era ideals about an individual's ability to change his or her fate. Urbanization led to new kinds of public recreation, including dance halls where different classes mingled together on dance floors and forged new social alliances along with the new dance steps. The nascent advertising industry began to link dancing to self-improvement, classiness, romance, grace, and personal style by using the names and images of new dance celebrities: exhibition ballroom dance teams who performed the latest social dances in cabarets. Women advocating for greater freedom in public spaces began appearing at dances unescorted, where, according to Malnig, new social rules "now allowed women to 'choose' a male partner for an hour or two, indulging in Grizzly Bear holds or tango dips, then discarding that partner at will."[5] New dance styles are commonly credited with inspiring radical changes in women's dress during this period, encouraging designers to do away with corsets and heavy fabrics to allow for greater ease of movement.[6] Rail travel increased the speed with which new dances spread. The new recording industry offered much cheaper alternatives to live music, increasing the number of people who had access to dance music, and also provided another means through which dances could be disseminated. Not only was the music itself the vehicle through which dances migrated, but dance instructions also found new homes on record jackets and even oral instructions on the records themselves.[7] New ideologies associated with the Progressive Era led people to believe that they could improve their social status as well as their physical and emotional well-being, thus encouraging dance both as a healthy form of exercise and recreation and as a potential site for social mobility. All these social changes converged to help create a radically different kind of social dance practice in twentieth-century America than that enjoyed by previous generations of upper- and middle-class society at private balls.

Not only did new dance practices emerge at this time, but a rapidly growing dance industry surfaced as well. Although the United States in the nineteenth century had some dancing masters who earned their living teaching and many publishers who counted on the sale of dance manuals for financial profit, it was not until the 1910s that a network of commerce emerged to sustain and capitalize on the growing dance craze. Dance teachers, public dance halls, record labels, dance clothing manufacturers, dancing schools, dance literature, professional dance performers, and dance impresarios competed to entice the growing dance public to purchase their products and services. The large-scale business of social dance had arrived. The ballroom dance industry was closely linked to the advertising industry and the emergence of consumer culture, and its success depended on the linking of dance lessons to broader cultural needs and desires. In the terms of the anthropologist Edward Myers, dance studios imbued dance lessons with exchange value by endowing them with relevant cultural values and meanings.[8] These early marketing strategies focused on linking ballroom dance lessons to higher social status. As popularity in structured partner dance waned later in the twentieth century, dance studios began to emphasize improved self-confidence, social interaction, physical dexterity, and life enjoyment as the benefits to be derived from dance lessons. But the model for turning social dance into commerce was established by the mid-1910s.

Central to this new business were the dance stars, expert practitioners of social dance who were hired to perform in restaurants and nightclubs around the country. Such notable couples included Vernon and Irene Castle as well as Maurice Mouvet and Florence Walton.[9] Their performances drew crowds to the nightclubs in which they performed, and their endorsement of a new dance increased its popularity. Their images were used to sell not only related products, such as records and dance manuals, but also goods entirely outside the sphere of dance, including hats and soap. Just as businesses counted on these celebrities to promote their products, so too did the exhibition ballroom dancers depend on the endorsements to increase their star status. And both relied on the dancing public's economic and popular support. The triangular dependency of these three aspects of the ballroom dance industry—the multitude of dance-related businesses, the performing dance celebrities, and the social dance public—was clearly evident in the mid-1910s.

The dance stars were performing not on stages to distant audiences but among the patrons of intimate cabarets and restaurants in which the audience danced before and after the show, imitating the moves of the performers with their own bodies. These celebrities were popular as performers because they demonstrated, despite theatrical embellishments, how one was supposed to look when performing the fashionable social dances. The dance historian Linda Tomko writes about the new cabarets:

> Patrons watched the exhibition dancers' performances from their seats, and then stepped onto the same floor the performers had only recently vacated. Patrons themselves thus became the subjects for examination, evaluation, and possibly emulation by other observing diners. . . . This was a context that rendered quotidian dancing an instance of performance, while performance came to be an activity available to any sociable body.[10]

Vernon and Irene Castle. From Vernon and Irene Castle, Modern Dancing *(New York: Harper & Brothers, 1914).*

THE CASTLE WALK

Vernon and Irene Castle demonstrating the Castle Walk in an intimate setting where audience members can take to the floor and mimic their steps. From Vernon and Irene Castle, Modern Dancing *(New York: Harper & Brothers, 1914).*

Tomko's observations offer further evidence that, at the inception of the modern ballroom dance industry, market forces encouraged the blurring of boundaries between social and theatrical ballroom dance, supporting a general conflation between the practices of its general public and dance stars. Although cabaret ballroom performances are not nearly as popular now, in the early twenty-first century, as they were in the 1910s (with cruise ships offering the largest employment opportunities for contemporary cabaret ballroom dance couples), the precedent set by the early ballroom dance industry is still prominent even in twenty-first-century DanceSport competition. Intimacy of performance space and the use of celebrities in marketing social dance in both periods promote a sense of continuity between social and theatrical dance.

STAMPING OUT IMPROVISATION

The new dances of the early twentieth century were characterized by individual choice—not only in the order and direction of steps, but in the style and variation of the steps themselves. This tendency to foreground improvisation and playfulness, clearly in evidence at the emergence of the modern ballroom dance industry, is nearly absent from twenty-first-century social ballroom dance. The reasons for this rift are multiple, but efforts to eliminate such unpredictability were already in evidence during the modern dance craze. According to the dance scholar Danielle Robinson, who has done extensive archival research in order to reconstruct early-twentieth-century social dances, the qualities of creativity and spontaneity were most prevalent in ragtime or animal dances. Improvisation, however, was largely eliminated from these dances through the standardization process imposed by the dance industry. Robinson's comparison of the ragtime dances of the 1910s to the modern dances of the same period illustrates how the transformation of the turkey trot into the one-step resulted in the elimination of the unpredictability essential to the original ragtime dance, producing a "refined" modern dance that adhered to the industry's ideals about grace, civility, and propriety.

Such terms, at times implying distinctions of class between dancers who were refined and those who were not, also stood in for racial difference. Robinson argues that such changes in the dances were a result of efforts to distance the dances from their African American origins. She links improvisation in the ragtime dances specifically to African American social dance practices of the period. As these dances gained popularity, their white practitioners minimized such critical characteristics as improvisation, torso isolations, and angular patterns created by the bodies moving through space. Pointing out that these very qualities are defining elements of African-derived dance practices, Robinson argues that those performing the "refined" modern dances were distancing themselves from the black creative innovators of these dances.[11]

In fact, the erasure of its African heritage was so successful that by the 1930s, ballroom dance was unequivocally recognized as a white form. In her analysis of the role racial politics played in thwarting the advancement of black performers during the 1930s, the dance scholar Brenda Dixon Gottschild demonstrates how successfully blackness had been erased from the history of theatrical ballroom dance. She argues that the ballroom adagio (ballroom dancing incorporating lifts from ballet pas de deux) performers Harold Norton and Margot Webb were actually denied professional advancement because they were black performers of a white idiom. Gottschild demonstrates that Norton and Margot faced even greater prejudice than black jazz or tap dancers of the same period because they had crossed over into a genre that was regarded as European and white. Although they were by all accounts superb performers of ballroom dance—whose movement privileges grace, control, and fluidity—their mastery of it did not grant them access to white opportunity. They were always fighting expectations that their dancing should follow traditions of dance with which their race was associated, such as the lindy hop, tap, or jazz. Few theater owners or audiences recognized either that black artists could perform other kinds of dance or that ballroom dancing itself was infused with elements derived from black social dance.

Although Robinson demonstrates that the refinement process of the ballroom dance industry during the 1910s had racial motivations, she is careful to stress that economic pressures were also crucial factors in determining how the new dances were taught. She argues that "in their efforts to commodify ragtime dancing, modern dance professionals sharply decreased its improvisation and, thus, its opportunities for self-expression, spontaneity, and individuality."[12] In order to appeal to mass markets, the dances were standardized and endorsed by the newly crowned dance celebrities. But even though racial prejudices and marketing viability may have inspired social dance's transformation from ragtime to modern ballroom dance, refined modern dancing was packaged for sale in class terms. Mastery of proper dancing technique was always aligned with an elevated class position.

Marketing social dance as a means of improving or sustaining class status was hardly new to the modern dance era. Throughout the nineteenth century, the Dodworth Family Dancing Schools in New York instructed thousands of children as part of their training to enter high society.[13] According to the historian Rosetta O'Neill, Allen Dodworth was motivated by the moral conviction that American society could be saved through teaching "proper" dancing. Working against common public opinion that dance was closely aligned with impropriety, sexual immorality, social vulgarity, and the devil himself, Dodworth preached that dance could shield children from these same moral deficiencies through its lessons of physical and social grace. Explicit social etiquette was integrated into his curriculum, but it was the enduring values embedded in the dances themselves—kindness, respect for others, and courteousness—that were assumed to instill high moral standards in his pupils. For example, the vertical posture, controlled and light quality of movement, and close attention to the actions of the entire group were skills that could be transferred to other social situations, aiding in the creation of upright, moral citizens. Dodworth's nephew rejected the ragtime dances of the 1910s, scorning their lower-class origins and what he assumed to be their implicit lack of morals, an attitude that ultimately contributed to the closing of Dodworth schools in 1920. But his uncle's precedent proved valuable for ragtime proponents who would likewise counter accusations of immorality by arguing that proper training actually improved the very moral character critics of dance feared would lead to wide social unravel.

Antidance treatises were commonly issued throughout the nineteenth century, but twentieth-century ragtime provoked a renewed outcry from dance adversaries.[14] The physical proximity of men and women, the sexual desire implied by the movements of their torsos and hips, and general anxiety about whites enjoying dances clearly linked to black society sparked heated debate about the appropriateness of ragtime dancing for middle- and upper-class white Americans. Many critics focused on protecting the sexual purity of American women, assuming that the intoxication of dancing necessarily led down a steep slope of sexual immodesty that would end in prostitution. The newly created ballroom dance celebrities, then, became central figures who redefined and marketed the ragtime dances (along with waltzes, tangos, and other ballroom dances) for the upwardly mobile white public.

Irene and Vernon Castle were the most widely recognized dance celebrities of this era. Their exhibitions, instruction manual, and dance school regulating for thousands of American adults (not the children who had been Dodworth's target pupils) the proper technique for the new dances. The Castles played a vital role in redeeming ragtime dancing as an acceptable activity for middle- and upper-class white Americans. "We were clean-cut; we were married and when we danced there was nothing suggestive about it," Irene Castle writes in her autobiography. "If Vernon had looked into my eyes with smoldering passion during the tango, we both would have burst out laughing."[15] The Castles' success in marketing their brand of elegant, wholesome, white dancing was remarkable, inspiring millions to learn their signature dance, the Castle Walk. Their popularity had as much to do with a public image that downplayed sexuality and vulgarity as it did with the charm of their style. According to the musicologist Susan Cook, their rival dancer Maurice Mouvet did not enjoy the same financial success as Vernon Castle because he represented a more deviant form of masculinity than the stoicism embraced by Vernon Castle.[16] The Castles wrote that their instruction manual "shows that dancing, properly executed, is neither vulgar nor immodest, but, on the contrary, the personification of refinement, grace, and modesty. Our aim is to uplift dancing, purify it, and place it before the public in its proper light."[17] "Purification" meant eliminating movements and postures that were considered black or lower class.

The Castles contributed significantly to the early standardization of ballroom dancing, but not all social dancers followed their doctrines. Declarations such as one made by the Castles' manager, Elizabeth Marbury, that "the One Step as taught at Castle House eliminates all hoppings, all contortions of the body, all flouncing of the elbows, all twisting of the arms, and, above everything else, all fantastic dips" enumerate for readers those actions *not to embody* on the dance floor.[18] Ironically, Marbury's need to distance the Castle's one-step from improvisational ragtime through vivid description of ragtime's core characteristics attests to its persistence as popular social practice contemporaneous with the modern dances. Although modern ballroom dancing differed from the previous century's social dance practices in the increased freedom and improvisational choices it allowed individual dancers, the budding ballroom dance industry was already working to control and eliminate those very qualities.

THE ARTHUR MURRAY EMPIRE

The commercialization of social ballroom dance intensified over the next decades as a former student of and teacher for the Castles engineered one of the most successful business strategies of the twentieth century. Murray Teichman, who changed his name to Arthur Murray to distance himself from his German origins, began selling mail-order dancing lessons in 1920. By 1925 Murray was netting $35,000 annually and the now famous Murray footprints had trotted into more than five million American mailboxes.[19] Whereas the influence of any individual teacher had previously been limited to his or her geographical locale, Arthur Murray reached millions of pupils through the ingenuity of his business plan. More personal and complete than other instructional dance manuals, Murray's mail-order lessons substituted for live teachers across the nation. His lessons included simple instructions that were at once thorough and accessible, basic exercises for practicing each technique, gentle encouragement for moving on to the next stage in his program, and the trademark Murray footprints—paper footsteps that could be placed on the floor for each student to follow. Murray's dance program hinged on its simplicity, on the similarity of all the dances to one another, and on the relative ease with which each successive dance could be mastered once the foundation was set. The success of Murray's mail-order business standardized ballroom dancing steps and techniques across the country at the same time it simplified the dances by eliminating major differences among them in character and technique.

If Murray's mail-order business dealt a major blow to regional differences and individual expression in social ballroom dance, his franchises—the first of which opened in 1938—were ten times more powerful in their ability to homogenize

Arthur and Kathryn Murray. Photo courtesy of Arthur Murray International, Inc.

social dance practices. By 1946, the seventy-two Arthur Murray schools had collectively grossed almost $20 million. Murray's franchises replicated the successful business model of his first studio. It was not Murray's personal skill as a dancer or a teacher that lent credibility to his name, but rather the Arthur Murray system for teaching dance. Each studio that bore his name taught identical steps, followed the same lesson plans, employed the same teaching methods, used the same language and physical décor, and aimed to hire a staff that could be expected to engage clients with the Murray etiquette. Like the modern dance industry of the 1910s, the Murray studios strove to improve the marketability of the dances they taught and similarly distanced their products from their non-white origins. Dances had to be simple and stable enough to be uniform at all Murray locations, which meant that improvisation and variation were not part of the program. But the choices about what kinds of steps and techniques to include and exclude had as much to do with racial assumptions of the time as it did with consistency of his product. Particularly while the segregated South defined race relations nationwide, blackness and lower-class status were continuously conflated. Marketing the Murray system as one that improved or secured class status meant that it had to consciously distance itself from the black origins of the dances it taught.

Murray dance manuals from the 1930s, 1940s, and 1950s, expanded versions of his original mail-order instructional program, clearly demonstrate that Murray was seeking to appeal to an upwardly mobile, white clientele. The jacket of his 1942 *How to Become a Good Dancer,* for example, touts the fact that Murray dancers are business leaders, leaders in high society, and royalty: the Duke of Windsor, Kay Francis, Rudy Vallee, James Roosevelt, and Elizabeth Arden. Readers could assume that if they were to master the skills in his book (available for a mere $1.98), they too would rise to join other Murray students in positions of social and economic power. Murray's manual is primarily devoted to the foxtrot, waltz, tango, and rumba, which he claims are the most popular dances of the day. He dedicates only one or two pages to each of five other dances—samba, conga, Varsovienne, jitterbug, and lindy hop. Most historical accounts claim that by the 1940s swing had become the most popular American social dance form.[20] Though Murray's instruction on the foxtrot is sufficient to teach a reader to adequately perform the dance, his explanations for the jitterbug and lindy hop (closely related dance styles that would eventually be grouped together under the umbrella term "swing dance") are insufficient for even rudimentary competency. Such an imbalance suggests that Murray was consciously distancing his curriculum from the dance practices of African Americans, the inventors of lindy hop and swing dancing. The mention of maids and chaperones at dances and the exclusively white models dressed in upper-class attire who appear in the book's illustrations offer further confirmation that dancing the Murray way was for the wealthy and white. Likewise, the exclusively white dancers on the popular 1950s television show *The Arthur Murray Party* were dressed formally—the men in white tie and tails, the women in long formal gowns.

Selling dancing as a means of social mobility also contributed to the elimination of improvisation from the dances. Performing a higher-class position was serious business and could not be approached tentatively if one wanted to be convincing. In his 1925 manual, Murray wrote, "the secret of being a good leader in dancing is to know EXACTLY how to do each step,—and then dance in a decided manner. You must be SURE OF WHAT YOU ARE DOING" (emphasis in original).[21] Precision and confidence, not playfulness or open-ended moves, projected the high-class image his students sought.

Murray's ingenious marketing through television, media manipulation, advertising, and dance manual publication created a Murray brand name that came to be associated with social transformation through the performance of class status on the dance floor. Learning to dance the Murray way implied elegance, social acceptance, and exclusiveness. It had very little to do, however, with actual skill in dancing. Many great dancers were employed by the Murray enterprise, including the phenomenal performers featured on his television series. However, this performance style had very little to do with what was actually taught in the Murray schools. Stuart Ross's 1946 exposé in *Dance Magazine* reveals how the Murray schools were structured to maximize profit, regardless of their effectiveness in actually teaching students to dance. Ross's article, entitled "I Taught for Arthur Murray: High Pressure Ballyhoo Has Turned Ballroom Dancing into a Multi-million Dollar Business," is an insider's account of the Murray system based on the two years the author spent teaching at one of his schools.

Ross exposes Murray's corporate priorities, divulging that at his job interview he was tested on his ability to sell, but never on his ability to dance. Ross explains how each lesson was carefully engineered to convince students of the need for further instruction. First, teachers insisted that students needed to learn at least twenty steps in seven or eight dances in order to be accomplished dancers. Furthermore, each dance course was designed to ensure that its students did not feel competent enough to declare their education complete. Ross writes, "Without discouraging him too much, I had to make the student feel self-conscious enough about his dancing so that he would readily see the need for more lessons."[22] Several Arthur Murray teachers recall that the importation of the English medal system in the early 1950s aided tremendously in this project to instill in their student body a regenerating desire to purchase more lessons.[23] By dividing the syllabus into levels (bronze, silver, and gold) and specifying technical skills that had to be mastered to pass onto the next grade, teachers could more readily sell larger packages of dance lessons. Able to secure the trust of students through the intimacy of private lessons, instructors were able to carefully bal-

Boa-constrictor grip
Besides looking resolved to do or die, Jack's hold hikes up Nanon's dress higher than the designer intended.

The listless droop
Dancing like a lump of lead may seem sophisticated to you, but not to your partner.

The show-off
Jack Haley impersonates Dippy Dan, who adores deep knee bends and tricky steps.

Pull 'em in!
If you want to look like a pair of comic characters, pull your partner forward so that the derrière waves in the breeze.

The great American gesture
After you've streamlined your rhythm the Murray way, don't ruin the effect by girdle tugging.

The yoo-hoo stance
She's so busy waving to her acquaintances. Flirts are a pain in the neck to masculine pride.

Illustration of "Don'ts on the Dance Floor," written by Arthur Murray and demonstrated by Jack Haley and Nanon Millis. Originally published in Liberty Magazine. *Reprinted in* Murray-Go-Round, *ed. Kathryn Murray and Arthur Murray (1954).*

ance encouragement and criticism so that students internalized the drive for self-improvement. As each objective was met, it was quickly replaced by a new aspiration. Ross concludes:

> The publicity may have proved invaluable from a business standpoint, but it seems that the pocketbook of the student of ballroom dancing has suffered considerably in financing this exploitation. Murray, with his highly publicized name, lavishly appointed studios and slick sales techniques has created an attractive illusion, but has he really helped the student of ballroom dancing?[24]

If, as Ross suggests, Murray students did not learn much about dancing, what were they trained to do? Students learned a repertoire of predetermined steps from which they could select and arrange in limited combinations. They certainly did not learn techniques for inventing their own steps or guidelines for improvisation. The Murray business strategy depended then, as it does today, on maintaining the illusion that the power and privilege associated with Murray dance knowledge can be accessed only through purchase of his products. Validating the improvisational innovations of just any dance student would have significantly lowered the value of the Murray dance steps. A student in one of the Boston franchises reported that one studio owner went to such lengths to heighten the value and mystify the source of Murray dance knowledge that he kept their gold-star manual (which described the most advanced steps) locked in a safe. Whether or not this practice is common, the story speaks to the efforts of franchisees to inflate the value of the Murray knowledge and their fear that circulation of one book could bankrupt the entire business.

As Arthur Murray was building his empire, public confusion between staged versions of social dance and social dancing continued to support ballroom dance as business. If the cabarets had conflated social and theatrical dance through proximity, dance films of the 1930s, 1940s, and 1950s furthered the illusion that ordinary social dance and elaborately choreographed performance were one and the same activity. Each time Fred Astaire won over the heart of a reluctant Ginger Rogers by sweeping her up in a flurry of pivots, dips, and syncopated time steps, audiences forgot (since the film never showed) how many shoes were bloodied in the studio to create the appearance of impromptu courtship. And if film furthered the illusion of intimacy between dance stars and their public, the medium of television, where idols were dancing right in viewers' own homes, only intensified it. *The Arthur Murray Party*, which proved an invaluable marketing boon for Arthur Murray Studios, featured professional dancers performing theatrical dance routines as if this were the ordinary fare at any Arthur Murray Dance School.

As with any successful business model, the Arthur Murray franchise was soon copied by other dance entrepreneurs. Its biggest rival was the Fred Astaire Studios, founded in 1947 by Charles Casanave in association with one of the nation's most famous dance stars. As the enterprise did not begin teaching ballroom dancing until after Astaire sold his interest in the school in the 1950s, there is little evidence that the Fred Astaire Studios syllabus or teaching methods had much to do with the actor's own theatrical dance practices. Fred Astaire Studios use methods virtually identical to those of the Arthur Murray Studios, including high-pressure sales tactics, private instruction, and a copyrighted syllabus of predetermined steps. At the turn of the millennium, Fred Astaire Studios boasted more than one hundred schools in North America,[25] while more than two hundred Murray schools were thriving throughout the United States, Canada, Australia, South Africa, Japan, Germany, Israel, Italy, and Puerto Rico.[26] Several small chain studios have since blossomed in the United States, as have many independently run ballroom dance schools, most operating more or less through the business model perfected by Arthur Murray. Though each new studio may teach a slightly different repertoire of steps, the basic formula of teaching steps, rather than techniques for discovering or creating one's own steps, has remained constant.

THE ENGLISH STYLE DEFINED

As Arthur Murray was building his dance empire in the United States, a very different process of standardization was taking place in England. American ragtime dancing traveled to Europe and England during World War I primarily through U.S. soldiers enjoying their off-duty nights in dance halls, setting the new dances loose to spread with contagious fury. English dance teachers, like their American counterparts, were anxious to regulate and tame these new innovations. Like the American ragtime dance reformation, the English crusade was couched in terms of propriety, morality, and decency, which only thinly veiled the obvious economic concerns: if dancing became a free-form frenzy with no standards or techniques, dance teachers would soon be out of jobs. Though the effects of the rising popularity of ragtime and subsequent jazz dancing on the ballroom dance industry may have been similar in America and Britain, the reaction of the British dance teachers was radically different on at least one count. American dance teachers were not able to overcome huge geographic distances and American individualism to agree on uniform standards for dancing. Although some U.S. dance organizations, such as the American National Association of Masters of Dancing and the American Society of Professors of Dancing, banded together between World War I and the depression in attempts to regulate dancing through licensing and standardized exams, these organizations did not have nearly the impact on the American dance industry that similar efforts had in England.[27] Their British counterparts overcame rivalries and differences to form a unified front to fight the epidemic. English dance teachers standardized the ballroom dances by committee.

The process of standardizing ballroom dancing is chronicled by Philip J. S. Richardson in *A History of English Ballroom Dancing*. As editor of the *Dancing Times,* the periodical that convened many of the meetings at which the English style of dance was defined, Richardson most likely overstates the inclusiveness of these events and underplays any rival attempts to otherwise define or resist the standardization process. Such bias notwithstanding, Richardson's records are rich in details about crucial events in the history of DanceSport development. The steps, rules, techniques, and conventions that were defined at these meetings became the foundation for what is practiced in English Style ballroom dancing today.[28]

The process of English dance standardization began to take on significant scope in May 1920, when the first Informal Conference was held in London. An announcement in the *Dancing Times,* England's foremost dance periodical, invited all dance teachers in the country to attend. According to Richardson, who was appointed chair of the committee by the two hundred teachers present, it was the "most representative gathering of teachers of ballroom dancing" ever convened in England.[29] The Russian Revolution was still fresh in the public's memory, and Richardson compared the new dance practices brought from America to the bolshevik values that led to the overthrow of the Russian crown as a tactic for rallying support for dance reform.[30] By making the debate over dance style a matter of national security and political stability, Richardson was able to mobilize British dance teachers to take up the project of standardizing ballroom dancing as a matter of national pride. A subcommittee, which reported to each subsequent Informal Conference, was formed to define the basic steps of the most popular dances of the day. These first committees devised basic descriptions and step lists for the one-step, waltz, foxtrot, and tango.

It was the formation of the ballroom branch of the Imperial Society of Teachers of Dancing in 1924 that had the greatest impact on British ballroom dance standardization. According to Richardson, it "had as great an influence on ballroom dancing as did the founding of the 'Académie Royale' by Louis XIV of France on the ballet."[31] Once sanctioned by the Imperial Society, the ballroom branch formed a committee to develop a syllabus and examination standards. The syllabus and technique the committee developed became the national standard at the Great Conference held in 1929 by the *Dancing Times.* Although this conference united teachers from several different organizations, the Imperial Society's syllabus prevailed, and it was adopted by all other associations. Aside from endorsing the Imperial Society's syllabus, the 1929 conference produced the Official Board of Ballroom Dancing, later the British Dance Council. The council currently serves as the governing body for ballroom dancing throughout Great Britain. Although this board represented several dance teachers' associations, the Imperial Society has had the strongest influence on its policies since its inception.

Evidence that the standardization process was motivated by the dance teachers' economic concerns is clear. Richardson explains that the Great Conference of 1929 was convened in response to

> a desire that, without interfering with the domestic policies of the various associations, it should be possible for all teachers to work on more or less uniform lines and so gain greater confidence with the public. It was urged in support, that there was a general complaint from the public that unless two people had been to the same teacher, they could not dance together with ease.[32]

English dance teachers put aside individual market competition in hopes of gaining greater legitimacy and respect for the entire industry by sharing their knowledge and developing a common vocabulary. Their efforts at cooperation for the benefit of all dance teachers (or at least those participating in the conferences) is evident in the resolution of the 1929 conference, which stated that "no individual teacher should 'exploit' a 'new dance,' but . . . the teachers as a whole, through this committee, should agree upon any new dance that was thought to be desirable."[33] Their reaction was radically different from that of U.S. dance teachers, who in the American tradition of entrepreneurship and capitalist market competition continued to develop rival styles of dance. The English coalition of independent dance teachers also contrasted starkly with Arthur Murray's model of hiring and training teachers to disseminate the style and steps he dictated. The English process of dance regulation was, however, similar to the American in its racial and class motivations. Richardson states repeatedly that each conference reiterated its mission to curb "freakish and objectionable" dancing. "Freak" steps are not defined by Richardson, although the resolution passed at First Conference specified "particularly dips and steps in which the feet are raised high off the ground."[34] Judgments about acceptable and unacceptable dancing were certainly closely linked to class concerns. In Britain's rigid class system, anxiety about being perceived as coming from a lower class than one's birthright probably motivated continual policing of proper and improper dancing. Dips and kicks appeared too low class for the ballroom dancing public.

While English social life was not as racially charged as that of the United States in the 1920s, there is no way to read the standardization of these dances without taking into consideration the history of British imperialist conquest and regulation of "colored" bodies abroad. The need to prescribe behavior for colonized peoples in everyday life was reflected in the efforts to redefine these newly colonized dances. Movement of nonwhite bodies and nonwhite movement practices had to be carefully ordered by British rule in order to ensure continued domination and submission. Cleaning up improvisational black dances for inclusion in white ballroom dancing included physical regulation of race-related and potentially disruptive movements, particularly improvisational elements. Richardson's history of the quickstep offers an example. He explains that the Charleston, "said to have its origin among the coloured folk of South Carolina,"[35] took England by storm in 1925 and 1926. The unpredictability of its wild "kicks and capers" led to a campaign to tame it: P.C.Q. ("Please Charleston Quietly") signs appeared in all the dance halls. It was not until the chaos of the lower-class black dance form was tamed by white dancers that the Charleston was incorporated into quicktime foxtrot, and by 1927 the new dance, "quicktime foxtrot and Charleston" (later shortened to quickstep), replaced the one-step in the ballroom competitions and Imperial Society syllabus. The beguine, from Martinique, was proposed to the Imperial Society in 1932 but was rejected as a ballroom dance because "it was danced . . . with a peculiar undulation of the whole body and the partners were not in actual contact."[36] Isolated movement of the torso, suggested by Richardson's description, was not tolerated by English Style ballroom dancing in the 1930s, nor was individual improvisation separated from a partner. Such qualities are precisely those that link the dances to African-derived movement practices. Judgments about which moves and dances were granted entry into the newly regulated ballroom schools may have had as much to do with maintaining the illusion that ballroom dancing was classy and white as it did with the economics of marketing dance.

Pursuit of class and classiness in the ballroom, however, had radically different expressions in England and the United States. In England, where performance of class could rarely change one's class position, extensive ballroom dancing lessons were not regarded as the key to social success. In fact, some evidence suggests that fastidious study of dance technique became the pastime of the upper-working and lower-middle classes—not the upper classes or aristocracy. Richardson notes a crucial distinction between two types of ballroom dancers, whose divergent styles and interests had become undeniably apparent by 1930. First was the restaurant dancer—the dancer who enjoyed dancing as part of an evening of dining, listening to music, and conversing with friends. Dancing was no more important to this dancer than the other social activities of the night, which, according to Richardson, meant that he did not take his dancing seriously. The Palais or competition dancer, on the other hand, was a serious student of dancing who considered dancing his central focus.[37] "To him the dance was everything: the music must be a slave of the dance—not a sister."[38] Competition dancers required the spacious floors of the public dance halls and music in strict tempo so that they could execute their carefully practiced steps with exactitude and precision. Whereas the restaurant dancer was willing to adapt his or her movements to a small space or to drastically different styles of music, the competition dancer required that the space and music adapt to him. Larger floors and predictable music enabled the competition dancer to develop skill in length of stride and smoothness of movement, though such consistency inhibited development of improvisational skills.

The restaurant dancer, who was improvising movement as part of a social event, was not the focus of the English dancing societies. "It will be seen that the development of the 'English style' was in the hands of the frequenter of the Palais and the public dance hall, and not in those of the smart West Enders,"[39] writes Richardson. The distinction between Palais and restaurant dancer is more than that between competition and social dancer; it is also one of class. The "smart West Enders" were of a higher class than the competition dancers. Richardson writes that the dance Palais were built in response to "the young man and the young woman who could not afford to visit the smart hotels and restaurants [and who] wanted a modern programme and up-to-date band."[40] The result of this focus on Palais and competition dancing rather than restaurant dancing was that social improvisation, as in American dance, was largely eliminated from ballroom dance practice. However, the class image and class status of participants engaged in ballroom dance courses continued to be drastically different in the United States and England. Whereas in America mastery of social ballroom dancing signaled an elevated class position, intense focus on the new development of competition ballroom dancing in England more often confirmed one's distance from higher class positions.

American ballroom dancing schools rarely focused on competition as the goal for their students in the 1930s, 1940s, or 1950s. Instead, students were encouraged to improve their dancing skills as a means of improving their popularity and class status. Murray's books include as much detailed instruction on (upper-class white) etiquette as they do on dance technique. Although the high prices of Murray dance courses suggest that students at the Arthur Murray schools were wealthy, the instruction books were likely purchased by those who could not afford dance lessons.[41] Instead, they bought *Arthur Murray's Dance Secrets,* believing that social mobility could be enabled through daily practice of proper dance posture. Unlike English technique books, such as Imperial Society vice president Victor Silvester's *Modern Ballroom Dancing,* which is written as a reference book for the student of an English dance teacher, Murray's books are intended as a substitute for the actual dance teacher.[42] Although etiquette is implied in the movement itself (female deference to male authority, for example), the fact that there is no corollary etiquette section in Silvester's book suggests that English dance manuals could not function as guides for social behavior. In the relatively static English class system, there was no substitute for family pedigree. Class status could not be secured through a dance manual. In America, however, where upward class mobility remains a dream that still motivates the American work ethic, dancing was sold as a commodity that enabled consumers to climb the social ladder. The dance steps changed with each new edition published, but the etiquette instructions varied minimally over the different Murray manuals. The Murray dancer is defined not by mastery of a certain body of dance steps, but rather by his or her mastery of a set of behavioral codes on and off the dance floor. The English dancer, on the other hand, is defined by his or her command over a certain set of movement techniques approved by the royally sanctioned dance society.

Fred Astaire's Hollywood appearances with Ginger Rogers throughout the 1930s also contributed to the association of ballroom dancing with upper-class status in American popular opinion. Astaire's typical upper-class character, with little to do all day but dance his way into his co-star's heart, conflated upper-class leisure, romance, and ballroom dancing. The image of Fred Astaire in his white tie and tails, with Ginger Rogers elegantly coiffed and in a long gown dripping with feathers, still reigns supreme three-quarters of a century later as the perfect union of romance, class, and dance. The popularity of Astaire and Rogers films—ten RKO pictures in total—attested to and helped solidify the function of ballroom dancing in the American imagination—the ultimate means through which to achieve a classy romantic union that ensured both marital bliss and elevated social status.

By 1930 the structure of the British Official Board of Ballroom Dancing was firmly in place. Over the next several years rules for competitions were set, definitions distinguishing the amateur from the professional dancer were established, and the technique was refined. A medal system of teaching was established wherein different steps were ordered into three levels according to difficulty. Students were encouraged to study and test out of each successive level as a means of measuring progress. Multi-couple dance competitions at which all contestants appeared on the floor at the same time and the winners were selected through a process of elimination became the standard. Though it was certainly not the only dance teachers' organization in the country, the Imperial Society of Teachers of Dancing became a major crusader for the English Style and promoted it worldwide. Imperial Society teachers taught their dance style not only in England, but on the European continent, in South Africa, and in Australia. The technique book on English Style ballroom dancing by Victor Silvester, founding member of the Imperial Society's ballroom branch, was so successful that it was translated into Japanese in 1931. Philip Richardson recalls that his paper the *Dancing Times* was (illegally) translated into Japanese during this same period. Promotion of the English style of dance as superior to other national styles became a major project of the Imperial Society. In Silvester's 1936 edition of *Theory and Technique of Ballroom Dancing,* he states that "it is this attention to detail and the technical precision with which all these points have been worked out, that have made the English style of ballroom dancing the best in the world, and the aspiration of the Continental nations."[43] In 1948, Silvester wrote in the introduction to *Modern Ballroom Dancing* that "the English style (as it is known on the Continent) has been copied and taught by practically every good dance teacher throughout the world because it is admittedly the best."[44]

There is little modesty in British texts about using dancing to further England's international prestige. Given the competitive history of English-French relations on and off the dance floor, it is likely that institutionalization of a distinctly English style of dancing was partially motivated by a desire to establish an English form that could challenge France's reputation as the premier center for dance. Silvester's description of "modern" ballroom technique in his 1936 *Theory and Technique of Ballroom Dancing* emphasizes the "naturalness" of ballroom movements. In direct contrast to ballet, Silvester stresses the neutral position of the legs and feet (as opposed to ballet turnout) and the use of pressure through the entire foot to generate movement (rather than ballet's preference for dancing on the toes). Though the old style of ballroom and sequence dancing utilized ballet technique, modern ballroom dancing, according to Silvester, applies the laws of mechanics to the human body, producing the most "comfortable" and "natural" movement. Silvester continues his treatise by saying that "the most natural and comfortable is always the most graceful and requires the minimum effort."[45] By Silvester's logic, since modern ballroom dancing is the most "natural" and therefore the most graceful form of movement, it is superior to ballet.

In contrast to Silvester's rejection of ballet, Arthur Murray's books build on ballet technique, emphasizing turnout, the five positions of the feet, and dancing on the balls of the feet as recently as 1959. Though Murray's dependence on ballet technique may have furthered his attempts to align ballroom dancing with upper-class values, the English insistence on "naturalizing" ballroom dance allowed them to disguise the specific white English culture out of which formal ballroom dancing developed. Modern ballroom dance, promoted as the universal physics of human motion, eclipsed the particular racial, national, and class politics that defined the form. The English were remarkably successful in their project to export this "universal" style to almost every country in which Western-style ballroom dancing was taught—in Europe, Asia, Australia, and parts of the African continent. By the early 1960s, their efforts had reached North America, and English Style ballroom dance started to permeate the American and Canadian dance scenes.

DEVELOPMENT OF AN AMERICAN
NATIONAL COMPETITION SYSTEM

Despite the success of the franchise system and its power to repress improvisation, individuality and regional difference still marked American Style ballroom dancing in the 1950s. According to Frank Regan, who was teaching ballroom dance at Arthur Murray Studios at the time, different styles of waltz and foxtrot were in evidence at regional competitions and social dances at the Roseland Ballroom in New York and the Harvest Moon Balls in New York and Chicago.[46]

Skippy Blair, who was teaching at an Arthur Murray studio in California during the same period, also attests to a vibrant practice of American style dancing on the West Coast.[47] The continued presence in the 1950s of lindy hop and jitterbug, products of the Harlem nightclub culture of the 1920s that swept the entire nation in the 1930s and 1940s, offers another example of vibrant American social dance culture outside of homogenizing studios. Although Arthur Murray Studios taught versions of these dances in the 1950s, briefly outlined in his techniques books, multiple swing styles continued to develop more quickly than the Murray system could codify them, and swing dancing remained a live dance form outside the franchise system. Today there are dozens of named styles of swing dancing practiced in different regions of the country, promoted and preserved by swing clubs operating only on the periphery of the ballroom dance industry. Some of these dances include the Carolina shag, the Dallas push, the Houston whip, DC hand dancing, West Coast swing, St. Louis shag, collegiate shag, Balboa, country swing, Hollywood style lindy hop, and Savoy style lindy hop.[48] Such a multiplicity of swing styles reflects a continued point of resistance to the ballroom studio system.

The 1950s explosion of Latin dance offers another prominent example of the growth of American dance outside the studio structure. Footage of mambo dancers from the Palladium, the New York nightclub that regularly featured the legendary bands of Tito Puente, Tito Rodriguez, and Machito, reveals creativity, spontaneity, and improvisation by the dancers in attendance.[49] Mambo and cha cha dancing replaced swing during this new American dance craze, particularly in New York and other U.S. cities with large immigrant populations from the Caribbean. Much like the ragtime dance craze, which was inspired by early jazz music, the Latin dance craze of the 1950s, fueled by the fusion of Caribbean music with jazz, reflected the improvisational character of the music in its dances. Even more revolutionary than the swing breakaway, in which partners were connected only by one hand and could momentarily improvise independently, mambo dancing included extended periods of solo dancing during which partners improvised without even touching each other. Partnered steps were often adapted from swing but featured radically different qualities. Energy was more tightly bound rather than freely directed outward, focus much more internal. Tension was created by the measured release of a leg flick or a head toss, its force doubled by its quick return to the tight kinesphere of a body trying to contain the multiplicity of rhythms it sought to reproduce. Hips, shoulders, and torsos were featured, in addition to the rapid footwork that had characterized swing as well. In response to the primacy of interlocking percussive rhythms in the music, dancers developed different syncopations, sustaining postures and then breaking out at unexpected moments. By the 1960s the Latin dance explosion had simmered down, displaced by another radical revolution in American social dance—the era of the twist, the frug, the pony, and an endless number of fad dances that shifted the focus away from individual partnerships to the lone individual.

In the late 1950s, there were a few isolated pockets of exiled dancers from Great Britain teaching English Style ballroom dancing in North America. In the Los Angeles area, Ken and Sheila Sloan had a significant following, as did Archie Dixon and Dorothy Webster, who were teaching English Style dancing for Arthur Murray Studios in Toronto. Likewise, there were a few competitions being held on this continent similar to those in England, including John Morton's California Star Ball, currently the oldest running competition on the American DanceSport circuit. There were some large Arthur Murray competitions run in Pittsburgh, and the popular Harvest Moon Ball was held in New York and in Chicago. But Arthur Murray Studios mainly focused on preparing their students for social dancing or showcase events—evenings in which each student would perform a choreographed routine with his or her teacher. Dance competitions were infrequent, and, outside of the franchise systems, little was organized on a national scale.

But in the early 1960s, English Style dancing and its competitive focus began to make major inroads into the U.S. market. The Imperial Society of Teachers of Dancing began running one competition a year in the United States to promote English Style dancing. A U.S. branch of the Imperial Society was formed in 1961 and incorporated in 1967. By 1962, the NDCA, which currently serves as the governing body for United States ballroom dance competitions, was granted membership into the International Council of Ballroom Dancing (ICBD), now called the World Dance and Dance Sport Council. This move marked the United States' entry into the circuit of competitions in English Style ballroom dancing being conducted worldwide.

In 1965, the Arthur Murray Corporation organized a United States tour for Bill and Bobbie Irvine, at the time the world champions of English Style ballroom dancing. As they recounted in their autobiography, the Irvines gave lectures and demonstrations in dozens of U.S. cities, introducing thousands of American dancers to the English Style for the first time. Their recollections reveal the major differences in technique still prevalent at that time between American and English dancers. Bill Irvine writes, "They had no idea of how to use the foot. They didn't believe you could put down your heel on the floor; they had been taught to dance forward on the toes only. The limitations this invoked can be imagined. . . . There was no lack of enthusiasm from the pupils—simply a lack of knowledge."[50] Murray technique was still based heavily on ballet turnout and rising high on the toes, as opposed to the English technique, which required full use of the foot, heels landing first on many steps. But scarcely five years later, when the Irvines wrote their memoir, English Style dancing, by that time renamed International Style, had become considerably more prevalent in U.S. dancing schools. Irvine wrote in 1970, "We re-arranged the teaching syllabus for them on a subsequent trip, and re-organized the teaching manual. We go regularly now to teach and demonstrate, and I'm happy to say that International Style ballroom dancing has taken a firm hold on the dancing public of the U.S.A."[51]

The English style of dancing and competition system began to grow in the United States at the exact moment ballroom dancing was at its nadir as a social activity. Throughout the first half of the twentieth century, ballroom dancing was a popular form of social dancing in America, particularly among the white middle and upper classes. Ballroom dance teachers thrived on being able to regulate and instruct proper dance technique, which was coveted as a physical marker of a highly desirable class position. However, Chubby Checker's 1960 appearance on *American Bandstand* in an infectious new social dance that could be done without a partner or formal instruction represented and stimulated a revolution in social dancing whose effects are still gyrating in nightclubs across the nation. The twist and its subsequent variations altered the role of the ballroom industry in American society. Not only did the dances themselves take on dramatically different form—individual freedom, explicit sexuality, and disorganized movement rupturing the aesthetics of social dance—but the social significance of dance shifted as well. Although social dance had always been associated with courtship, new dance practices reflected changing sexual mores. Social dance became a prelude to an uncommitted sexual encounter rather than

Bill and Bobbie Irvine, M.B.E., competing in Latin. Royal Albert Hall, London, 1968. Photo by Henryk Blotnicki, Sweden.

an overture to marriage. But, more significant than these shifting romantic messages, mastery of a codified set of dance techniques and steps lost their power to signify elevated social class position. No longer were dance masters those who held the secret to social success; instead, they threatened to become antiquated conservatives trying to rein in America's sexual and social revolutions.[52]

U.S. ballroom dance studios were receptive to the importation of the English competition style at this historical moment, I argue, because it allowed them to shift their focus away from contemporary social dance, which didn't seem to need teachers anymore, and toward competitive performances of social dance. The outdated reference to organized heterosexual courtship and performance of class status through a strictly defined leader-follower partnership was not such a liability in the competitive context. Convincing new students that ballroom dancing was a valuable social skill may have been difficult in the cultural climate of the 1960s, but competition dancing was often an easier sell. In competition, the artifice of performance was already assumed. Under its auspices, the disjuncture between new social trends on the dance floor and the performance of ballroom dance in competition may not have needed explanation. If an investment in studying ballroom dancing could be created without relying on its usefulness for courtship or as a marker of class status in social settings, then the American ballroom dance industry could survive the radical individualism, political upheaval, and sexual revolution of the 1960s. Ballroom dance competitions offered students a new forum in which to be recognized for their mastery of refined movement. Ballroom dancing's stage was transposed from social floors to competition settings. As agility on the ballroom floor became less important for acceptance into elite social circles, dance teachers could no longer rely on external social pressures to motivate pupils' continuation of dancing lessons. The desire to perfect one's waltzing skills had to be manufactured from within the industry. It was not until the disco craze of the mid-1970s, marked by John Travolta's 1977 appearance in *Saturday Night Fever,* that "touch" dancing once again became a popular American pastime. Though ballroom studios did not hesitate to capitalize on this fad and seized the opportunity to lure the general public back in for hustle dance lessons, the introduction of competition dancing had already made serious headway in restructuring the American ballroom dance industry.

Until the 1960s, American dance competitions were primarily locally based events at dance halls or clubs, where the best social dancers competed for recognition. When Arthur Murray's syllabus had been distributed nationally but enacted locally, there was still some room for regional variation. When this English system of national and international competition was adopted by U.S. dance schools in the 1960s, however, variation was further diminished. Dancers began traveling to compete together in nationally organized competitions, sharing space and mimicking the winners of each competition in hopes of improving their own rankings. The introduction of English Style ballroom dancing brought with it the legacy of a thirty-year development as a competitive dance form largely divorced from social dance practices. The English Style had been remarkably successful as a competition form because it defined such clear standards for measuring achievement, methods for comparing skill, and techniques for teaching standardized steps. Improvisation, creativity, and musical interpretation did not lend themselves well to the competition format, but mastery of skill—which the English system had perfected—did. The English dance techniques and competition system were attractive to American competition organizers because they included established standards by which skill and success at a national and international level could be measured.

A national circuit of dance competitions began to emerge in the United States with formats and rules modeled on the English system. Early competitions run by the ISTD in the United States promoted only English Style ballroom dancing and offered no categories for American styles of ballroom. But American styles of ballroom dancing did not entirely disappear, especially those promoted by the large franchise studios. U.S. teachers adapted American Style dancing to fit the English competition system. Fred Astaire and Arthur Murray studios began to hold competitions modeled after the British, in which all couples danced on the floor simultaneously and winners were selected through a process of elimination. This new format eclipsed the single-couple showcases that had been the norm at large studio events. They also adopted the English medal system for defining dance level and syllabus standards. But such an overlay of the English system of competition, which required that one's skill be judged against uniform standards, onto American Style ballroom dancing, which was still characterized by individuality and regional variation, produced something that was neither highly competitive nor socially interactive. Since playfulness, improvisation, and creativity could not be judged in the English group competition format, adapting American Style ballroom dancing to this system meant that individual steps had to be codified. Particular steps, however, were not the essence of these American dances; their adaptability to particular situations through improvisation figured much more prominently than did specific vocabulary. Because the competition format did not reward improvisation and could not support radical stylistic variations, teachers began applying simplified English technique to the American steps. Thus, an entirely new style of American dance emerged—competitive American Style ballroom dance—that preserved neither the playfulness and social qualities of earlier American dances nor the technical rigor and structure of the English Style.[53]

When interest in social ballroom dancing started to revive, fueled by the disco craze of the mid-1970s, and then soared in the 1990s, few teachers or studios recognized the incongruity of teaching social dancing based on the new teaching methods, which were designed to produce successful competition results. They continued to teach American Style social dancing using the new priorities that had been established for competition. Though the popularity of the new competition dancing, renamed DanceSport by 1990 in order to improve its chances of inclusion in the Olympic Games, grew, hand in hand with general revivals of partner social dancing, the dance industry began to rely more heavily on conflation of the two styles in order to sell both.

Primarily because teaching competitive ballroom dance has proved to be so much more profitable than teaching social dance, the industry rhetoric implies that social ballroom dancing is merely poorly executed DanceSport.[54] Whereas competitive ballroom dancing was once a polished and flamboyant version of the popular social form, social ballroom dance has now become a stylization of DanceSport. Before DanceSport, innovation in social dance happened on the social dance floor, and ballrooms such as the Savoy and the Palladium were legendary for their roles in the developments of swing and mambo respectively. Now creativity in ballroom dance is largely fueled by pressure to excel in competitive dancing; new moves "trickle down" to social dance floors as DanceSport competitors teach their social students new rumba and foxtrot variations. Social ballroom dancers now look to DanceSport competitors for inspiration and guidance. However, the two are no longer, if they ever were, the same form. DanceSport may represent social dance, it may be inspired by social dance, but it is not the same genre of dance any more than ballet is still the same form of dance once practiced by the French nobility. But the DanceSport industry is rife with confusion on this subject. Its structure perpetuates this myth that Dance-Sport is the highest pinnacle on a continuum of social dance.

CONTEMPORARY CONFLATION OF SOCIAL AND COMPETITIVE DANCE

Historical continuity between social dance and DanceSport, rather than their disjuncture, dominates the dance industry's public rhetoric. "Histories" of DanceSport included on countless studio Web sites and in promotional literature are little more than origin stories, distilling the history of foxtrot or rumba to a single person or nation credited with its invention (Harry Fox in the case of the former, Cuba for the latter) and the date of its introduction into American ballrooms (1914 for the foxtrot, 1930 for the rumba). None of these histories ever explains the transition from these early examples to the contemporary DanceSport versions. The elision helps maintain the fantasy that the two practices are one and the same. Television programs featuring DanceSport may devote broadcast time to linking the dancing performed in competition to social practices of the early twentieth century.[55] Brief historical synopses do little, however, to draw out any visual resemblance between historical footage of social dancing and the dramatic DanceSport competition with which it is juxtaposed. Viewers unfamiliar with competition dancing tend to see only a connection in name between International Style cha cha and the dance practiced at the Palladium in the 1950s. And yet sustaining the illusion that DanceSport is only a more highly developed version of these social dance forms is one of the industry's primary marketing strategies.

The success of theatrical ballroom dance performed in competition or on-stage depends on the emotional potency of the social dance fantasies maintained by spectators. Part of the viewing pleasure is in envisioning oneself into the scene and in the fantasy that this movement form—unlike ballet, for example— is accessible to the common viewer. During the 2000 PBS broadcast *Champion-ship Ballroom Dancing,* the celebrity co-host, Sandy Duncan, commented while the U.S. national champions performed a theatrical waltz adagio, "the truth is, anybody can go and learn the basics." To prove her point, Duncan appeared at the program's conclusion dancing with her teenage son, who seemed mark-edly ordinary against the backdrop of DanceSport Glamour mavens. While obviously not on par with the professional dancers, he showed off an enthusi-astic social swing and was joined on the floor by the rest of the audience in the traditional closing scene, where the audience in the ballroom and at home in their living rooms are invited to "join us" on the dance floor. Other traditions of concert and theatrical dance rarely end with an invitation for viewers to join the performers on stage, relying instead on maintaining distinctions between the extraordinary human beings capable of performing such spectacular physi-cal feats and the ordinary bodies of the spectators. Such attempts to emphasize continuity between these two groups and downplay the chasm between social and competitive ballroom dance represents a crucial apparatus of the Glam-our Machine. The potency of a DanceSport performance depends on implying that during the very next song it could be you—the viewer—out there on that dance floor, holding that beautiful woman in your arms, or swooping back into that debonair man's strong hold. Indeed, most American DanceSport competi-tions are organized so that social dancing is integrated into the event's structure, general dancing by the audience alternating with rounds of competition. The performance of courtship and courtship itself are intentionally allied, their dis-tinction obfuscated.

Aided by popular histories that place social and competitive dance on a con-tinuum and by media conflation of romance in social dance with performance-based representations of social dance, studios themselves encourage the mar-riage of these divergent practices as a necessary tool for their own economic survival. In order to attract new clients, studios rely on American interest in social ballroom dance classes, usually propelled by a lingering ideology that one should know how to waltz and foxtrot to be a cultured member of society and by a vague impression that coordinating one's movements with another body and with music would be enjoyable. However, the social dancer is rarely the ballroom dance teacher's preferred student. Students usually embark on a social dance program with the expectation that they will take a few lessons, learn how to dance, and leave the studio in a month or two. From a business perspective, studios and teachers are deeply invested in altering this plan. In addition to instilling perpetual self-doubt in students' perceptions of their own abilities, ballroom studios use two other strategies to retain students indefinitely: they insist that dance literacy requires mastery of a dozen dances, and they introduce students to competition. The first of these strategies explains how ballroom dance studios have kept alive a number of social dances that would have otherwise died out when the music lost popularity and nightclub owners opted for smaller, less expensive dance floors. The second tactic is, however, more closely linked to the Glamour Machine. If a teacher can sell a student on competition dancing, that student will have to spend years taking dance lessons to master the difficult competition technique. This is the hook that keeps the two ends of the industry co-dependent. Teaching only social dancing is rarely profitable enough, and new competitive students are usually only gleaned from social dance classes. Very few students enter the studio as aspiring competitors.[56] It is only through calculated encouragement by their personal dance teacher that new students are persuaded to enter newcomer categories of competition, initiating them into the DanceSport lifestyle. Given that studios hope to turn every social dance student into a competitor, it is not surprising that DanceSport technique is taught even to beginning social dancers, promising a smooth transition from social to competition floor. There are some ballroom studios that teach only social dance, and a very few that can survive offering instruction in DanceSport alone, but most teach both, literally, side by side. Competitive and social dancers are invariably brushing up against each other in studios across America. In some studios it is not unusual for national DanceSport champions to be receiving coaching at the same time as a beginner couple who has come in to take a few foxtrot lessons before a friend's wedding. This juxtaposition in space between the competitive and social aspects of the business represents their continual interdependence.[57]

Although I have argued that confusion between theatrical and social dance has been used as a marketing tool of the ballroom dance industry throughout the twentieth century, the current obfuscation runs deeper than mere public perception. Teachers of social ballroom dance are primarily DanceSport competitors and rarely participate in social dancing themselves. There are few opportunities for professionals to dance socially with each other (they are generally forbidden to do so at studio events), and thus most tend to think of social ballroom dance as work, not play. Though most teachers of ballroom dance are engaged in ongoing education to improve their own skills, their training is almost exclusively in DanceSport, not social dance. Ballroom dance teachers have little motivation to invest in social ballroom dancing lessons when their own careers are measured by success as DanceSport competitors. Therefore, ballroom dance teachers apply DanceSport technique when teaching social ball-room dance, with little awareness that, for example, expansive gestures that are effective on the competition floor are not appropriate in the social setting, where subtlety and improvisational play are more useful.

The problems created by the juxtaposition of social ballroom dancing with DanceSport have been exacerbated by the increased participation of immigrants from countries with little tradition of social ballroom dance. The recent growth of American DanceSport, particularly in International Style competition, has been fueled by an influx of immigrants from Eastern Europe eager to continue practicing this sport, a popular recreation for youth in their home countries. DanceSport programs were widely supported by Communist governments in Eastern Europe. Though not as heavily subsidized after the dissolution of the USSR, the infrastructure for teaching large classes of children is still in place. The prevalence of these "dance clubs" in most major cities, coupled with new cultural permission to strive for personal excellence through individual com-petition, enables DanceSport to thrive in Eastern Europe.[58] Children who im-migrated from these countries began competing in America as amateurs, and young-adult immigrants entered the industry as teachers of dancing, their jobs in American dance schools allowing them to support their own DanceSport passion. This flood of immigrant participation throughout the 1990s, while rais-ing the standard of American DanceSport competition, has further confused the social/competitive dance distinction. Most of these immigrants have no experience with social ballroom dancing, coming out of programs geared ex-clusively to DanceSport. However, they are dropped into the American dance industry to teach social dancing, with little training or explanation of the dif-ferences between competition and social forms.[59]

Few immigrant or American ballroom dance teachers are conscious of a clear differentiation between social ballroom dance and DanceSport, most often re-producing the industry rhetoric that suggests continuity between the foxtrot danced socially and that seen on the competition floor. The closest rhetorical differentiation made is between International Style (standing in for competition dancing) and American Style (more readily associated with social dancing). Al-though this distinction does accurately reflect the different contexts in which the two styles developed, the International Style having been clearly defined as a competition form much earlier than the American Style, failure to recog-nize that either could be a social or competitive form causes further confusion. Both are practiced in the competitive context, although International Style is al-most universally recognized as the more serious, technical, and implicitly higher form. Therefore, the linking of American Style to social dancing further rein-forces the misperception that social dancing is just inferior competition danc-ing. Lacking alternative models, most teachers eliminate the difficult points of DanceSport technique for their social students.

Because the ballroom dance industry so successfully obscures and elides the distinction between social dance and DanceSport, I will take some time here to clarify their differing priorities. An audience fifty or even ten feet away cannot see the same kinds of subtlety in movement as a partner who is six inches away. Thus, theatrical representations are usually exaggerated, suggesting rather than enacting a flirtation or embrace. The way a physical connection looks to an outside viewer and the way it feels to participants can differ radically, influencing the kinds of choices that are made in different contexts. Is this move to be felt or seen? A social dancer, who needs only for his partner to feel the sensation of his caress, will make a much smaller gesture than a competitor, who hopes distant viewers will be able to read the intensity of his embrace. In competition, expansive movements are practical both for capturing attention when audience members are seated at a great distance and for outshining dozens of other competitors simultaneously attempting to draw in viewers' eyes. Social dancers often imitate these exaggerated gestures, but with a tentativeness that betrays their own misgivings about their appropriateness in a social situation. A sweeping arm gesture, which in competition might have the effect of presenting one's body for spectacular consumption, may appear ritualized and awkward when a social dancer thrusts his or her arms out perpendicular to his body. The posture practiced in the Standard category of DanceSport competition, which requires vertical lift and an outward poise so that the partners are stretching away from each other in a locked embrace, is effective in competition because it draws attention to the dancers' imposing use of space. By simultaneously maintaining a close position in the lower half of the body, they can move deftly and smoothly with tremendous speed and power while still maintaining an expansive and calm appearance. On a social dance floor, however, such avaricious possession of precious space is usually rude and impractical, not to mention unromantic. Misapplication of these DanceSport technique to social dance often results in physical postures or gestures that appear absurd, graceless, or incongruous, further reinforcing the perceived hierarchy and implicit value judgment about "inferior" social ballroom dance and "superior" competitive dancing.

The transposition of concepts from competition to social floors in the Latin category often appears similarly misguided. Hip movement is only one of many elements that characterize the Latin dances in competition. The supple movement of the rib cage, changes in the timing and direction of hip rotation, and the use of counterweight to produce fast changes of direction fall out of social iterations of ballroom Latin, leaving only exaggerated hip action to mark it "Latin." In their attempts to mimic the competitors, social ballroom dancers (and many dance teachers) fail to recognize that they are copying effects only producible through application of ten other techniques their bodies are not yet prepared to execute.

The distinction between social dance and performance of social dance often boils down to whether sight or touch is privileged. In fact, differing expectations about the relative value of optic and haptic in these two environments intensifies their impact in both. Witnessing the intimacy of a scene that appears to be directed at tactile sensations can be just as thrilling as experiencing that caress. The frame of the social nightclub makes viewing the spectacle more appealing because the setting suggests transgression. Illicit public display of affection and corollary witnessing of clandestine intimacy intensifies the experience on both sides. The viewer feels the pleasure of stumbling upon a secret, and the couple's flirtations are strengthened by the knowledge that someone might be watching.

Removed from the frame of the social, the effect of these same movements would be entirely different. The same movements billed as a performance under bright lights on a stage would likely be unremarkable. This kind of intimacy can be closely approximated in a theatrical context only by film, where the close distance and illusion of overseeing an intimate moment can be replicated. The thrill of this forbidden spill over between the sense of sight and touch happens in performance as well. A touch that is theatrical, meant only to represent courtship and not to enact it, can be experienced at a very personal and intimate level. A dancer performing or teaching may experience sexual or emotional arousal not intended by the physical touch enacted. Knowledge that these feelings are ostensibly forbidden (this is just acting or business) can intensify reaction to the touch. At the same time, the feeling of arousal can make the portrayal of romance even more convincing to the audience. These crossover experiences of sight and touch notwithstanding, however, social dance is primarily structured for kinesthetic pleasure on the part of the practitioners, and performance-oriented dance events are designed to give the audience visual delight.

Many skills useful in DanceSport are not relevant to social ballroom dancing, but there is one skill only tangentially pertinent to DanceSport that is crucial for social dancing—improvisation. Although social ballroom dancers do not employ extensive improvisation in their practice, social dance forms such as salsa and West Coast swing foreground spontaneous reaction to the music and one's partner.[60] Dancers make choices about how and when to move in the moment of execution. Improvisation is the point. Excitement is generated out of uncertainty. Not being able to predict precisely the next moves of the musicians or of one's partner makes each decision that brings all three into harmony deliciously rewarding. The best social salsa and swing dancers not only are skilled at responding to a human partner, but also know equally well how to partner the music. Many dancers are masterful musical interpreters, matching percussion accents and melodic crescendos with their own physical repartee. Such skills are admired not because a dancer has planned in advance which movements will compliment which measure of music, but precisely because he or she has not. The dance scholar Susan Foster describes the pleasure of watching improvisational concert dance when she writes, "Unanticipated trajectories, landings, and traversals create stunning kinesthetic paradoxes as one compares what the body might have done with what it actually did."[61] Spectators of improvisational social dance likewise compare the spontaneous decisions of the dancers with other possible choices, the elegance or cleverness of each move strengthened through the contrast. The expert improvisational dancer can instantaneously recognize musical patterns, evaluate the available spatial parameters, and seamlessly communicate with his or her partner in order to perform stunning combinations of grace and dexterity that an inexpert observer might swear had been rehearsed beforehand.

Although improvisation may dazzle onlookers in a social dance club, it rarely works as a successful strategy for staged performance of social dance. The stage and competition frame set up different audience expectations from those produced by the frame of a nightclub, and improvisation in the formal setting is rarely readable as such. Removed from the social dance floor, where it is clearly framed as improvisation by the surrounding dancers, the casual spectators, the dim lights, and the intimate focus, a skillful improvisation may seem unremarkable when presented on a stage. An audience of a performance expects a well-rehearsed routine, neatly worked out to match the music. Whereas in the social setting spectators may have just witnessed the dancers' introduction and can be assured that their interactions are unrehearsed, an audience of theatrical performance has no similar validation that significant movement choices are being made in the moment of execution. The clear separation between audience and spectators in performance genres often obscures the viewers' ability to read improvisational structures.

For DanceSport competitors, spontaneous creation of new combinations and moves on the competition floor seems too risky. Dancers have only a few seconds to convince each judge of their superior skill. There is no room for error. Such calculation is in stark contrast to social dancing, which invites, even expects, experimentation, failed signals, and creative mistakes. Even though DanceSport competition offers minimal opportunity for improvisation, spontaneous improvisational choices are periodically in evidence. For example, if a dancer interacts with an audience member, another competitor, or judge during the competition, the crowd erupts in cheers. Occasionally, competitors will dance briefly with their opponents after a collision, intentionally chase a camera man, or caress a judge. These moments delight the audience because they offer rare insight into the dancers' impromptu decisions. Much more commonly, however, improvisational decisions are not apparent to an audience in performance. Doing one fewer turn because of poor balance, adjusting a trajectory because of an unexpected obstacle, or changing the choreography owing to a memory lapse are supposed to be hidden choices.

Although I have discussed multiple reasons for the disappearance of improvisation from the ballroom dances as they were codified for sale in the ballroom dance industry, including motivations based on both economic and racial assumptions, the contemporary conflation of DanceSport with social ballroom dancing continues to drive improvisation out of social ballroom dance. Because the ballroom dance industry is primarily run by DanceSport aficionados, the low value placed on improvisation in competitive ballroom dance is transposed to social ballrooms. Social ballroom dancers (or at least the leader in each partnership) are taught how to make improvisational choices only in the order of steps executed. Although social dancers may enjoy more improvisational choice than DanceSport competitors typically employ, many other improvisational possibilities are potentially available to social dancers. Each social ballroom dance could be taught in a manner that encouraged play, musical interpretation, creative expression, and innovation. Each dance has a basic rhythm and several basic patterns. Dancers could vary these steps, extend them, develop them, alter the rhythm, or change them in any way as long as the deviations from the norm could be followed. A step works in social dancing if an experienced leader can get an experienced follower to do the step even if she has never seen it before. She must know how to respond to weight shifts, how to connect her center to his, how to turn, and particular conventions of the dance, but she needn't know the specific move before he leads her into it. These are precisely the conventions that enable improvisational salsa and West Coast swing dancers to converse on the dance floor, even when they are unfamiliar with each other's dance vocabulary. Because these two social dance communities place a high value on improvisation (although they are certainly not the only dance forms to do so), I will compare salsa and West Coast swing to ballroom dance in order to highlight the difference between improvisational social dance and social ballroom dance.

IMPROVISATION IN SALSA AND WEST COAST SWING

Although both salsa and West Coast swing have competitive and performance versions, each community is centered on social practice as the primary pursuit of even its most skilled dancers. Many DanceSport champions have little experience or skill in social dancing; salsa and West Coast swing champions, on the other hand, prove themselves accomplished social dancers before entering competition. The congresses and competitions held by swing and salsa societies foreground social dancing. Bands and deejays play until 4 A.M., with competitions and shows serving only as intermissions in the central business of social dancing. In contrast, ballroom dance events feature hours of competition with infrequent interludes of social dancing that are only tangential to the primary focus of competition. On the one hand, the separation of social and performance-based genres has led ballroom dancers to develop more sophisticated techniques for spectacular display than either salsa or West Coast dancers. However, their corollary focus on social dancing has allowed salsa and West Coast swing dancers to cultivate more advanced strategies for improvisational exchange. Codification of any dance form for economic profit always produces some loss of creativity and variety in the practice; however, both the salsa and West Coast swing industries produce social dancers who are active in the process of recreating and developing a vibrant dance practice.

This difference is reflected in and reproduced by the contrasting structure of competition in these industries. For example, events sanctioned by the World Swing Dance Council place a high priority on Jack and Jill competitions, contests in which the partners are assigned to each other as the competition begins (as opposed to the DanceSport convention of partnerships entering a competition only after months of rehearsal together), forcing improvisation between the partners, who may be strangers. The swing competition circuit also highlights a category called "strictly swing," in which dancers can choose their partners but not the music. They are not expected to do preset choreography and are judged on how well they improvise to the particular selection of the deejay. Judges for both these categories place a high value on clever musical interpretation. Given the structure of DanceSport competitions, which allot judges

Social dancers improvising at the West Coast Salsa Congress. Los Angeles, California, May 2005. Photo by Roy Amemiya, Salsaholics.com.

less time to watch each individual performance, evaluating for improvisational musical interpretation is rarely practical. Because DanceSport judges have less than two minutes to judge between six and twenty-four couples simultaneously, the subtlety of improvisation is overlooked in deference to speed, dynamic changes, and visual impact. Improvisation choices in DanceSport are primarily in floorcraft, the art of fitting one's routine into the ever-shifting paths of space that open and close as other competitors simultaneously negotiate the same floor. Although musical interpretation could be foregrounded in social ballroom dance, teaching skills for changing steps to match the accents of a particular musical selection is not practical in the current studio system, in which multiple private lessons are taught in the same space. Because up to twenty teachers might be sharing the same floor and stereo, students are trained to respond to the drone of "a-5-6-7-8" rather than to the subtleties of a piano riff or the blare of trumpets.

The salsa and West Coast swing communities are centered around the practice of one major dance (and several less complex minor dances), whereas ballroom dance socials invariably require that participants be versed in upward of ten different dances. The sheer number of dances that even a beginning student is required to know in order to enjoy a social ballroom dance party severely limits the time he or she has left to develop improvisational skills. Practitioners' resources are spread so thin, it's not surprising that ballroom dances are often reduced to their steps. Teaching all students the same basic patterns is the fastest way to get them dancing together, setting a precedent that is hard to reverse once the students might be ready to apply techniques that could develop improvisational skills.

Instead of training advanced social ballroom dancers in exchanging rhythms, extending patterns, or creating their own variations, the ballroom dance industry turns to DanceSport for the expression of more advanced social dance moves. Competitors use preset choreography, enabling them to do steps that, although still requiring initiation on the part of one and reaction on the part of another, can only be successfully completed when practiced and agreed upon beforehand. Sudden stops in extended body lines, for example, are not practical on a social dance floor, where both partners must be prepared for the unexpected, keeping their bodies in constant motion to absorb sudden changes of momentum. The adaptation of these theatrical partnered moves for social dance inhibits individual, interactive, spontaneous creativity. Many ballroom dance studios teach choreography as social dance. In other words, they teach amalgamations that are not leadable and can be executed only by two people who have memorized the same combination. Studios have resorted to social dance choreography for at least two reasons. The first is that many of the popular moves professionals execute require more skill than most social dancers will ever have. In response to the desire of students to mimic the champions, dance teachers invent moves that look similar but don't physically upset the partnership when executed incorrectly. Leading and following require the sharing of weight and energy between partners. Advanced moves often depend more heavily on partnership for balance, leaving the dancer more vulnerable to being pulled off-balance or even injury by an incorrect response. Modifying these moves and turning them into solo choreography, where the dancers are responsible only for their own weight, makes the moves safer and possible for less advanced dancers. Social dancers can get a taste of advanced moves without actually acquiring the skill necessary to execute them accurately.

Another reason ballroom dance studios teach choreography as social dance is that ballroom dance maintains no convention for initiating solo dancing. Competition Latin routines are danced almost 50 percent of the time without touching one's partner. Competitors will dance side by side in unison, face each other for playful exchange, run away from each other, or dance around each other, all without a physical connection. These kinds of partnering relationships are central to DanceSport, but they are all pre-choreographed for competition, any adjustments in direction being established through visual leads. Salsa and West Coast swing both have techniques for interspersing solo work into the structure of social dancing. In salsa, the leader can release his partner anytime during the dance to allow for solo "shine" work. The dancers will face each other for several measures, playing with fancy footwork and body rhythms in a tradition reminiscent of Afro-Cuban rumba, before reconnecting for more partner work. West Coast swing dancers do not usually release connection entirely, but the leader does reduce tension in the connected hand to invite play from his partner. Each improvises footwork and body styling until the leader reestablishes tension in the connected hand by moving back into a new move. But there is no convention similar to either in social ballroom dance. Ballroom dancers are not taught that improvisation or play is an option, or that the follower has any opportunity to insert her voice into the dance. Ballroom dancers rationalize that leading is not possible without physical contact. But "leading" in the tradition of physical directives is no longer the point in this kind of solo work. It is about challenge and dialogue, each partner offering his or her own interpretation of the music to the other in an exchange of one-upmanship.

This difference represents a larger divide between the roles of leader and follower as conceptualized in ballroom dance when compared to other social partner dance forms. In ballroom, the leader determines the steps a couple executes, as well as their order, direction, and rhythm. He will likely execute the same repertoire of steps no matter whom he dances with. The only unknown factors are whether he will crash into anyone and whether she will follow. There is little expectation that she will significantly influence the dance, change the steps, or react unexpectedly to his lead and create new moves. Though the man is still expected to lead the majority of the moves in salsa and West Coast swing, there are also conventions in both these forms for the follower to alter the style, feel, even the entire composition of the dance. Despite its machismo, which characterizes the culture out of which it evolved, salsa has a structure that allows the female salsera more agency than the female ballroom dancer is given. Because of the loose physical connection and consistent timing of salsa (each pattern finishing at the end of an eight-beat phrase), a follower can syncopate her footwork; isolate her ribs, hips, shoulders, or head in rhythmic thrusts; change the direction of a step; or alter her body shape, all without changing the move her partner leads. And not only is solo shine work typical in salsa; supported shine work is also common, in which the man opens his legs to provide a stable base and offers his hands for support to his partner, who can then improvise her own swivels and syncopations, ending with a foot shooting between his legs or a slow, seductive body ripple.

West Coast swing allows the follower these same possibilities and more. She can even "hijack" most moves he leads and alter their direction or change the length of the pattern by extending it to suit her mood. This is accomplished through a technique that requires a light connection throughout so that each partner is sensitive to receiving information. This possibility for either member of the partnership to ad-lib within a structure in which the man leads the majority of the patterns is enabled by the fact that every pattern, no matter how extended or altered, always ends and begins the same way. Every pattern ends with an anchor in which both partners establish a connection by stretching their centers slightly away from one another. The dance is contained in a "slot" where the follower moves back and forth on a straight line, passing the leader, who generally stays in the center. The rigidity of this structure ironically enables freedom of improvisation because both partners know they cannot start a new pattern until they have anchored at the end of the slot. The dance works as a conversation rather than a dictation. West Coast swing dancers are so chauvinistic about the sophisticated ability of both partners to improvise that, in the words of popular writer Eve Babitz, "people who do West Coast Swing think it's so great that all other dances would *be* West Coast Swing, if only people *knew*" (emphasis in original).[62]

Despite the absence of freedom in improvisational structure, social ballroom dance as it is currently practiced is an enjoyable social activity for many practitioners, offering them opportunities for social interaction, exercise, accomplishment, emotional release, and even artistic expression. Many people prefer the small degree of freedom and creativity allowed in ballroom dance in contrast to the more unpredictable practices of West Coast swing or salsa. Ballroom dance still offers them some amount of improvisational freedom in contrast to round dancing, for example, which utilizes ballroom dance steps performed in a set order specified by the caller, who organizes the entire group to execute the same steps at the same time. Social ballroom dancers may be specifically drawn to its strict structure—the reams of rules written down in technique books for each step about direction, amount of turn, angle of foot placement, rotation of body, sway of body, elevation of the body, degree of foot pressure, precedes, and follows. Ballroom dance can readily be defined by its propensity for formulas, and one's success can be measured by the precision with which one applies them. Many social ballroom dancers will admit that they enjoy ballroom dancing precisely because social interaction under its auspices is governed by rules justified by the laws of physics.[63]

Those students of ballroom dance, however, who come seeking the emotional high produced from the interactive experience of improvisational social dancing are rarely satisfied. Instead, the industry relies on transforming this interest into a desire for perfection of competition technique. The drive to maximize profit margins, though not the only explanation for the continued omission of improvisation from social dance programs, is a compelling factor. Sale of interactive creativity is much harder to sustain. One can create a venue in which the interaction is promoted and shape the atmosphere so that the music and the décor invite it, but such business endeavors do not produce the profits of Arthur Murray International. The West Coast swing community, which is centered around playful improvisational movement, does not generate the profits typical of DanceSport. Few teachers of West Coast swing make their living teaching full-time, in contrast to the thousands of full-time ballroom dance teachers working in the United States. Aside from a few star teachers, only the dance organizers and the music industry make a significant profit in West Coast swing. Nor are vast numbers of salsa teachers able to support themselves through teaching. Salsa is rapidly becoming the most popular dance of the twenty-first century, but the number of salsa teachers is increasing just as quickly. Strong value on individual improvisation encourages students who have been dancing for only a year to start teaching their own style, flooding the market with new salsa classes. Those salsa dancers who do earn a living selling their skills are often forced to eliminate the very qualities that define it—regional style differences, playful improvisation, musicality, and creativity—in order to appeal to market forces. Large-scale attempts to standardize salsa and certify teachers, such as the World Salsa Federation, rely on the models created by the ballroom dance industry, essentially reproducing social ballroom dance under the name of salsa.

PERFORMANCE OF SOCIAL CLASSIFICATION

In theory, the social ballroom dance industry could be restructured to emphasize improvisation, musicality, and individual expression. Such a reconceptualization, however, might transform ballroom dance into something that warrants a new name. Throughout the twentieth century, ballroom dance has been defined by its promise of upward class mobility. I have argued that the suppression of improvisation in ballroom dancing is closely linked to its performance of upper-class status. The wildness and absence of formal dance education apparent in what looks like unrefined improvisation marks the distance of improvisational social dancers from ballroom social dancers. This stark class divide is represented in the film *Dirty Dancing* through the contrast between the refined ballroom dancing practiced by the wealthy patrons in the main ballrooms of the resort and the "dirty dancing" enjoyed by the working-class staff in their own quarters. Though overt sexuality—hip grinds and full body dips—is a major factor in marking the informal dancing as unacceptable for the high-class patrons, it is also the unpredictability of its structure that marks its lower-class status. This example is one of many that attests to the fact that upper-class status and highly improvisational movement have never been able to coexist under the name ballroom dance.

If precision, refinement, and discipline have trumped improvisational play throughout the history of ballroom dance, perhaps this is because ballroom dance is not really a social form as I have defined the term. I distinguish social dance from a performance genre by the priority each places on the experience of the participants versus that of the viewers. Social dances are for the pleasure of the dancers foremost, and performances are focused on audience impact. I have already illustrated many ways in which social ballroom dance is a unique genre of social dance, one that fails to value the improvisation, musicality, and play that characterize so many other social dance practices. I will now take my argument one step farther to suggest that all ballroom dance, even in its social expression, is more about its effect on viewers than the experience of the dancers, linking it more closely with performance-based representations of social dance than with other social dance practices.

Ballroom dance is always performative, always conscious of how it is locating its practitioners on social grids. To dance ballroom at all is to mark oneself above the masses untrained in "proper" dance technique. But once inside the ballroom dance community, everyone is carefully evaluating and reevaluating where they, and others, fit on endless grids of classification and ordination. Competitors are most obviously ranked by level and placement. But even social dance students know who is studying at the bronze, silver, or gold level. Each step one executes on the social dance floor is already marked, its performance marking the dancer. But classification is more complex than merely a three-tiered system. Those who know that dance is more than just the steps, those who are studying the hallowed technique, also know that if they execute a bronze-level step with more finesse than those silver-level dancers plodding through the moves, then they will be classified as one of those who *really know how to dance.* The selectiveness implied by mastery of the complicated Dance-Sport technique is embraced by even its beginning students. All ballroom dance practitioners believe they are studying *real* dancing, as opposed to the inferior shuffling of those ignorant folks who haven't seen "good" dancing. This arrogance is crucial to the production of Glamour. Glamour promises to be selective in naming its ambassadors, and those who seek its validation disdain those who know nothing of its seduction, hoping that separating themselves into a higher category of dancer will raise their own ranking on the Glamour scale.

Performance of Glamour class position is crucial at any ballroom dance social. Competitors on a social dance floor will dance their competition routines regardless of how inappropriate the context, just to make sure that everyone can identify their status as competitive dancers, people who obviously invest much more time and money in their studies than the social dancers who come out once a week to clutter up the dance floor. International Style dancers are likewise determined to stand out from the crowd, to be distinguished from the "less serious" American Style dancers, whose technique books are not nearly as full of details about contra body movement (CBM) and contra body movement position (CBMP). They are confident that most American Style dancers don't even know the difference. (CBM is rotation of the opposite side of the body toward the moving leg, usually to initiate rotation, and CBMP is a position of the foot when it steps on or across the line of the other foot.) And if they don't know this basic distinction, how can they *really dance,* the logic suggests. And then there are the professional dancers at any social dance—those who have just finished a six-week training course and think they are the next Fred Astaire because they have just been hired by the studio bearing his name, as well as those who have been in the business for ten years. They must all make sure they are distinguishable as professional dancers. Their livelihood is dependent on convincing everyone else at the dance that they know more than the amateurs, that their dance knowledge is worth $60–$100 an hour. Where each participant fits on this grid dictates what kind of partners (and potential mates) they can dance with, what kind of friends they will associate with, and where they fit on the Glamour scale.

It is not just classification that prevails at any (even social) performance of ballroom dance, but anxiety about classification. Performance of social ballroom dance may no longer offer the same kind of universally recognized markers of social position it did in the first half of the twentieth century. But for everyone inside the ballroom dance community versed in the physical codes that mark ordination on dance classification scales, social status is read through mastery of ballroom dance technique. Every dance is an exhibition of skill and status. Just like the competition system, in which an amazing performance recognized by the right judges could catapult a dancer to the top of the system, any social dance performance could change one's position. The weight placed on social status within this system is due in part to the vast range of social positions its participants occupy outside the ballroom.[64] Much more heterogeneous than other dance communities, such as West Coast swing, which is overwhelmingly white and middle class, or even salsa, which is predominantly Latino working and lower middle class, the ballroom dance industry relies on the coalescence of people from radically different economic, educational, racial, ethnic, and social positions. Economically, the industry rests on the financial support of a few monetary elite. The "work" of the industry—the dancing, teaching, and performing—is primarily done by working-class Americans, gay men, and Eastern European immigrants, three groups that lie just outside the mainstream of American culture. The bulk of the social dance students and many of those who get caught in the competitive circuit are middle-class Americans who are seeking some excitement and romance outside their own social strata. It is the convergence of all of these groups seeking a change in their social position that results in dancing that is always, even in its social expression, about performance.

The reasons contemporary social ballroom dance has little to do with social *dancing* as I have defined it are multiple, all of them are key to explaining the phenomenon of Glamour. The evolution of this style of social ballroom dance has been influenced by the heterogeneity of its social constituents, its history as mediator of class and race mobility, and the business strategies adopted by a profit-driven industry. The shift from an industry that taught popular social dances to one that perfected and stylized outdated partner dances for competition has been crucial in shaping its Glamour Machine. Though Glamour was certainly a component of modern ballroom dancing in the early twentieth century, its promise of transformation was more modest in scope. Julie Malnig suggests "that for working-class women [in the 1910s] adopting styles of dress, behaviors, and movement styles was a way of experimenting with alternative forms of social identity and independence to better oneself within one's *own* community or class."[65] Social mobility may not actually be any more attainable today than it was a century ago, but the illusion that radical social transformation is possible has intensified in recent decades as interaction among people in different social strata has increased.[66] DanceSport participants may be setting higher aspirations for their own social mobility, ultimately contributing to greater disappointment when their expectations are not met and driving them to gloss over this shortfall through the cartoonish grandiosity of competition dancing. If social ballroom dancing has traditionally meant performing a higher-class position, competition ballroom dancing has come to signify performing that performance of a higher-class position, the doubled layer inviting hyperbolic theatricality. It is this extreme exaggeration of performance that defines contemporary American DanceSport, its references to social interaction and courtship deeply buried by the promises of mystical transformation of the Glamorous body each time the ballroom dancer steps onto a polished wood floor.

three

Brownface: Representations
of Latinness in Latin Dance

An overwhelming stench hovers in the air as a DanceSport competitor lathers brown body paint onto her naked body. She squirms under the sting of chemicals burning her freshly shaved legs. Every fair-skinned dancer has tested a dozen self-tanning products before settling on one that stains her skin dark enough to "pass" as a professional Latin DanceSport competitor. Central to the transformation of a mere human body to that of a Glamorous DanceSport star is the ritual of painting light skin a deep bronze. At $27 a bottle, the German-made Profi-Tan-intensive-Latin-Color is a popular product of choice. After three generous coats of the bronze elixir have been absorbed into the skin, her "brownface" is complete, and this dancer is ready to withstand an entire evening of competition cha chas.

Although competitive ballroom dancers are not the only consumers of self-tanning products, the prevalence of artificially darkened white skin in Dance-Sport Latin competitions invites examination into the relationship between ballroom "Latin" dances and their ethnic referents. I introduce the term brownface, not a word used in the DanceSport industry, in order to call attention to the racial and potentially racist consequences of this practice. Many colleagues in the dance business deny that the use of tanning cream has anything to do with race. It is stage makeup, they insist, designed to give pale skin a healthy glow under harsh bright lights, an interpretation supported by the fact that bodybuilders and beauty contestants also use tanning creams when displaying their bodies for formal evaluation. Others point out that tanned white skin has become associated with wealth and leisure in late industrial American culture, where most people work in doors, out of the sun.[1] Whether it comes from tanning booths or bottles, the dark skin of DanceSport celebrities aligns it with other sites of upper-class recreation. There is no denying that the ballroom obsession with artificially darkened skin is closely linked to the image of classiness and athleticism it projects, and its role in producing Glamour involves more than just a reference to race. Admittedly, both DanceSport Standard and Latin dancers use some form of dark makeup for competition. But it is in the Latin category, where women's legs, bellies, and backs and men's chests are exposed, that the use of such products is most pronounced and widespread. Whether this practice evolved because costuming in the Latin category has gradually exposed more flesh or through a conscious attempt on the part of competitors to look more "Latin," its effects are racially charged. Race is never just about skin color, but no single factor is more central in determining racial categorization. In America's racially fraught sociopolitical climate, there is no way to read the practice of brownface, particularly that of the Latin DanceSport competitors, that does not in some way have to do with race and the ethnic and national groups invoked by its visual marking.

DanceSport Latin is a stylization of social ballroom dances that, although inspired by Afro-Caribbean and Latin social dance practices, were popularized and defined in the West. After five to seven decades of revision at the hands of English, European, and American dancers, the DanceSport versions of the Latin dances bear little in common with contemporary or historical practices in Latin America. Much like the conflation of social and performance versions of ballroom dance I discuss in chapter 2, the rhetoric of dance teachers and media representatives continues to rely on a close association between DanceSport's Latin division and dancing practiced in Latin America. This chapter focuses on the racial implications of such representations of Latinness in DanceSport. I begin with an historical excavation of how these Latin dances entered Dance-Sport competition, revisiting much of the narrative outlined in chapter 2, in which I argued that the elimination of improvisation from the ballroom dances was linked to marketability, class mobility, and racial prejudice. Now I concentrate more specifically on the racial implications of codifying dance practices from Latin American cultures for consumption in the ballroom dance industry. I proceed with a close reading of how DanceSport choreography performs racial positions, examining the extent to which gender and sexuality contribute to racial discourse. Comparing DanceSport Latin to blackface minstrelsy allows me to unpack how brownface functions for DanceSport competitors and spectators as a means of negotiating their own racial and class positions as well as of mediating cultural anxiety about public displays of sexuality. I also explore how brownface obscures African historical antecedents to DanceSport. Using salsa as a specific case study, I consider stylistic differences between ballroom Latin dance and social dance practiced in Latino communities, citing both ethnographic research in clubs as well as the representation of salsa in film, salsa competition, and controversies in the emerging salsa dance industry as points of comparison to DanceSport. I call into question the racial divisions invoked by the common dichotomy of studio versus street dancers and their mutually exclusive dominion over technique and *sabor* (flavor). My comparison of studio and street dancers expands my analysis of differences between social dance and

2001–2002 U.S. National Professional Latin Champions Slavik Kryklyvyy & Karina Smirnoff. California Open, Costa Mesa, CA, February 2003. Photo © 2003 by Jonathan S. Marion.

its theatrical representation, bringing new issues to the forefront through the specifically racialized context of Latin dance.

Such disparate lines of investigation allow me to expose various ways in which representations of Latinness in DanceSport serve the Glamour Machine. Brownface hides the history of actual racial discrimination out of which these dances were born and substitutes for that real-world inequality the illusion that racial and ethnic difference can be slipped on and off like a fashion accessory, its impact only as long-lasting as this season's hairstyle. And it contributes to the fantasies invoked by the Glamour Machine by projecting differences of class and gender onto the performance of ethnic Otherness.

MIGRATION, APPROPRIATION, AND
RE-CREATION OF LATIN DANCE

In chapter 2, I discussed how the development of a ballroom dance industry and its subsequent focus on competition was both aided by and contributed to a refinement process that virtually eliminated improvisation from ragtime and swing dances and distanced them from their lower-class black origins. The Latin dances that gained popularity in Western ballrooms were similarly revised and codified by ballroom dance teachers for many of the same reasons, the result of which was the elimination of improvisation in favor of a more marketable set of preestablished steps. In contrast to such dances as the foxtrot or swing, which became acceptable in the ballroom only after references to the black culture out of which they emerged had been sufficiently erased, Latin dances were popular precisely because they capitalized on their reference to non-Western, nonwhite culture. The fact that neither the dances nor the cultural values they alleged to portray were those practiced in the countries that inspired their ballroom counterparts seemed of little concern to Latin dance practitioners in the West. The ballroom versions of Latin dances are Western appropriations with only limited similarity to forms practiced in Latin America and that rely extensively on Western stereotypes of Latinness for their emotional and aesthetic appeal.[2]

The postcolonial scholar Marta Savigliano has identified the Western appropriation of Latin dance as one of the myriad forms of cultural imperialism in which "Passion"—which she identifies as a form of "emotional capital"—is extracted from the third world for sale in the first. Savigliano's theory of exoticism is based on her examination of the global circulation of tango, the first Latin dance to make a significant and lasting appearance in European and American ballrooms. The year 1913 is often singled out as the height of this tango mania. The sudden popularity among the cultural elite of Paris of what had been a lower-class dance form associated with violence and prostitution in Argentina created an atmosphere of scandal that further heightened its appeal. Tango's allure was not only the movement itself, which was reputed to be more passionate, crude, and sexually suggestive than that of other popular ballroom dances, but the mythology in which the dance was packaged, its underworldly origins generating a simultaneous fascination and repulsion Western tango consumers could not resist. In fact, the idea of tango—its mythologized origins in the brothels, its boiling passion, its image of domination and rebellion—proved to be more profitable and marketable than the dance itself. Tango students in Europe were either unprepared to learn the complexities of the dance, ill-informed about the technique, or uninterested in the movement style practiced in Argentina. Instead, a proliferation of new dances circulating under the same name emerged as dance teachers codified and redefined the dance for Western consumption. Westernized tangos were similar enough to other ballroom dances to be mastered without extensive study, referencing the Western fantasy of tango as exotic Other primarily by adopting only those elements most easily appropriated, such as clothing or gestures:

> All theories and technical courses stressed that, when dancing tango, attitudes, gestures, and proper conversation were far more important than the actual steps. In this manner, dance masters attempted to compensate for the actual difficulties of the dance, fearing the resistance of their potential students.[3]

Staged versions of tango in European cabarets introduced further confusion, stretching even further the range of movement styles now practiced under the rubric of tango. Savigliano describes these changes in theatrical tango performances:

> The original choreography had been stylized into glamorous, almost balletic, postures (extended arms, stretched torsos and necks, light feet) and rough apache-like figures (deep dips, backward bends, dizzying sways) with marching walks in between. In general, to dance in a tango style meant to combine in a piece both airy elegance and tumultuous earthiness, the result being an effect of sensuality and passion. The tension and contrasts observed in the Argentinean tango were overdone and misinterpreted, and the result was a grotesque mismatching of qualities.[4]

Almost one hundred years later, the multiplicity of tangos is still flourishing. Dozens of countries prefix their own versions: American, English, French, Filipino, Taiwanese, and Argentine tango are but a few of the most prominent styles. Aside from the name and the music (which by the 1930s had been so severely altered by Europeans who standardized the rhythm into a march that it was barely recognizable to Argentineans), the dances were linked only by reference to Latin passion. Just as profound as the changes made in the dance itself were the effects of the tango's export on the Argentinean people. Though tango's success abroad may have helped to increase Argentina's international visibility, it also reduced the country's international identity to a global symbol of passion, likely diminishing rather than increasing the country's economic and political status. Furthermore, differences within Argentina were elided, particularly those of race and class, as tango, which before its export had been a dance of the dark-skinned working class, became a symbol for all of Argentina. The popularity of tango as a commodity in the global economy of Passion further reinforced the Latino and Latina stereotypes, securing Argentina's position in the pan-Latin fantasy propagated by the West. This process of cultural imperialism was repeated, only with slight variation, with each new Latin dance that was admitted into the ballroom.

Although the English tango was accepted as one of the Standard ballroom dances in the early 1920s, other Latin dances were added into the English competition system relatively late. Although samba and rumba experienced surges of popularity on English social dance floors during the 1920s and 1930s, these Latin dances were not initially included in the competition or examination systems. Partially because of disagreements about how to standardize these new dances, which, perhaps even more than the ragtime dances, were based on rhythmical improvisation, new Latin dances were not included in English Style ballroom competitions until the late 1950s. At that time, Brazilian samba, Cuban rumba and cha cha, American jive, and Spanish paso doble were grouped together into a new category called Latin and American Dancing. The names referred to an imagined ethnic origin, the identification of which seemed to guarantee authenticity in the Western imagination. This category was soon included at all competitions in addition to the classic ballroom dances (waltz, tango, foxtrot, quickstep, and finally Viennese waltz, added in the 1960s to even out both categories at five dances each). Though the reputed national origins of each of these dances in the new Latin and American (later shortened to Latin American) category are still touted in the publicity materials of every ballroom dance school and society, the dances that were adopted by the British ballroom dancers bore little resemblance to their counterparts in their reputed countries of origin even at the moment of their importation or appropriation. Like the tango, each of these dances changed markedly in its new cultural context owing in part to market forces, the differing physical predispositions of its new practitioners, new class contexts, and varying cultural values.

The Latin dances were primarily introduced to the British dancing public through the efforts of a single couple, Doris Lavelle and Pierre Zurcher Margolie, known to most as Monsieur Pierre.[5] Their authority on Latin dancing was attributed to numerous research trips to Paris (where Pierre, who was French, had been living), the portal through which Latin dances were made fashionable in Europe, and later research trips to Cuba, New York, and Brazil. Despite their efforts to study the Latin dances in indigenous contexts and to translate these observations into a teaching system faithful to their observations, drastic reinterpretation was unavoidable. A dance practice is much more than a list of footsteps and rhythm charts. The culture and values of its practitioners are embedded in the postures, gestures, and dynamics of the dance. It was impossible for a single European couple, who were themselves foreigners to Latin culture, to transmit the choreographic and social essences of several different Latin cultures to an entire nation of British ballroom dancers. Pierre and Lavelle were not equipped for such a monumental task. The British public, moreover, was not interested in cross-cultural immersion. Recontextualized in European ballrooms among waltzes and foxtrots, Latin dances were adapted by English bodies to adhere to their own culture's ideals and values. Postures were straightened, rhythms were simplified, and steps were named and categorized. Perhaps the most convincing evidence of the need to modify the dances to English tastes can be found in Pierre's own texts. In the preface to his 1948 technique book *Latin and American Dancing,* he states, "For several years my problem has not been to teach Latin and American Dances, but to try and convince the dancing public—and the teachers—that these dances are no more difficult than the English ones."[6] Such a project suggests that Pierre emphasized similarities to European dances and downplayed differences and in so doing drastically altered the Latin dances so that his English students would readily accept them. Pierre seemed aware of his public's limited ability to grasp movement techniques too foreign to their own culture and spoke with respect uncommon in Westerners of his time of the skills possessed by Cuban dancers: "The name Rumba in Cuba is used only for the very fast version seen on the stage or as exhibition, and is so super-rhythmic that it is quite beyond the reach of any European dancer."[7]

The new Latin dances promoted by the Imperial Society shared little in common with those Lavelle and Pierre had observed. Improvisation was eliminated, and their technical character was ignored when it differed too drastically from the already well-defined ballroom technique. The dancer Frank Regan, for example, claims that the application of the ballroom hold to these Latin dances prevented the English from properly executing them.[8] Although the closed-couple hold had originally been imported from Europe, Caribbean dancers adapted it to make it tight and small, lower and more compact than the classical ballroom hold, which was itself exaggerated for British competition. English dancers who attempted a Cuban rumba or cha cha with their higher and broader dance frame ultimately generated a new movement form.

Even before their export to Europe, all Latin American dance was, to use a term coined by the eminent Cuban scholar Fernando Ortiz, the product of "transculturation"—the merging of elements from two or more cultures.[9] African rhythms, brought to the Americas by slaves, transformed as they met with European melodies and Indigenous instruments, resulting in numerous and varied musical styles throughout Central and South America and the Caribbean. New dances likewise evolved that combined elements from African dances, such as pelvic and torso isolations and the primacy of improvisation, with European closed couple partnering techniques. The migration of dances such as the samba or rumba to Europe and America and their subsequent syncretization with previously established ballroom dances were hardly new or isolated events. They were merely another instance of transculturation, the process through which these dances were created in their countries of origin. The problem I highlight here is not that Latin dance continues to grow and change in new locations, but that the new forms keep the same names, leading to confusion and contestation over who and what defines Latin dance. I will proceed with a brief explanation of how each of these dances entered the DanceSport Latin division, focusing extensively on the dance that is considered the foundation of all other Latin ballroom dances: the rumba.

Rumba

Ballroom dance teachers routinely describe rumba as "the Cuban dance of love." The dance commonly referred to as rumba in Cuba today, however, looks so dissimilar to that performed at DanceSport competitions that even the most undiscerning viewer is perplexed.[10] The ballroom styles are characterized by long graceful strides on straight legs as bodies twist and melt into picturesque poses reminiscent of an ice skating duet. The man's hands are almost always in contact with the woman's flesh as he spirals and stretches her vertical torso, breaking from this erect posture only for deep splits and long back bends, each one carefully planned and painstakingly rehearsed. The Cuban forms are danced with knees flexed, torsos pitched forward, feet barely scuffling out and back under each dancer's body to match quick, subtle movements of the arms as the hips maintain a graceful undulation. Rarely do the dancers make physical contact; rather, they engage in a taunting approach and retreat in their clever play of torso and pelvic isolations, which, although spontaneously improvised, maintain a vigilant adherence to the *clave* rhythm (the guiding percussive pattern for Afro-Cuban music). Even the melodic love ballads used by ballroom dancers depart so sharply from the complex percussive rumbas heard in Cuba that no one would confuse the musical styles. The two rumbas appear to have little in common except their name.

Although most historians of ballroom dance have perfunctorily dismissed the discrepancy, usually explaining it away by stating that the ballroom rumba is actually based on the Cuban *son,* a Cuban ballroom dance that utilizes closed couple partnering, historians of Cuban rumba have not been so willing to ignore the problem. In fact, they have been the ones to recognize there *is* a problem that these dissimilar dance practices share the same name.[11] In an effort to combat this problem, several scholars of Cuban music have proposed specific terminology to differentiate the rumba traditions. Isabelle Leymarie, for example, advocates for use of "authentic rumba" or "rumba brava" in contrast to "rumba de salon" or "ballroom rumba."[12] Robin Moore likewise distinguishes between "traditional rumba" (which he sometimes calls "folkloric" or "street") and "commercial rumba," which includes ballroom styles.[13] Although these new names help to draw attention to the multiplicity of rumba practices, each set of terms also privileges one tradition over the other. Leymarie's choice of "authentic" for the Cuban practice implies that ballroom rumba is inauthentic and therefore less valid, a reversal of status that is not likely to bring about mutual respect and

Latin competitors Jonathan Roberts & Anna Trebunskaya in a pose illustrating the tender intimacy and elongated lines of DanceSport rumba. United States DanceSport Championships, Hollywood, FL, September 2005. Photo © 2005 by Jonathan S. Marion.

understanding. Moore's use of the word "traditional" is likewise problematic because it suggests that rumba must stay frozen in time as a historical artifact that cannot continue to develop as a modern art form. Even my own use of the term Cuban rumba in opposition to ballroom rumba falsely implies that Cubans had nothing to do with the development of rumba danced in ballrooms and that ballroom-style rumba can never be danced in Cuba.[14] The inadequacy of our vocabulary to resolve these issues only underscores the indictments revealed by examination of rumba's history—rumba was born out of racial conflict within Cuba and its interaction with global economies of exoticism.

Most sources concur that rumba evolved in communities of poor blacks living in the ports of Havana and Matanzas in the mid-nineteenth century. This "rumba complex," as it has been named by musicologists, included three styles of rumba: *yambú, guaguancó,* and *columbia.* All three sub-genres of rumba drew heavily on dance traditions imported by slaves from Africa, although the hybridization of dances from distant African tribes and their reformulation as rumba was a uniquely Cuban phenomenon. Both the *yambú* and *guaguancó* styles of rumba are danced by a single male-female couple. The two perform a stylized display of courtship while the rest of the group comments on and contributes to their interaction through song. The *yambú* is celebrated for its slow, sensu-

Neri Torres and Johanner Artola dancing rumba guaguancó *during a 2004 performance of* ¡Guaguancó, Oyelo Bien!, *choreographed by Neri Torres for* IFE-ILE *Afro-Cuban Dance and Music Ensemble. Note how the forward incline of the torsos, flexed knees, and internal focus contrast with the elongated body lines of DanceSport rumba.* © 2004 CB *Fountain—SalsaFoto.*

ous, and stately interaction, whereas the faster *guaguancó* can be easily identified through frequent use of the *vacunao*—a thrust of the man's pelvis (or foot, arm, or any other limb) in a symbolic attempt to possess her through figurative penetration. The female dancer shows her skill by protecting herself from his *vacunao* by quickly covering her pelvic region with her hands or skirt. The *columbia* form of rumba is traditionally danced as a solo competition among men, who vie to outdo each other through display of their athletic and rhythmic prowess in dazzling exhibitions of fast footwork and acrobatics.[15]

Clearly derivative of African music and dance, rumba was derided, rejected, and even outlawed by the white Cuban elite in the early twentieth century, a direct result of the prevailing climate of white supremacy.[16] Simultaneously, Cuban rumba was appropriated by white Cuban performers in a blackface theater tradition called *teatro vernáculo* popular in Cuba between 1860 and 1930. The musicologist Robin Moore argues that these performances marked the beginning of a commercial rumba practice that departed significantly from the traditional rumba. European instruments were substituted for the African percussion ensemble used in traditional rumba, and a wide variety of musical styles, including the *son,* were incorporated into the new hybridized rumbas. Moore proposes that the rumba dance was likewise adapted, mocked, redefined, and transformed on *teatro vernáculo* stages.[17] Moore's scholarship on this topic demonstrates that, counter to the common assumption that ballroom-style rumba is a Western misinterpretation of a Latin dance practice, commercial cooptation of the Afro-Cuban rumba began on the island of Cuba itself.

Throughout the 1920s, as cosmopolitan Europeans and Americans focused their attention on black art and culture, the popularity of Afro-Cuban dance and music began to grow. Inspired by the Harlem Renaissance in New York and Negrophilia in Paris, white Cubans reinvented Afro-Cuban culture to suit Western fantasy by launching American and European tours in which they claimed to represent Afro-Cuban music and dance. Few of these artists, however, had any experience with or interest in traditional Afro-Cuban music or dance. Instead, they extended and accelerated the convention established in the *teatro vernáculo* of incorporating multiple musical styles into their hybridized rumbas. As the previously scorned rumba was embraced by the white Cuban elite, parallel histories of rumba began to proliferate.

During the 1920s and 30s, an astounding array of Cuban music, including varieties of *son, danzón, guajira,* and *guaracha,* enjoyed international popularity, almost always under the label "rumba."[18] Moore writes:

> Publishers and performers in the United States and Europe began to appropriate the term rumba (or rhumba), using it as a generic label for Latin American-influenced composition. Largely unaware of traditional rumba and unclear as to its differences from commercial rumba, they applied the term

indiscriminately. The earlier semiotic expansion for the term rumba within Cuba—that is, its gradual association with all Afrocuban dance music rather than with specific genres—soon paled in comparison with the diversity of music and dancers later called rumba on the international market. Any song or composition drawing even the most tangential inspiration from Latin America was suddenly a potential rumba.[19]

The practice of marketing all Cuban music as "rumba" was not only simpler for the Western consumers, who could not generally distinguish one Latin musical style from another. It also enabled promoters to profit from rumba's association with Afro-Cuban culture without any actual knowledge of or contact with it being required. Though most Cuban music and dance styles reflect a combination of European and African influences, rumba incorporated fewer European elements than many other styles. As one of the most "African" of the Cuban musical traditions, it was both more exciting as an exotic commodity in Europe and more threatening to white Cubans. By exporting *son* under the name rumba, white Cubans could profit from rumba's exotic appeal without "dirtying" themselves with what they considered the crude vulgarity of Cuba's black underclass rumba.

By the 1930s, the popularity of rumba shows in Europe and America had so successfully determined what travelers expected to see while vacationing in Cuba that the Cuban tourist industry was compelled to stage rumba shows to meet expectations shaped abroad. After its international tour, the commercial rumba, which was born in Cuba's *teatro vernáculo* and spent its adolescence maturing in Paris nightclubs, returned home to Cuba, this time to be embodied and disseminated by a new population. Whereas commercial rumbas had previously been performed almost exclusively by white dancers, by the 1930s mulatto and black performers were more commonly employed in the booming tourist nightclubs of Havana. So if the distinction between traditional rumba and commercial rumba had been one of black versus white, the racial distinction broke down in the 1930s. When mulatto and black performers entered the tourist industry, their performances resembled those of the European commercial tourist trade more closely than traditional Afro-Cuban rumba. Although some cabaret rumba dancers of this era drew on movement vocabulary from *rumba guaguancó* and *rumba columbia,* they recontextualized it alongside movements borrowed from *son, danzón,* conga, paso doble, tango, jazz, Santería ceremonies, and even ballet. Examples of cabaret rumba from this era have been preserved in dozens of Mexican *rumbera* films, which feature almost exclusively white actresses playing sexually alluring, but morally reprehensible, mulatta rumba dancers.[20] Evidence from these films and the substantial archival work of Robin Moore documenting stage shows reveals that cabaret rumba varied greatly in the many venues in which it was performed across Cuba, North America, and

Europe. Furthermore, all these performances departed drastically from traditional Afro-Cuban rumba, but no one has documented how these cabaret rumbas affected the social practice of ballroom-style rumba that developed parallel to it. Many of these cabaret rumba performances (particularly those preserved on film) consisted of solo female dancing with almost no partnering. How did the cult of commercial stage rumba tradition influence the development of social rumba danced by couples in American ballrooms?

Most histories of American ballroom dance suggest that the *son,* a popular ballroom dance of the (white) Cuban middle class throughout the nineteenth and early twentieth centuries, was the basis for the American Style rumba.[21] Arthur Murray's 1938 dance manual, for example, identifies his rumba as the Cuban *son.* A 1943 rumba manual published by the American Rumba Committee also identifies the "American Rumba" as an adaptation of the Cuban *son.* Nonetheless, these texts suggest that the transition from Cuban *son* to American rumba involved more than a change of name. According to the American Rumba Committee, "Son, as danced by the Cubans, consists of but few steps which are repeated endlessly and in Closed Position. Dance teachers of the United States added to it so-called 'open' figures where the dancers separate, pass around each other, and turn under each other's arms."[22] Whereas the *son* may have been accepted by white Cubans primarily because its use of the European closed dance position distanced it from its African-based rhythms, American consumers rejected the closed dance position and reasserted in its place the freedom of individual movement more typical of the Cuban rumbas. The committee further explains that the introduction of the Cuban rumba to the American dance scene in 1932 "was noted for three things: 1. The steps were all extremely short. 2. They were taken on the whole flat of the foot. 3. There was a decided hip movement as the steps were taken."[23] Not particularly specific, these three characteristics are common to all Cuban dance styles of the period and do not help to narrow the search for the source of American rumba, except that they highlight the key points at which all Cuban dances departed from American ballroom dances of the period, which were taken with long strides onto the ball of the foot with no visible swaying of the hips. The Cuban *son* probably formed the basis for American rumba, but a great variety of Cuban dances likely served as inspiration for the inventions of American dance teachers who classified any dance step that included hip movement as "rumba." By 1947, Arthur Murray clarifies that "Americans refer to all Cuban music as 'Rumba.' But there are more variations of tempo and style in the Rumba than in the Fox Trot."[24] He goes on to note tempo differences in the bolero, *canción bolero, bolero son, danzón, danzonette,* "*guajero*" (probably *guajira*), *son montuno,* and *guaracha.* His inclusion of such a vast array of musical styles offers further evidence that American rumba was comprised of elements from many different Cuban dances.

The new rumba (called American rumba in the United States and the box

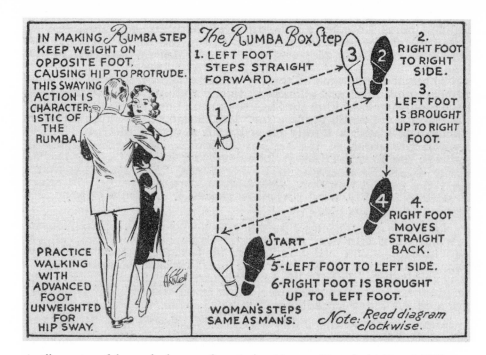

An illustration of the rumba box step from Arthur Murray, "Everybody's Dancin'," New York Daily Mirror *(1951). Ballroom studios still teach this box as the foundation for American Style rumba. Drawing by Lou Hanlon. Courtesy of Arthur Murray International.*

or square rumba in Europe) was practiced similarly in American and European ballrooms until 1947, when Pierre first traveled to Cuba. Upon his return to England, he lobbied for a complete revision of the rumba as taught by English dancing societies. Most controversial was the new rhythm he insisted upon after having been trained by the Cuban dance teachers Pepe and Suzy Rivera.[25] Whereas the rumba had previously been danced in European and American ballrooms using either a rhythm of slow-quick-quick (step on the first beat, hold the second beat, and then step on beats 3 and 4 of each measure) or quick-quick-slow (step on the first three beats of the measure and then hold the fourth beat of the measure), Pierre argued that the rhythm should be more accurately counted 2-3-4-hold 1 (starting the pattern on the second beat of each measure).[26] He dispensed with the box that had been traced by the dancers' feet in the basic pattern of the square rumba and taught a new rumba basic involving a forward-and-back check that roughly followed the path of a lightening bolt on the floor. In 1948 Pierre began promoting his new import as the "Cuban System of Ballroom Rumba." It was eventually adopted by the Imperial Society of Teachers of Dancing in 1955 as the official English Style and today remains the standard for International Style DanceSport.[27]

While Pierre's quest to recover the "authentic Cuban rumba" may have been motivated by an awareness that ballroom dancers had misinterpreted the Cuban dance, his own voyage to Cuba did not lead him to the traditional Afro-Cuban rumba, which was still practiced almost exclusively in black communities. Pierre shared the racial attitudes of his day and would not have sought out black dance teachers on his journey. Although he was undoubtedly exposed to commercial rumba shows performed by black dancers, he did not bring the exhibition styles back with him to England. Few historians of ballroom dance, however, have been able to identify what Pierre was studying in 1947 and on subsequent trips to Cuba in the 1950s. The English dancer and author Frank Borrows suggests that the new "Cuban System Rumba" was actually mambo:

> About 1950 a new style of playing Cuban music was noted. It appeared that Cuban orchestras had been influenced by swing, and the off beats began to be accented. This style of playing was called Mambo and the new Mambo dance was presented at an International Dance Congress by Monsieur Pierre. The basis of this dance was that the steps were taken on counts 2.3 and 4 of the bar. The Mambo made little headway here but had greater success in the U.S.A. and on the Continent. . . . Meanwhile the Mambo counted 2.3.4 was presented here again under the name "Systemo Cubana" [sic] or Cuban System Rumba. This time it met with greater success.[28]

Borrows makes an important point that is rarely recognized today: the Cuban System Rumba (which later became the English Style rumba and then the International Style rumba) and the American mambo were actually the same dance in the early 1950s. The basic step pattern and timing of both are still exactly the same, although their drastic departure in speed and movement quality tends to obscure their fundamental likeness. Although Borrows provides an important clue that Pierre and Lavelle likely studied in Cuba the same dance that became popular as mambo in the United States, he does not identify its Cuban name. One might assume that Cuban System Rumba is actually based on the Cuban mambo, but the dance codified as mambo in the United States differed markedly from that called mambo in Cuba, which was comprised of a small side step and tap of the opposite foot accompanied by a hip twist or pelvic pulse, danced facing but not touching a partner.[29] Although the disjuncture between the Cuban and American mambo, which is danced in a closed hold with short forward and backward steps, is nearly as great as that between the Cuban and American rumbas, it may be more straightforward to explain. Cuban dancers commonly incorporated the Cuban *son* when dancing to mambo music, likely resulting in the renaming of this fast *son* as mambo dancing in the United States. Thus, it seems most likely that both the American mambo and the Cuban System Rumba developed from (mis)interpretations of the Cuban *son*. The foot patterns are similar, and the new rhythm Pierre brought back from Cuba is similar to (although not exactly the same as) the *contratiempo* rhythm used in Cuba to dance the *son*. Significantly, the mambo captured the interest of English dancers only when Pierre presented it the dance under the name "rumba." The idea of rumba, the most forbidden and exotic of Cuban dances due in equal parts to its explicit sexual pantomime and its origins in the black underclass, had for decades stimulated the Western imagination.

When traditional Afro-Cuban rumba was embraced by Fidel Castro's government in the 1980s as a symbol of national culture, Cuban folklore groups began to export the genre abroad. This new export of rumba out of Cuba, this time in a form closely resembling the early Afro-Cuban tradition, continued the dialogue that has been in existence for almost a century among the various rumbas practiced worldwide. Although there is virtually no technical similarity in the movement styles of Afro-Cuban folklore dancers and DanceSport competitors (aside from the emphasis on hip movement), the story told through traditional Afro-Cuban rumba has recolored DanceSport rumba choreography. The narrative embodied by Afro-Cuban rumba—the unending chase of a flirtatious woman by a boasting man whose advances are continuously foiled by her dexterity and grace—can also be seen in ballroom rumba. The female ballroom dancer alternately accepts and rejects the advances of her male pursuer in a steady sequence of swoons and retreats. Is it possible that the ballroom dancer's rapid closing of her legs in fan position, the sudden covering of her feminine jewels after inviting contemplation of her inner right thigh is a remnant of her deft reply to his *vacunao* in *guaguancó*? Perhaps the rumbas of the ballroom and the Afro-Cuban street tradition are not as utterly unrelated as they first appear to be. It is naive to conclude that these rumbas have only a name in common. They share a complex history that reveals both a deeply troubling racist legacy and the resilience of rumba for its capacity to reassert vital characteristics throughout a century of appropriation, recontextualization, and transculturation.

Cha Cha

During their 1951–1952 trip to Cuba and New York, Pierre and Lavelle likely encountered an early version of cha cha chá, which is reputed to have been invented by the Cuban violinist Enrique Jorrín that same year.[30] As mambo music increased in tempo, many dancers became frustrated with the frenetic pace. Jorrín noticed that dancers responded well to the third section of *danzón* music, dancing a modified *son* in which they added two extra steps, shuffling their feet in a triplet. Jorrín created a new musical genre based on that slowed-down *danzón,* naming it after the sound of the dancers' feet marking time to the music. By the mid-1950s, both the name and the dance had become so popular that cha cha chá threatened to overtake mambo as the most popular Latin dance in America. The American dance studios quickly added the new dance into their programs, shortening the name to cha cha to facilitate its teaching.[31] Even today, dancers trained by descendents of this studio system refer to the dance as "cha cha," in contrast to those who learned around Latin musicians and still refer to the genre as cha cha chá. Meanwhile, Pierre and Lavelle took the cha cha chá back to England and devised a syllabus similar to the one they wrote for Cuban system rumba. The English cha cha cha (the name lost the accent mark but usually retained the final "cha" except when the dance was referred to casually as "cha") written by Pierre and Lavelle became the basis for that used today in DanceSport.

Samba

In 1953 Pierre and Lavelle toured Brazil to invigorate the English samba with "authentic" flavor, as they had done with the rumba. A version of samba had been danced in American and English ballrooms since the 1920s and enjoyed a burst of renewed popularity after the release of the 1933 film *Flying Down to Rio*, in which Fred Astaire and Gingers Rogers appear dancing "the carioca," represented as a national Brazilian dance craze. The term Carioca refers to a resident of Rio de Janeiro, so the word might have been associated with a style of Brazilian dance practiced in the capital city, but the film version featured steps invented in Hollywood. Elements from the theatrical number were incorporated into the potpourri that was being danced as samba in ballrooms, which also included steps from the Brazilian *maxixe,* bossa nova, and samba. During their trip to Brazil, Pierre and Lavelle were confronted with the vast diversity of dances encompassed by the name samba, each marked by regional and class differences. Unable to find agreement among their informants about which version was the "true" samba, the travelers mixed and matched steps from *gafieras* (working-class dance halls) and rival samba schools. According to Lavelle's diaries, they adapted the "most ballroom-like and teachable steps" for their revised samba syllabus.[32]

Paso Doble

Although radically different from the dances of the same names that inspired them, the English rumba, samba, and cha cha cha have at least some historical precedent in Latin American social dance. The remaining two dances included in the "Latin American" category have an even more tenuous relationship to Latin American cultures. The English paso doble represents a Spanish bullfight, wherein the dancers perform movements imitating the matador (the male dancer) and his cape (the female dancer), interspersed between movements borrowed from flamenco and Spanish paso doble. Despite the Spanish sources, their constellation into the dance now performed by DanceSport competitors actually occurred in France in the 1920s, a dance that was imported to England by Pierre when he arrived from Paris.[33] Although there is a Spanish folk dance called the paso doble from which many of the marching movements in the French/English paso doble are drawn, the DanceSport version seems to have developed more of its character in France than Spain, the French ancestry attested to by the words still used to name its steps. A slippage between dances from Latin American cultures and the reference to Spanish culture in the paso doble seems to allow for the unquestioned inclusion of the paso doble in the Latin American category of DanceSport.

Jive

The addition of jive, the English version of swing, to the Latin category represents the most blatant reconceptualization of "Latin America" for DanceSport purposes. The fact that the division was originally called Latin and American dancing may help to clear up the non sequitur in nomenclature, but it does not fully explain why jive was included in this category at all. Jive was codified after World War II soldiers brought jitterbug dancing to Europe and English dance societies set about taming it for inclusion in their syllabus.[34] The unpredictability of African American–derived swing rhythms and their accompanying dances offended many English ballroom dance teachers. The outcry was similar to that over ragtime syncopations, the presence of both in respectable ballrooms denounced as vulgar and uncouth. Richardson wrote that the English youth were dancing to swing and boogie-woogie music in "a mad frenzy of indescribable movements." He quotes Alex Moore, another ballroom dance luminary, speaking about an English jitterbug contest held in 1940 (which, he points out, was not sanctioned by the Official Board): "[It] was about the most disgusting and degrading sight I have ever seen in a ballroom."[35] Unable to ward off the inevitable swing invasion from America, the English dance teachers embarked on their "refinement" project, defining acceptable and unacceptable steps for jitterbug just as they had done for ragtime dances, this time sanctioning a new name—jive—for the properly disciplined dance.

Jive was categorized with the Latin dances partly through an accident of historical timing. It was standardized for entry into competition during the same period as the new Latin dances were, and all the newcomers were grouped together under a new heading. It was also the similar perception of wildness, primitiveness, and blackness that contributed to the classification of the tamed swing with the newly disciplined Latin dances. Dance literature of the time reveals references not only to the blackness of these dances, but to the sexuality and uncivilized behavior that they purportedly engendered. Richardson, for example, writes in 1946, "The true rumba seems to have been a native dance of Cuba, purely Negroid in origin and with no trace of Spanish ancestry. It was a wild and lascivious dance with many suggestive hip movements."[36] Arthur

Murray's 1942 dance manual similarly states that "La Conga" practiced in ballrooms had been adapted from dances practiced by "colored natives" in Cuba: "Remember—it originated with, and for generations has been danced by, simple natives. And if they learn it, you certainly can!"[37] Although foxtrot, quickstep, and tango were also offspring of dances created by African descendants living in the diaspora, I believe the continued presence of black and dark bodies dancing the Latin and swing dances in the Americans into the 1950s contributed to their similar grouping into the new category of Latin American competition.

TRANSATLANTIC ENCOUNTERS:
ENGLAND AND AMERICA

In addition to the teachings of Doris Lavelle and Pierre, the British Latin dance luminary Walter Laird has been profoundly influential in defining the style of DanceSport Latin. Laird's technique book, *Technique of Latin Dancing,* first published in 1964, is still revered today as the ultimate repository of knowledge for ballroom dancers. His detailed descriptions of basic actions have been continuously studied by contemporary DanceSport competitors, and his status as the grandfather of all Latin dance is undisputed in the ballroom dance community.[38] Although Latin American DanceSport has changed drastically since the 1960s, its radical shifts of style distinguishing it markedly from the ballroom division of competition, the technique Laird developed is perhaps the only constant standard by which to measure a dancer's quality and ability. The DanceSport champion Lorna Lee (who competed in the 1960s and 1970s) spoke about authenticity in Latin dancing when I interviewed her:

> One of the . . . roots of the authenticity of Latin American is that the weight is taken on the inside edges of the feet, and . . . most of the steps are danced with the ball flat footwork. . . . If you extend the feet too much to the point where they go too very high on the toe like a ballet dancer pointing the feet, the weight is taken out of the foot, and the body action or the body weight becomes far too high. And therefore the authenticity of the dance is lost, because it should be down, grounded onto the floor with the weight towards the . . . inside edges of the balls of the feet, which is how our technique is written.

Lee's comments suggest that her understanding of authenticity in Latin American dance comes from the written work of Lavelle and Laird, rather than from any indigenous dancing she might have observed. For example, later in the interview she criticizes the privileging in current Latin American competitions of "entertainment value and impact in the show and the quick eye picking up the speed" at the expense of "those things that we're taught in the very, very beginning of dancing." Yet, when she bemoans the displacement of the "hip twist" by "the drama and all the exaggerated, abstract lines," the move to which she refers—a basic figure in DanceSport rumba—is one so named and defined by Lavelle and Pierre.

I am not belittling the crisis Lee identifies in Latin DanceSport—a need for clear standards by which to judge a competitive form. However, to turn to Lavelle and Laird as the final authorities on Latin American dance tends to obscure the radical transformation these dances endured on their transatlantic journeys, the colonial history of Europe in Latin America, and the potential consequences of such cavalier appropriation of dances across national boundaries. To judge a dance form in competition, standards against which to measure the right and wrong way to dance must be established. It is not the standards I am calling into question, but the cultural hubris with which the Western ballroom dance industry disseminates its definitions, provoking dismissal of all other possible versions of Latin dance.

Both the International Style and the American Style of DanceSport Latin as practiced in the United States are modeled on and largely determined by this English history of DanceSport. Though American access to Latin American social dance practices may have been more direct, particularly in New York, where a large population of immigrants from the Caribbean was dancing to the new hybrid Latin-jazz music, the contemporary American ballroom dance industry models its Latin technique on the English system. Several American-based dancers who witnessed the development of the American DanceSport industry

Latin competitors Vaidotas Skimelis and Jurga Pupelyte push abstract lines to new levels of daring. Yankee Classic, Boston, Massachusetts, June 2005. Photo © 2005 by Jonathan S. Marion.

in the 1960s recalled how other versions of Latin dance were slighted in favor of the English technique. Felix Chavez, for example, recalls a competition he entered in Los Angeles in 1965:

> And I'll never forget one competition, it was called the Windsor Ball. It was one of the big ones. English people were running it. And we were dancing Latin. We were favored to win in Latin. And another couple from Downey was favored to be second and then, you know, so forth and so forth. So we went, it was about 1,000 roughly, maybe about 1,000–1,500 people in the whole place, and we started doing the Latin and we finished. They announced the winners, and they announced another couple that were from San Francisco. And the people went [*single clap*]. Total silence in the whole room. Total silence. They announced the second-place winners. Same thing. Total silence. Third-place winners. Total silence. We came in fourth—bedlam. Everybody stood up and started screaming and yelling. It was amazing. And the fifth-place couple also, everybody stood up and yelled and screamed and yelled. I mean it was obvious. And it was English judges from England that were judging that, they'd say it was too cabaret, too jazzy, too all that. But it was Latin. Angela and I had been studying with Cuba's number 1 Latin dancer and he'd taught us the true Latin movement, which few do now. And we were doing it, we were doing all that stuff, and they still judged it against it, 'cause they judge against hip action.[39]

Although the audience clearly favored Chavez and his partner, the English-trained judges ranked the couples according to the standards defined in the English technique books. Although English Style Latin has developed markedly since 1965, no new definitive technique has been accepted by the DanceSport industry.

Owing to geographic proximity and an influx of Cuban and Puerto Rican immigrants into the United States during the 1960s and 1970s, American dancers had easier access to Latin American social dance practices than did English dance teachers. Thus, it was often through American dancers that new developments in Latin DanceSport were brokered. Although the English publicly disdained American Style Latin dancing, many American dancers recall that their interpretations of Latin dance were nevertheless appropriated by English teachers. American DanceSport Latin competitors entering British competitions in the 1970s recount that the English were fascinated with their dancing. Frank Regan (who, although Scottish born and raised, trained and competed in the United States) describes his first English competition:

> And we did well, only because we were so different they couldn't help but notice us, and I guess they wanted to see what we were doing so they kept

bringing us back. . . . So anyway, I do recall after coming off the floor—the first year I went over I was third in the Rising Star, so I came off the floor, and this woman called Nina Hunt who trained a lot of the English couples, said to me as I came off the floor, "Frank, I've got all your material on film. You'll see it next year when you come back." So you know I took that as a sort of a left-handed compliment. It wasn't just me, it was Vernon Brock as well and Bobby Medeiros and Sam [Sodano], they filmed all our stuff. And it was after that that the English Latin began to undergo a transformation. It all began to transform and by the mid-1980s, it began to look like what we had been doing here. Needless to say they've taken all the credit for it, as they always do with everything.[40]

Frank Regan's story is consistent with those of other American competitors of his generation, all of whom claim to have been mavericks on the international scene.[41] Consistent with Regan's jibe about the British taking all the credit for innovation in dancing, little of this history is remembered in DanceSport folklore. The weak history of American success in international DanceSport competition and the dubious position of American Style Rhythm today have erased any memory of America's contribution to Latin DanceSport development.

Although the early development of ballroom Latin as a form distinctly different from the Latin American social dance practices from which it was drawn may have had as much to do with cultural difference in physicality as it did with more overt imperialistic tendencies, continued resistance to change in the Latin dances has been equally motivated by economic concerns. The English are deeply invested in maintaining their status as the authorities on ballroom and Latin dance in order to sustain their careers. The ballroom Latin dancer turned salsero Enio Cordoba recounted the efforts made by his mentor, Bobby Medeiros, in introducing European dance teachers to the dancing of ethnic Latinos in Miami nightclubs in the 1980s. Medeiros's crusade to bring International Style Latin closer to the styles practiced in Latin nightclubs met with resistance in the DanceSport industry, particularly in England. According to Cordoba, Medeiros was not invited to teach in England, although he did lecture all over Europe, promoting the use of music with Latin percussion instrumentation in DanceSport Latin competition instead of the pop music common at the time. Cordoba recalls that Walter Laird himself explained the English resistance to changing the Latin technique: "The minute they [English teachers] can't teach it, all the work dries up over there and everyone flies West."[42] The American DanceSport industry, largely built by exiled British dance teachers, continues to bow to the English monopoly on Latin dance technique.

Admittedly, DanceSport Latin style has undergone radical changes over the past ten years. Marketing Latin as hip, young, contemporary, and exciting is equally important to, if not more crucial than, emphasizing its Latinness. But these developments have been largely instigated by Eastern European dancers, not by Latinos. Recent developments in Latin dance, including greater speed, flexibility, balance, use of space, and complicated partnering tricks, produce performances that, although often captivating to watch, generally take the dances further from the dances of Latin American origin with which they share their names. Although the Latin category in DanceSport competition shares at least equal status (and perhaps higher, at least amongst the youth) with the Standard category, this is not a parity built on an equal relationship between the West and Latin America. Migration of the Latin dances to DanceSport competition floors occurred under a form of cultural imperialism that relied on and reinforced global stereotypes of primitive, wild, sexual, Latin Others.

DANCESPORT'S RACIAL LOGIC

Despite the gradual recognition of the legacy of cultural appropriation in which it is embedded, DanceSport still represents to many a utopian community in which peoples from different races, classes, and nationalities come together through their common love of dance. From this frequently embraced romantic point of view, the participation of dancers from former Soviet bloc countries, Western Europe, Asia, Australia, and the United States demonstrates the power of DanceSport to unify people across national and racial boundaries.[43] Writing for *Dancing USA,* the dancer Neil Clover insists that "never once in history has political rationalization ever accomplished what a few soft-spoken ballroom dancers did in recent years—penetrated 40 foreign frontiers with genuine, sincere, real honest-to-goodness common ground—ballroom dance."[44] The celebration of Latin culture, as exemplified in the Latin dances, alongside references to aristocratic European culture, as portrayed in the Standard dances, appears to provide further evidence that DanceSport equally validates the cultures of varied ethnic groups. In fact, DanceSport Latin might even deconstruct racial categories when read through the lens of performativity theory.[45] If the racial position "Latin" can be established through DanceSport performance, it follows that racial identity can be assumed by any individual versed in those particular codes of movement, irrespective of genetics. Such a reading offers DanceSport lovers a seemingly liberal angle from which to market DanceSport's position in racial politics.

Such an image of a multinational, multiethnic melting pot, however, serves to obscure the Eurocentric and white-dominated systems of logic by which the industry is structured. DanceSport's history is inseparable from the legacy of Western imperialism and colonialism out of which it evolved. In the words of Ellen Gainor, writing about the irony of ballroom dance as a metaphor for equality in a play set in 1950s South Africa, "Every country and people that participate in this artistic communion do so because they have embraced British regulations and aesthetic values for ballroom dance, bowing to a form of cultural imperialism built on an illusion of equality and internationalism."[46] The representation of Latin in DanceSport performances relies on and reproduces stereotypes derived from a racially fraught history of Euro-American relations with Latin America. The very existence of a category called "Latin dance," in which dances from different countries with radically different histories and physical practices are lumped together, reveals the Eurocentric perspective of this discourse. I am not suggesting conscious racist intent or actions on the part of particular individuals, but I hope to highlight how the representations of race produced by DanceSport interact with larger racial discourses circulating in American society.

The definition of race itself is a hotly contested subject, but the demarcation of Latino/Latina as a racial category is even more ambiguous than that of most other racial identities.[47] Race, which contemporary scholars commonly agree to be a cultural construction, continues to function, as it has throughout history, as if it had a basis in categorical biological difference.[48] It is generally assumed that race can be read by looking at the human body. Though numerous counter-examples of its transparent visibility can be found, such misreadings of racial identity are cited as the anomaly, the exception that proves the rule.[49] Race, it is believed, can be determined by physical characteristics: skin shade, eye shape, nose contours, hair texture, eye color, and so on. Although gross physical variation exists within racial groups, to classify Latinos by such visible markers proves even more problematic than most other projects of racial categorization because Latin America is defined by its mix of European, Indigenous American, and African peoples. Latinos are white, brown, black, and dozens of mestizo shades in between. Many demographic questionnaires, including the U.S. Census of 2000, now include the question of "Hispanic/NonHispanic" origin as separate from race, recognizing that Latinos are of varied racial backgrounds. Though such efforts to increase specificity in racial and ethnic identity in official reports may on some levels help increase sensitivity to cultural differences, to treat the category of Hispanic or Latino as if it did not still function as a racial group is to ignore the racism people of Latin American descent often suffer.

To contend that Latino or Hispanic is not a "real" racial category is hardly a sustainable argument: there is no such thing as a "real" racial category, at least as defined by essential biological differences. Race comes to have significance in the way in which a society constructs it as a meaningful way in which to group people into hierarchical categories. Within Latin America, Latino as a racial categorization has little meaning because everyone born in the Caribbean and in Central and South America falls under this label. Instead, categories such as black, white, and mulatto are significant. It is only outside Latin America that the concept of "Latino" takes on a racial meaning. So, although I admit that Latino is a complicated racial category, because its constituents have radically different experiences of racism depending on their skin color as well as a variety of other socioeconomic factors, the frequency with which it functions as a single ethnic type cannot be ignored. The practice of brownface reinforces the perception of Latin as a visually legible racial category.

The naming of the two divisions of DanceSport already sets up a binary in which Latin is a deviation from the Western standard. Broadly speaking, the Standard dances are those of European or American descent, and the Latin dances are those of Latin American descent. Such a sweeping statement glosses over the complicated historical trajectories already mentioned; however, the categorical distinction is maintained in performance. The image portrayed by the Standard couple bears much in common with representations of whiteness as discussed in literature from the field of whiteness studies. The cultural critic Richard Dyer examines visual representations of white people in and by Western culture in his book *White*. His analysis reveals that the white race is constructed as powerful, good, clean, godly, wealthy, light, universal, and invisible. Central to his theory is the notion that whiteness is able to transcend particular bodies and stand in for all humanity. DanceSport Standard portrays many of these same values, exemplified in the lavish costumes, his chivalry, her extolled beauty, their unison movement. All these "old-fashioned" markers appearing to transcend specific individual identity, perhaps even racial identity. But upon even cursory examination it becomes clear that this notion of romance is derived from white, European, aristocratic society. The couple's costumes and the graceful restraint of their movements refer to a specifically white romantic notion of eternal bliss. Aesthetic values are very similar to those of classical ballet—the most highly regarded of the Western aristocratic dance forms. These values include vertical movement, light use of body weight, concealment of effort, flowing movement, and poses foregrounding the extension and length of muscles and body lines.

This representation of whiteness is partially enabled by the corollary racial position that is represented in the Latin division of competition. These two categories are always juxtaposed at competitions, neither one ever appearing without the other.[50] If the Standard performance represents whiteness, the Latin performance signals a racial identity that is Other to this white standard. Consistent with representations of Otherness examined by postcolonial theorists, DanceSport's version of Latin reveals much more about Western desires than actual experiences of individuals who consider themselves ethnically or racially Latino.[51] A reading of the movements performed in Latin DanceSport reveals how this Other racial identity contrasts with the white Western racial positions in Standard ballroom practices.

In contrast to the Standard dances, which require the couple to be in a closed dance position (pressed against each other in a perpetual embrace), Latin dances can be performed in a wider range of body positions, allowing for more varia-

Seven-time U.S. Standard Champions Jonathan Wilkins and Katusha Demidova. Blackpool Dance Festival, England, May 2005. Photo © 2005 by Jonathan S. Marion.

tions in choreography and personal expression. The Latin dance performances appear to be more physically and emotionally expressive owing to the greater range of body shapes and movement choices available. This freedom also encourages interpretations of Latin as more "primitive" because its technique and choreography are less formally structured than that of the Standard dances. For example, almost every Standard variation has been named and recorded in textbooks. Though certainly more homogenous and strictly regulated than social dance practices in Latin America, advanced Latin DanceSport choreography is being reinvented each year by its practitioners. This relative choreographic freedom in the Latin category provides possibilities for nonwhiteness to be read as more creative and innovative. But this same quality leaves Latin dance open to accusations of being less disciplined and controlled than the "refined" Standard dances. If the Standard dances represent a romantic fairy tale of civilized Western culture, the Latin dances represent a primitive mode of human expression, one that is overly sexual, emotional, and physical. Though neither of these identities is located in time or place, they are contextualized by their relationship to each other. If the Standard dancer is Western, civilized, aristocratic, and white, the Latin dancer is by contrast non-Western, uncivilized, savage, and nonwhite.

The representation of race in the ballroom is not, however, quite as simple as this white/ nonwhite dichotomy suggests.[52] The brownface of the Latin dancers marks their difference not only from the Standard dancers in the ballroom, but from the Latino dancers—salseros, tangueros, sambistas—outside the ballrooms as well. Beyond skin color, DanceSport athletes also perform their difference from ethnic Latinos through a movement technique recognizably different from contemporary Latin American social dance practices.[53] So even though ballroom Latin dancers and club salsa dancers, for example, may both dance "Latin" to the same music, the two performances look very different. The ballroom Latin dancer might be characterized as appearing clean, controlled, and balanced (or, from a different perspective, stiff, sterile, and predictable) in contrast to the salsa dancer's rhythmical, playful, spontaneous, and free (or wild, messy, violent, and off-balance) style. Richard Dyer points out that tanned white skin is still recognizable as white.[54] He reminds his readers that someone who uses tanning products can borrow particular characteristics associated with a nonwhite ethnic group without forfeiting white racial privilege. Likewise, Latin ballroom dancing is still ballroom dancing. The ballroom Latin dancer borrows some of the passion and sexuality associated with Latin dancing without forfeiting the class and racial privilege by which ballroom dancing is defined. Neither the white dancers in bronze paint nor the English dances with Latin names become the racial Others they reference. They maintain their white privilege, always recognizable through display of the refined ballroom dance technique. Ballroom Latin dances and practitioners benefit from alignment with both "ex-

Latin competitor Jose DeCamps offers a cool foil for the wild expression of his partner Cheryl Burke. Embassy Ball, Irvine, California, September 2005. Photo © 2005 by Jonathan S. Marion.

otic" Latin culture and classy white society, siphoning off positive associations from each and sidestepping the discrimination or limitations experienced by members whose sociocultural location remains fixed.

GENDERING RACE, RACING GENDER

Through costuming, visual narrative, and a lead/follow dichotomy, the ballroom constructs what it means to be a man or to be a woman; each identity position comes into existence only through comparison to the other. Although same-sex dancing is not infrequent in practice, teaching, recreation, or the rogue single-sex ballroom dance competition, ballroom dancing is defined by a binary sex partnership.[55] Perhaps in response to the entry of same-sex couples in competitions, the National DanceSport Council of America now makes explicit this previously unspoken rule, stating that "a couple is defined as a male and a female."[56] The co-participation of men and women in equal numbers, at least on the competition floor, leads DanceSport proponents to tout gender parity as one of the sport's most appealing features. In an opening message on the International DanceSport Federation's Web site, the federation's president, Rudolf Bauman, brags that DanceSport is the only sport "where men and women compete on equal terms, and 100% gender parity."[57] Even to those who know nothing about the sexism experienced by women in this industry, this insistence on gender equality must be undermined by the accompanying pictures of the organization's presidium—eleven men, one woman, whose uniqueness is marked by the title "Mrs." in front of her name. Men listed have no similar designation (simply Keji Ukai as opposed to Mrs. Natasa Ambroz), reflecting how often female is seen as the deviation from the male norm in positions of power in this industry. DanceSport hardly looks like a candidate for endorsement even by essentialist feminists. Rather than promoting equality of men and women, the binary opposition of men and women tends to reinforce and even exaggerate sexism experienced in other sectors of society.

Gender on ballroom stages is always already raced, or at least marked by a category that invokes a raced discourse.[58] There is no movement that genders a ballroom dancer that does not also mark him or her as either a Standard or Latin dancer. There is no shoe or costume that genders a ballroom dancer that does not also signal his or her membership in either the Standard or the Latin category. If, as I have already suggested, Standard and Latin can be read as white and assimilated nonwhite racial positions, comparing the gender roles in these dance styles can likewise be read for stereotypes of and even prescriptions for masculine and feminine behavior for each racial group. Though gender roles are consistent across the Standard and Latin dance styles in many ways, female Latin dancers differ from their Standard counterparts in their ability to initiate action, their physical position in space, and their role as object of spectacle.[59]

Because the female Standard dancer is always in closed dance position, she has no opportunity to initiate action. Though she is not passive (she must in fact be very active to react quickly enough to his movements), she does not participate in the decision-making process, which is the sole purview of the man. He determines where, when, and how the couple will move around the floor. Any input she does have, such as a gentle squeeze on his arm to warn him of oncoming traffic when he is moving backward, is masked so that he appears to be fully in charge. In contrast, the female Latin dancer, who is not required to stay in closed dance position, has the freedom to initiate action. Though the male Latin dancer leads movements executed jointly by the couple, Latin dancing includes solo choreography in which each person is responsible for initiating movement.

Her movements predetermined to a certain degree by the closed dance hold, the female Standard dancer appears in a limited number of physical positions in relationship to the man with whom she dances. She is always closer to him than she is to any other person on the dance floor. In addition, she never appears above him. He is always positioned in a dominating physical relationship, his vertical stature extending above hers. Although a female Latin dancer is also usually close to the man with whom she dances and lower than him in vertical space, this is not a rule. When the Latin couple separates, it is likely that each will be closer to another person on the dance floor than to each other. There are also many moments in the choreography when the vertical hierarchy is inverted and she appears above him. He may drop to his knees in a gesture of adoration; he may position himself underneath her to lift and frame her; or she may push him down beneath her in an act of playful one-upmanship. The narrative of the Latin male-female relationship is one in which there is often a teasing exchange of power consisting of moments in which both the man and the woman challenge, pursue, and reject the other partner.

In the Standard dances, the female partner is always framed as the object of spectacle. Her dress is bright and luminous, in contrast to his black tails. It is she who creates the exaggerated shape at the top of their bodies by stretching her upper back and head into his arms. He remains relatively vertical throughout the dance as his female partner creates shapes off his body. His focus and body position in these picture poses direct the viewer's eye to her. She is the spectacle. He is the frame. Although, in the Latin dances, the male and female roles are to a certain extent defined by this metaphor of the diamond and its case, Latin dancers are much more likely to transgress these boundaries. Men dancing Latin often make a spectacle of themselves, calling as much attention to their own bodies as to those of their partners. The sheer frequency of the criticism that a male Latin dancer is out-dancing his lady (a verb never used to describe a Standard dancer) reveals both the expectation that the woman should be the star of the show and the frequency with which this mandate is violated.

Rhythm competitor Emmanuel Pierre-Antoine on his knees in deference to his defiant partner Alexandra Gregoire. Yankee Classic, Boston 2004. Photo © 2004 by Jonathan S. Marion.

This man has taken on the traditionally female role of showing off flexibility and long body lines. The references to "primitiveness" in her costume are typical of DanceSport Latin. United States Ballroom Dance Championships, Miami, Florida, September 1999. Photo by David Mark.

Though all three of these differences in gender roles between the two styles can, to a certain extent, be attributed to different methods of establishing connection in the two styles (Standard dancers must remain in closed dance hold, whereas Latin dancers can utilize open positions), the contrast also produces a raced gender discourse. These differences seem to suggest that Latin women are feisty and difficult to tame, in contrast to their docile Western counterparts. They also imply that Latin men are more self-centered and sensual than stoic Standard (Western) men. Such a distinction suggests that ballroom Latin dancers may be promoting alternative models of masculinity and femininity. If Western femininity has been defined as (at least public performance of) passive obedience to male patriarchal rule, might the female Latin dancer suggest a way to realign femininity with the power to initiate action? Likewise, if Western masculinity has been defined through the renunciation of emotional or sensual expression, might the male Latin dancer be offering a new model for masculinity that unites his body and his emotions?

In her work on tango, Marta Savigliano has explored the ways in which seemingly binary gender roles prescribed by Latin dance subvert the active/passive dichotomy of male and female. She notes that if the men depicted in tango lyrics are always struggling to tame their women, the women must be engaged in constant rebellion, her agency apparent in his insistent need to reaffirm his position as dominator.[60] Although Savigliano's analysis is specific to tango in Argentina, such an interpretation might also be extended to gender in ballroom dance. DanceSport's Latin gentleman and lady may offer a model for how to break open restrictive gender codes so that they allow women to take more assertive action and men to enjoy being the object of romantic pursuit.

This performance of *latinidad* in the ballroom is, however, a Western invention, a projection of what has been excluded from Western masculine and feminine ideals onto a racial Other. Although DanceSport suggests a broadening of gender roles, their relegation to the space of raced Other has problematic consequences. These new gender roles get reified as Latin, not as possible gender roles for anyone of any racial identity to inhabit. Furthermore, the violation of Western gender roles in the Latin category can also be used to justify labeling nonwhite racial groups as savage because they do not adhere to the same behavioral codes for "lady" and "gentleman" as their Western counterparts. So the gendering of the racial positions actually marks them farther apart, and the racing of the gender positions continues to reinscribe hierarchies about whose version of masculinity or femininity is civilized. The narcissism and sensuality embodied by the male Latin dancer as well as the excessive passion and independence exhibited by the female Latin dancer offer a contrast to the "proper" gentlemen and ladies in white tie and tails.

Sexual desire is also represented differently in the Latin and the Standard dances. Coupledom is marked (at least on the dance floor) by a heterosexual pair in both styles, but the movements each partner displays align them both with very different traditions of sexuality. On the one hand, the Standard couple maintains an image of eternal domestic bliss in their unified complementary movement. Reference to sex is subtle, merely suggested by their frontal body contact which, although scandalous in the early nineteenth century when the waltz was first introduced into upper-class European ballrooms, is now rarely interpreted as sexually promiscuous. The Latin couple, on the other hand, is enacting an entirely different narrative of courtship. This is one in which sex is the main attraction, their gyrating hip actions not merely referencing but actually reenacting movements from sexual intercourse. This display may represent a more contemporary practice of courtship; however, the contrast of the Latin man and woman to their Standard counterparts also produces a raced discourse of sexuality.

In her public encouragement and enjoyment of sexual attention, the female Latin dancer violates Western standards of modesty and propriety. Such assertiveness could be read as lower class (more like the behavior of prostitutes than of ladies) or the hallmark of a modern feminist. But its marking as Latin has negative consequences for ethnic Latinos/Latinas. Aside from signaling her distance from Western proscriptions on public behavior, the image of the oversexed Latin dancer fuels a common stereotype that Latina women are sexually unrestrained. This stereotype has encouraged widespread discrimination when, for example, the purported unchecked passion of Latina women is linked to U.S. welfare bills. This misinformed logic was used in the 1994 political battle over California Proposition 187, a measure written to deny medical treatment and education to undocumented workers. Governor Pete Wilson capitalized on stereotypes of the Latin harlot to foster fears that illegal Mexican immigrants would drain the state budget through excessive dependency on publicly funded prenatal care.[61]

The performance of masculine sexual desire in the Latin category of Dance-Sport likewise feeds into negative stereotypes of Latino men. The film scholar Charles Ramírez Berg attributes the first portrayal of the now common "Latin lover" stereotype in Hollywood film to Rudolph Valentino's performance of tango in the 1921 film *The Four Horsemen of the Apocalypse*.[62] The violence associated with this scene, which concludes with Valentino throwing his partner to the ground after an aborted kiss, helped solidify American fantasies of Latin dance and the men who mastered it as sexually uncontrolled and dangerous. The figure of the Latin lover introduces a more complex picture of masculinity, beyond one of mere brutality. Valentino combined dominance, as represented by his role as aggressor in the scene, with the sensitivity and tenderness of a considerate dance partner. In an interview in *Dance Lover's Magazine,* Valentino advised that male tango students should remember "that the good dancer gives his exclusive attention to his partner."[63]

Valentino represented a masculinity that catered to the desires of women, not just those of men. This "woman-made man" was ridiculed throughout the media, and in 1927 the *Nation* published an article stating, "If it is true that man once shaped woman to be the creature of his desires and needs, then it is true that woman is now remodeling man. . . . The world is now fast becoming woman-made."[64] The scholar Gaylyn Studlar theorizes that Valentino's early career as a dancer, an already feminized identity in American society, forced him into a position of feminized masculinity that "defied normative American models."[65] He was ridiculed by heterosexual men as queer, but despite his transgression of normative masculinity, and perhaps precisely because Valentino challenged and redefined traditional gender roles, he became a sexual icon for American women. An analogous argument has been made by Marta Savigliano, who, in her analysis of tango lyrics, concludes that representations of Latin men usually confound American prescriptions of gender identity. They are macho in their violence and dominance over women, yet feminine in their interest in love.[66]

Male DanceSport Latin dancers similarly straddle the two poles of hyper-machismo and effeminacy. These men could be read as brutish and sexist in their continued need for physical control over women. They might also be considered as queer as drag queens in their exaggerated hip action and affected gestures. Perhaps this dual macho/effeminate image of the Latin male in general, and Latin dancers in particular, is what leads so many gay men to participate in the Latin division of DanceSport. It offers them an opportunity to negotiate their own complicated relationship to the masculine/feminine binary. Although few Standard male dancers identify themselves as homosexual, nearly half the professional male Latin competitors in the United States are openly gay. Values performed by Latin competitors seem to align with values in many pockets of gay culture, including exaggerated display of emotion and flamboyant, sensual body movement. There is a disjuncture, however, between the embrace of Latin dancing by gay men and the disavowal of homosexuality in many Latino communities. Although DanceSport has remained a predominantly white practice, the identification of gay men with Latin dancing has served to perpetuate both homophobia and racism. As more Latino communities in the United States and abroad begin to embrace DanceSport, the unlikely pairing of male homosexuality and Latin dancing forces both groups to deal with their prejudices about the other as they find themselves similarly ghettoized and must coalesce for survival. Gay Latino men find particular comfort in the ballroom, where the coexistence of their ethnic and sexual identity is accepted.[67] But such instances of coalition do not eclipse continued prejudice against gay men. Public knowledge about which male competitors are gay and which are straight also enables spectators to watch for signs from gay male dancers that their masculinity on the dance floor is "just a performance." "Real men" are those who love women, not those who only act the part. Hybrid performances of traditional heterosexual masculine ideals (strength, power, decision maker, supporter) and nontraditional masculine ideals (self-spectacularization, delicate movement, attention to aesthetics) help to expand and redefine notions of masculinity. Such realignments do little, however, to actually encourage open acceptance of homosexual identity because no gay male couples are represented in DanceSport performance.[68] Even if gay men find a space to resolve tensions at a personal level, they must still perform the role of heterosexual man on the competition floor.

Both gay and straight men's preoccupation with their own performance of masculinity on the dance floor begs the position of many scholars of performativity who contend that all identity, including that of gender, is a performance (see my discussion in chapter 1). Although DanceSport performance of gender identity could be read as a self-conscious parody of gender, a camp performance that highlights the performativity of all gendered identity, this is certainly not the predominant lens through which DanceSport is viewed by its own practitioners. In fact, DanceSport participants usually read the performance of gender in competition as merely an extension of gender roles assumed in heterosexual courtship off the dance floor, behaviors most assume to be universally recognized. Hazel Fletcher, a world-renowned English Latin coach, explained her perspective in a personal interview, which I quote at length.

HAZEL FLETCHER: I have no interest in what kind of sexuality you want to pursue off the dance floor, but when I'm judging, when I'm watching a dancing competition, I want to see a man dancing as a man with a woman dancing as a woman. I believe that in a great couple you shouldn't know whether the man is heterosexual or homosexual, it's of no interest. In other words, you could say I'm not anti-whatever they want to be in their private life, what I am anti is effeminacy on the floor, from a man. Or equally, you could say, butchness from women, because that doesn't define that sort of man/woman, him leading/her following, the role they're supposed to be playing.

JULIET MCMAINS: You say, "a man dancing as man, a woman dancing as a woman"—are there more ways to dance as a man and not look effeminate?

HF: Well, a lot of it comes down to very basic principles. How to stand, how they're using . . . even their footwork, to me, even to an angle of an ankle, or a position of the free leg in relation to the standing foot. If a man, without moving, if he puts his free leg in the wrong place, he can look effeminate. And that could offend as a judge in a way as much as bad technique or poor timing, because it doesn't define the role. I often relate to couples, to simplify it, a bit like if you asked a man and a woman to sit down. Now the man basically will probably sit with his legs apart and the woman will cross her knees, and that's something that we've either done without learning it, or it's something that girls have learned very young from their parents and every time you sit down you cross your legs. You behave like a lady. You don't sit there in a skirt with your legs open. It's something that the girls would have been taught from seven years old. If you relate it as simply as that on the competition floor . . . I get upset that we actually have to teach ladies to be feminine. I would—I think that they should have a sense of their own modesty, you might say, that they automatically don't want to do anything crude or vulgar.

JM: Is it possible that what's crude and vulgar for one person is not for another, and people have to learn the standard by which vulgarity is judged in this context?

HF: Well, I would like to think that we don't have to learn it, that it's an inbuilt thing, but, of course, well, everybody's acceptability of taste is different, isn't it? Yes. But, I generally think that if judges were actually talking about something that offends them after a competition from somebody— they would all find different words, but they would all have the same meaning. All our tastes are a little bit different, but what we want to see on the dance floor isn't that different, not really.

JM: Do you find there are just as many women who have to learn to be feminine as there are men who have to learn to be masculine? Or do you have. . . ?

HF: Well, I think half of the time they think they've got to learn it and they don't—it's related to what I said earlier. That if they fall back into what they're going to do in real life, like the mating game, if a man sees a woman across the room, is he gonna mince up to her on his tiptoes if he's really interested in her? *No.* He's gonna puff his chest up like a peacock and . . . body language, normal masculine, feminine, body language, the mating game. You know, I want to see it with taste—I don't want to see anything. . . . I like to see dancers being aware of sensuality. I don't want to see outright sex. I don't want to see groping and I don't want to see men caressing their own body with their hands, because that isn't a thing that a man normally does in life. But a woman will touch her own body. She will . . . that's not unnatural in life. So, I think a lot of it isn't learning, it's almost reminding the dancers of their own role in life.[69]

Fletcher goes on to admit that gender roles differ in some non-Western cultures (Japan being her main reference point); however, she continues to assert that gender, whether learned or innate, is basically natural and universal. She assumes that her definition of masculinity and femininity is universal because it is shared by other DanceSport judges, but she does not recognize that their agreement stems from their virtually identical training in the aesthetic codes of the Western and white dance industry.

Although masculinity in other Latin dance styles, such as salsa, is constructed similarly through many common conventions (e.g., his role as leader, supporter, taking up more space), many salsa dancers think all male DanceSport Latin dancers look gay. The subtle distinctions Fletcher finds so crucial in judging their adherence to masculine codes of DanceSport movement fail to register for salseros. Salsa dancers often cite the extension of the arms by men as effeminate, as well as the exaggerated hip movements and stretched feet. Though Fletcher likewise notes that too much hip movement or ankle articulation can make a man look less masculine, her tolerance for these qualities is much higher because they are conventions of the ballroom form. Class differences in gendered behavior may also contribute to the appraisal of male ballroom dancers, who aspire to perform a higher-class position than salseros, as effeminate. Many scholars have noted that upper-class masculinity appears less virile when judged by the standards of lower-class masculinity, which usually values strength over delicacy.[70] Ironically, many styles of salsa dance utilize techniques that male ballroom dancers eschew as being too feminine, such as articulation of the fingers and shoulders and swiveling steps in the feet. Although ballroom dancers rarely suggest that salsa dancers look gay, the use in each form of techniques condemned as effeminate by the other demonstrates that gender roles are culturally specific. Language commonly used in the ballroom industry, however, implies that masculinity and femininity as represented in DanceSport are natural and universal, further masking and perpetuating the legacy of Western cultural imperialism by failing to recognize the specificity of DanceSport's courtship reenactment.

BROWNFACE'S MINSTREL LEGACY

Though almost universally recognized today as intolerably racist, blackface minstrelsy was one of the most popular American entertainment forms throughout the century in which it was commonly practiced, approximately 1830 to 1930. During minstrel performance, white men painted their faces with burnt cork or greasepaint to perform skits in which black men were portrayed as stupid, lazy singing fools happy to entertain their masters with slapstick comedy. Though there are many dissimilarities between the brownface practiced in DanceSport competition and the blackface minstrelsy practiced in urban nineteenth-century America, I further interrogate brownface by examining the parallels between these two entertainment forms. In both practices, lighter-skinned performers paint their bodies darker in order to take on behavioral stereotypes ascribed to an ethnic group with darker skin and less social, political, and economic power. In the case of minstrelsy, performers were primarily Irish immigrants, not yet American enough to be considered white at the mid-nineteenth century, who blackened their skin in order to perform gross caricatures of African Americans. American DanceSport, which is a fringe activity compared to minstrelsy in antebellum America, is often practiced by Eastern European immigrants, who bronze their skin in order to perform what to many appears to be a gross caricature of Latinos. In both blackface and brownface, newly arrived light-skinned immigrant performers borrow and redefine cultural products—music and dance—of a minority ethnic group for their own profit.

Although the power imbalance between blacks and whites in antebellum America was much more acute than that between Latinos and whites in America today, theories that have been developed about how blackface functioned in its time can be useful for understanding how brownface is operative in contemporary America. The cultural historian David Roediger has argued that Irish minstrel actors and audiences were able to establish their own position as "white" by assuring their distance from blackness in minstrel performance. The imperfect mimicry of racial Others by blackface entertainers served to reify their racial difference. Although not a direct parallel, Eastern European DanceSport competitors may similarly be solidifying their own white status by performing distance from Latinos in brownface. Linda Mizejewski theorizes that Jewish and Eastern European Ziegfeld Girls performing in "café au lait" makeup (light-skinned blackface) in the 1920s likewise solidified their own white assimilation by invoking comparison with those whose skin color was too dark to be considered white.[71] Though Eastern European DanceSport competitors (many of whom are Jews who have been granted religious asylum in the United States) are not facing the same prejudices,[72] current cultural and political anxiety about Latino immigration specifically, and about the loss of white American cultural dominance more generally, may necessitate similar performances of racial distance.

Moreover, the popularity of both minstrelsy and DanceSport has forestalled the ability of minority ethnic groups to represent and commodify their own arts. It was not until well into the twentieth century that African American entertainers could easily perform anything other than happy-go-lucky Jim Crow and Zip Coon minstrel characters. Likewise, Latino artists have only recently begun to successfully perform and sell their own versions of Latin dancing in America. These emerging "authentic" Latin dance markets,[73] such as the rapidly growing global salsa community, rely heavily on a hypersexualized stereotype of Latin dance. So even though salsa offers an alternative to the DanceSport version of Latin dancing, it is still largely determined by expectations the ballroom dance industry has created about what defines "Latin" on the dance floor.

The cultural historian Eric Lott has suggested in his book *Love and Theft* that minstrelsy encompassed both a fascination with black culture and a simultaneous derision of it, a "dialectical flickering of racial insult and racial envy."[74] Richard Dyer underscores this point in his work on visual representations of whiteness when he points out that cosmetically darkened white skin can signal a desire to take on some of the characteristics ascribed to the darker racial group.[75]

This ambivalence toward Others, a desire to try on but not get too close to the racial Other, is also reflected in Latin dancing. Like the minstrel show that reveals more about white fantasies of black culture than about black culture itself according to Lott, DanceSport performances expose Western fantasies of what it means to be Latin.

The almost total absence of DanceSport in Latin American countries is perhaps the most convincing evidence that it is about Western, not Latin, culture. Most visually prominent in the DanceSport version of Latin is the hypersexualization of the performing bodies, underscored by the costuming, the visual narrative (constructed in moves that often mimic sexual seduction), and the discourse that surrounds both the teaching and the performance of this style of dance. Even a brief glance at the attire worn on the competition floor—little more than rhinestone-covered bathing suits for women and skin-tight pants with shirts open to the navel for men—reveals a visual discourse that is not about what Latin Americans and Latinos actually wear, but rather represents a theatricalized projection of what an exotic Other might look like.

Beyond the clothes, it is the visual narrative enacted in DanceSport Latin that produces the Latin stereotype embraced by the West. Each of the five International Style competition dances has its own character—the rumba is passionate, the cha cha is flirtatious, the samba is playful, the jive is exuberant, the paso doble is dramatic—but all tell a story of heterosexual courtship through social dance. However, as I discussed at length in chapter 2, DanceSport is not social dance. Although it developed out of Western social dance practices and is deeply intertwined with the social dance industry, DanceSport is highly stylized theatrical art/sport. In contrast to many partnered Latin American social dance forms in which improvisation and playfulness are central, DanceSport favors well-rehearsed routines carefully choreographed for maximum display of skill and spectacular effect. Seduction is practiced on the audiences and judges, not within the partnership. As in the ballet pas de deux, preference for long body lines often supersedes any tendency toward realism in these passionate embraces. But unlike ballet dancers, whose hips are showcased only as the point from which the legs and torso extend, ballroom Latin dancers isolate, gyrate, thrust, and roll the pelvis. This striking break with the prominent tradition of partnering in Western ballet helps to reify the Latin stereotype of excessively sexual, passionate, and emotional. Social dance in Latin America may be more sexually expressive than Western forms, but these qualities are so exaggerated in the DanceSport versions that they are not even recognizable to most Latinos as Latin dance.[76] Subtlety, playfulness, musicality, and improvisation have been virtually expelled from DanceSport Latin, leaving exaggerated sexual postures and gestures as what most prominently marks these dances as "Latin."[77]

Latin competitor Adriana Przybyl embraced by her partner Andrei Przybyl in a pose that foregrounds leg lines influenced by ballet. United States DanceSport Championships, Hollywood, Florida, September 2005. Photo © 2005 by Jonathan S. Marion.

The marking of sexuality in these dances as Other was probably crucial to their initial acceptance into Western ballrooms in the 1930s, 1940s, and 1950s. Western social dancers could embrace the sensuality and sexuality of Latin dances without owning them as part of their own culture. The contemporary media glut of explicit sexual imagery might suggest this argument is difficult to sustain when applied to DanceSport practiced in the twenty-first century. However, the overwhelming presence of sexual imagery in American society does not mean that American anxiety about sexuality has been resolved. Many observers and participants may find it more comfortable to project their sexuality onto the image of the Latin Other. Furthermore, displays of explicit sexuality are not considered "classy," the coveted label by which DanceSport aspires to be categorized. The American ballroom dance industry has always been invested in appealing to audiences who are, if not already upper class, at least upwardly mobile. Perhaps covering the nearly naked dancing bodies with something, even if it is only tanning cream, is enough to protect the industry from a looming downward spiral towards strip clubs and escort services. Brownface provides enough cover for DanceSport's version of Latin sexy to remain classy. Classy and sexy can be united under the safety of a brownface mask, where the professional dancer and conspiring audience can enjoy this erotic sexuality without forfeiting class status.[78]

Another reason that sexuality in DanceSport can only be expressed under cover of brownface is that such unproblematized displays of heterosexuality and unabashed erotic celebration of Western corporeal beauty are not generally accepted in high art. Ballroom costumes and aesthetics look more like those that appear in Las Vegas strip clubs than those of concert dancers. Without the historical momentum of ballet, the self-reflexive political probes of many modern dance choreographies, or the popular support of jazz dance, DanceSport struggles to secure its terpsichorean status. Although the tension between DanceSport's dual identity as sport and art has been heightened since its 1997 recognition as an official Olympic Sport, many ballroom dancers strive to be recognized as artists. They can justify the gaudy costumes and vulgar gestures by maintaining a fiction of authentic Latin dancing. Under the guise of ethnographic representation, third-world dance forms that might otherwise be read as low class in the American context can be transformed into high-class art. When many of these same dancers appear in front of the same judges to perform the Standard dances, the suggestion of sexuality is much more subtle. Women's legs are hidden under several layers of chiffon, and although male and female bodies are pressed closely together in full frontal contact, there is no grinding or pulsing of the pelvic region. At least this particular kind of sexuality is reserved only for brownface.

The performance of brownface is more complicated than simply a Western projection of sexuality onto an exotic Other. In American scholarship and popular discourse alike, the issue of class difference is far too often mapped onto ethnic and racial difference. A similar transposition from class to race is reproduced in DanceSport performance. Though the American ballroom dance industry has long been one that sells upper-class status and class mobility, the extreme class differences between its participants are rarely discussed. The economic foundation of the American DanceSport industry is pro-am competition—amateur dancers who pay their professional teachers to compete with them in the same circuit of competitions as top-level amateur and professional athletes. Most professional DanceSport competitors in America finance their expensive coaching and travel schedules by selling their services in pro-am competitions. For these pro-am students, DanceSport is a hobby—their professional reputation and economic stability lie elsewhere. DanceSport professionals, on the other hand, usually have little college education or significant earning potential outside the industry. Most come from working-class backgrounds, and many of them are recent immigrants striving to live out the American dream through success as DanceSport athletes. The dance community is hesitant to admit that Latin DanceSport professionals, who are masters of its classy movement technique, hail from the lower classes. Instead, they are marked by brownface as racially exotic Others. Properly tanned DanceSport professionals with superior movement technique are covered by a racial marker that stands in for the less visible signifier of class.[79]

The Latin studies scholar Celeste Frazer Delgado has posited that the West has entered into an era of transnational capitalism in which *latinidad,* exoticism, and primitiveness can function as floating signifiers that more often mark class differences than those of race.[80] Delgado's argument rests on the assumption that the expansion of capitalism to every corner of the globe no longer allows the category of "primitive Other" to function as a justification for capitalist expansion and exploitation of third-world cultures. Performances of primitiveness are no longer linked primarily to ethnicity, she argues. Instead, they relate just as often to class and to access to economic, political, and certain kinds of cultural resources. DanceSport Latin competitors are signifiers in this new global hierarchy, marking differences of social position through the convenient, if no longer directly relevant, physical marker of race. Just as blackness, according to David Roediger's analysis, came to symbolize for the new industrial worker all that industrialization had forced him to abandon but still longed for (leisure, sexuality, nature), there may be a way in which Latinness performed in DanceSport symbolizes for the new transnational citizen all that has been lost in the new era of transnational capitalism: visible markers of nationality, ethnicity, and social hierarchies.

If Latin dance is raced in order to hide the function of class difference, there are also ways in which class is used to disguise its racial history. The earliest practitioners of nearly every Latin dance form were African slaves or their descendants living in Latin America, yet all explicit reference to Africa has fallen out of these African-inspired dance forms as they are practiced in ballrooms.[81] "Cleaning up" the Latin dances for inclusion in the ballroom required that they cross both class and race boundaries. Tango, mambo, rumba, and samba were originally practiced by the darkest and poorest members of Latin communities.[82] This whitening and classing up required intellectual mastery of the movement, eliminating its unpredictable elements, and disciplining the body and the dance into organized footsteps and patterns of motion.[83] The ballroom forms are characterized by a straight spine, movement that is produced through the balanced transfer of weight from foot to foot, poses and body shapes in which the entire body is extended, foot positions that are clearly articulated, extreme tonedness throughout the body, and the prevalence of predetermined steps. Although Latin social dance forms practiced outside the ballroom are comprised of specific techniques that are particular to each, several commonalities are consistent across salsa, samba, rumba, and tango. In contrast to the DanceSport forms, they utilize a more dynamic and flexible spine, weight shifts propelled by core body movement (often resulting in weight suspended between the feet), flexed knees, the privileging of polyrhythms over body lines, improvisation closely linked to musical structures, and postures in which the buttocks are displayed.[84]

The cultural critic Richard Green has theorized that focus on the black "booty" and its reputedly substantial proportions has repeatedly appeared in negative representations of blackness in Western culture.[85] The technique for ballroom Latin dancing follows Western dance traditions that require tucking the butt under the body in order to enable more balanced and aerodynamic movement through space. Ballroom Latin includes poses in which the butt is thrust backward to showcase it, but its fundamental technique relies on a backside that is not posterior to the rest of the body. The bottom must be in a straight line with the rib cage, shoulders, feet, and head.[86] The hips are allowed to rotate on this vertical axis, but the butt must not protrude backward during traveling steps. This development enables sudden stops after very fast movements because the body weight is always balanced over one foot. However, relaxation (and thrusting outward) of the butt enables more polyrhythms within the body, an aesthetic that has been overshadowed by the drive to produce faster and more dynamic horizontal movement.

Contemporary practices of Latin dances outside the ballroom community celebrate the beauty of the buttocks. In the Argentine version of tango, torsos are inclined inward toward each other and butts lag behind, while both the

English and the American DanceSport styles require that the hips be pressed under and the torsos be stretched outward. In describing this distinction, Marta Savigliano points out that the more "refined" (i.e., higher-class and whiter) styles in which the torsos are balanced away from each other were coveted by elite Argentineans in the 1920s.[87] Hiding the buttocks appears to have been central in raising tango's class status and making it acceptable to white patrons.

Though swing is not considered a Latin dance by most, it is performed in the Latin category in DanceSport competitions. The obsession with 1940s-style swing dancing that swept American nightclubs in the 1990s was ripe with backsides hanging gleefully behind torsos as dancers whirled around in a near sitting position. Footage of Whitey's Lindy Hoppers, the Savoy Ballroom originals, reveals that this crouched position was the style in which the African American originators of swing dancing moved.[88] The emphasis on the backside may have been popular in black nightclubs, but the posture was straightened up by the social dance industry when swing entered white ballrooms. A 1950s Arthur Murray dance manual specifically warns, "Don't dance with your hips 'way back. . . . Dancing with hips 'way back is out of date."[89] The illustration of what *not* to do bears a striking similarity to the posture of the black lindy hoppers, suggesting that, as in the case of tango, making swing acceptable to white patrons required hiding the racially marked backside. Was the disappearance of the butt as a site of movement in European and American Latin dancing merely a technical development in the drive for maximum speed in this ever more virtuosic dance form? Or did it have something to do with the erasure of blackness from the history of Latin dancing? If the butt is indeed marked as black, as Richard Green suggests, I suspect that the absent butt in Western versions of Latin dances has as much to do with rewriting their racial history as with their technical development. It appears that Latin exoticism was marketable, but African exoticism was not.

Although awareness of the African ancestry of the Latin American dances has nearly dropped out of contemporary histories of DanceSport and its teaching, an anomaly appears in Victor Silvester and Philip J. S. Richardson's 1936 book *The Art of the Ballroom*. A chapter entitled "Jazz," written by Ivan Sanderson, who is, disturbingly, not a dancer or a historian but a zoologist, traces the African roots of the ballroom dances. The fact that he was a scientist trained to study animals, who in Silvester and Richardson's words "penetrated several hundreds of miles of unexplored jungle of West Africa where he came in contact with the original home of Jazz," reveals the deeply racist climate in which these dance forms were imported to Europe.[90] This six-page history not only credits "Negroes" with the inspiration for contemporary ballroom music and dance, but recognizes the invisibility that their cultural contribution has suffered under its appropriation by Western forces.

From that time [1925] until 1934 the Negro again took second place, though he provided all the novelty in dancing for which he was never been credited. New dances with extravagant names were (and still are) often advertised, most of which die without so much as being noticed, leaving no trace. The only examples that survive or exert any lasting influence on Jazz dancing as a whole, are those which are Negroid in origin like the Charleston, the Black Bottom, and the Rumba.[91]

This awareness of the dangers of cultural appropriation does not, unfortunately, penetrate the rest of the book, which recounts the history of ballroom dancing in Britain as if Africa and its people living in the diaspora ceased to develop concurrent cultural practices. The "Jazz" chapter was not included in subsequent editions and printings until 1977, when the book was reissued as *Modern Ballroom Dancing*. Sanderson's name has been erased from the book, Silvester posing as the sole author, an act of misappropriated credit which reproduces that of the African dancers about whom Sanderson wrote. The ghostly persistence of Sanderson's short essay even in the 1993 reissue of Silvester's book suggests awareness and perhaps even uneasiness about the erasure of blackness from Latin dancing.

BODILY PRESENCE

More poignant than the absence of the black butt in the discourse and technique is the absence of the black body in contemporary practice. There are alarmingly few black DanceSport competitors. Asians and a growing number of Latinos are beginning to participate in DanceSport competitions, but black bodies are almost entirely absent.[92] Those who represent the sport to the public are acutely aware of this fact and at times distort the demographics of DanceSport so the American public will not cry racism. The creators of the 1998 film *Dance with Me,* for example, invented a "South African" competition partnership by teaming up Rick Robinson and Maria Torres, two of the very few black competitors in the professional American DanceSport scene. Dancers were drawn from the ranks of American and Canadian DanceSport professionals to appear in the film's climactic "international" competition scene, under their own names and with their own partners, representing the country of origin of at least one member of the partnership, with the exception of Robinson and Torres.

During an interview, Torres expressed her own mixed feelings about this casting decision. On the one hand, she recognizes that positively representing an ethnic minority in a Hollywood film is in itself a victory to be celebrated. She laments, however, that neither she nor Robinson was representing either her or his own competition career or ethnic background. The film's producers may have felt compelled to reinvent the racial demographics of DanceSport competition in order to normalize their casting of the African American Vanessa Williams in the starring role as DanceSport champion, but the irony of choosing South Africa as a symbol of racial tolerance and diversity could not have failed to register with many viewers. Throughout the publicity surrounding the film, no DanceSport expert broached the sensitive topic of the lack of black interest in the sport. In an interview for the American DanceSport newspaper *Dance Beat,* two of the dancers who appeared in the competition scene stressed how realistic the director had tried to make it by seeking out the most highly ranked competitors: "They were looking for the top six and if somebody couldn't do it they went down the list."[93] There was no mention in the interview of why this pursuit to accurately represent DanceSport led to the fabrication of a South African couple. Although DanceSport Latin relies on the imagined racial difference of the Latin Other, explicit discussion of particularly raced bodies is apparently taboo for DanceSport ambassadors.

Though black interest in DanceSport remains minimal, increasing numbers of Latino dancers are entering the Latin divisions of DanceSport competitions in the United States. Latino ballroom dancers with whom I have discussed issues of cultural appropriation believe that they are working to change the system from within by introducing movements from authentic Latin dances into their DanceSport routines.[94] They believe they can take the best from both movement techniques and unite them on the ballroom floor. But the fact that these routines are being performed in the ballroom and evaluated by the DanceSport industry's rules and aesthetics already stacks the power differential on one side. Ethnic Latinos who perform their own Latinness in ballroom are often accused of exceeding the expectations of their own identity. The Latina DanceSport competitor Maria Torres, whose training also included Afro-Cuban dance, recalls that she was chastised by the judges as being "too authentic, too street, too Latin."[95] Judges were probably reacting to specific technical weaknesses, such as imprecise footwork, but their attribution of her low placement to the Latinness of her Latin dancing reveals how successfully Latinness has been construed as "undisciplined."[96] Torres's lack of attention to foot placement in her DanceSport performance, a skill relatively irrelevant in the Cuban context, gave the DanceSport judges grounds for lowering her marks. The challenge facing ballroom dancers attempting to import techniques from other Latin dances forms is to introduce these "authentic" movements without violating some cardinal aesthetic of DanceSport. So although one reading of Latino bodies performing Latin dances suggests that nonwhites are breaking into white systems of power, the racial politics in this system are changing very slowly. On many levels, these individuals are merely performing their own colonization and supporting their own subjugation to white power, further obscuring its work by allowing the white-dominated industry to use its Latino dancers as poster children for its multicultural image.

Not only do the Euro-Latin dances represent how assimilation into Western white culture occurs, they further model the correct way for nonwhite people to gain membership into Western culture. Much like the Japanese Takarazuka performances, which, according to the anthropologist Jennifer Robertson, model for colonized subjects the correct way to be Chinese under Japanese rule, DanceSport performs the correct way to be Latin under Western capitalist imperialism.[97] DanceSport not only mirrors how racial hierarchies function; it has a profound effect on Latino subject formation in a rapidly expanding global capitalist community. So, while DanceSport suggests that race doesn't matter by implying that anyone can inhabit a Latin racial position, it simultaneously reinforces under what circumstances race does matter. Race doesn't matter as long as you are not too different from white, as long as you mark your difference with quaint exoticism that does not challenge existing social hierarchies.

LATIN BINARIES: SALSA VERSUS DANCESPORT LATIN

Until recently, ballroom dancers have practiced Latin dances in their own studio and competition circles, invoking little interaction with Latin social dance practices enjoyed in Latin America or in Latin American diasporic communities. In recent years, however, multicultural awareness has led to the rising popularity of several "authentic" Latin dance forms, including Brazilian samba, Argentine tango, and Caribbean salsa. The visibility of these styles in stage shows, studio classes, and nightclubs has led to increased public awareness of and demand for these forms in the global market. The recent explosion of interest in Latin music, helped out by the crossover of Latino artists such as Marc Anthony, Gloria Estefan, and Jennifer Lopez to mainstream pop-music charts, has helped to fuel a concurrent Latin dance craze world-wide. DanceSport also received greater public attention when long-term campaigns to bring it to mainstream television audiences led to a series of network television broadcasts in the late 1990s and reality television shows featuring ballroom dance in 2005. The growing popularity of differing styles of Latin dance brings DanceSport Latin into heightened dialogue with alternative versions of the very dances performed by its champions.

The current historical moment differs from many other periods in which Latin dance was imported to the West, most notably because of the success of Latino entrepreneurs who, by opening their own studios, have begun to challenge the ballroom industry's monopoly on teaching Latin dance. Despite the increased visibility of a multiplicity of Latin dance forms, the representation of DanceSport Latin and its relationship to these "authentic" Latin dance styles continues to be haunted by a racist colonial history.

The 1998 film *Dance with Me,* starring Vanessa Williams and Cheyenne, dramatizes the opposition between International Style competitive ballroom Latin

Vanessa Williams dancing with Rick Valenzuela, who plays her dance partner in Dance with Me. *Boston, Massachusetts, November 1998. Photo by David Mark.*

and salsa. Although DanceSport and salsa share roots in Afro-Cuban dance, this film's representation of these two practices highlights their difference, an opposition that I will demonstrate relies on implied racial distinction. Not only does the film's portrayal of each dance form illustrate a contrasting style of movement, but these differences also extend to how the dances function in the protagonists lives. DanceSport Latin is about discipline and control, as represented in scenes where Ruby (Williams) attempts to master her body through hours of structured practice in the studio. Salsa, as introduced to Ruby by Rafael (Cheyenne), a Cuban who has come to Texas in search of his absent father, is portrayed as the expression of emotion through spontaneous physical response to music and another person. Whereas the practice of DanceSport Latin functions as the means through which Ruby earns a living and fulfills an American work ethic according to which personal satisfaction must be subjugated to professional success, salsa dancing, by contrast, becomes the vehicle through which she falls in love and recognizes the value of community. These two forms of Latin dance are diametrically opposed in the film: on the one hand, the structured, technical form for competition dancing, and on the other, the spontaneous, free form for social interaction. The world of DanceSport brings professional recognition and financial success but lacks emotional honesty. The world of salsa clubs and parties offers personal interactions of friendship, community, and romantic love, but no economic stability. Not merely an invention of the filmmakers, this representation of a polar binary between the two communities accurately captures many of the tropes used by dancers to represent themselves and each other.

The conclusion of the film suggests a triumph of salsa over ballroom. Ruby's choice of a romantic relationship with Rafael over a career as a DanceSport champion implies that the values embraced by salsa dancing (friendship, love, familial responsibility, and community) win out over those of DanceSport (competition, professional development, and financial success). In the final scene of the film, however, Ruby and Rafael are pictured teaching in the same ballroom dance studio in which they met. They have brought some of the salsa dancers and musicians from the club into the studio, but love and salsa are not enough to shield the happy couple from the necessity of earning a living. Although the film champions the values Rafael brings from his authentic Latin culture, the couple chooses not to return to Cuba, but rather to sustain these values as they continue to live in America.

Their choice parallels that facing many Latino salseros in the United States who are now earning a living teaching, performing, and competing in salsa. No longer is salsa merely a social form shared among family and friends. Its burgeoning popularity has precipitated (and been precipitated by) an ever growing salsa dance industry, which, although not named in the film, was absolutely crucial to its production. Los Angeles salsa dancers and teachers were used extensively as cast and choreographers, yet the term "salsa" was not mentioned once in the film. Nor was the varied ethnic and national makeup of its cast acknowledged.[98] Instead, the film represents a generic Latin dance embraced by a generic Latin community whose nominal identity as Cuban must have been undermined by the fact that the Cuban lead was played by a music star readily identifiable to the American public as Puerto Rican. Although this elision underscores how salsa can enable a Latino identity that transcends national identity, the film's failure to name or distinguish among different Latin dance styles falsely implies that Latin dance enjoyed by Latin people exists outside structure, education, and commerce.[99] Still emergent when this film was made, the new salsa dance industry may constitute the largest percentage of social dance commerce worldwide. Consumers from Anchorage to Zagreb are salsa mad, purchasing salsa dance classes, videos, magazines, shoes, and music as well as entrance to clubs, congresses, and shows at a fever pitch. Salsa dancers who acquired their skills by growing up in a culture in which salsa music and dance are part of everyday life cannot rely on the methods by which they learned for the basis of a successful teaching business. Because until recently there was little precedent in Latin America for teaching social dance in formal classes, salsa professionals have relied heavily on the models created by the ballroom dance industry for counting their rhythms, breaking down actions, and naming their steps. Even Eddie Torres, New York's "King of Mambo" and its most influential mambo and salsa teacher, credits the ballroom dancer June Laberta with teaching him music and dance theory.[100] While salseros have readily borrowed from the ballroom dance industry, they have simultaneously struggled to distinguish salsa from ballroom Latin. Celebrating the African roots of salsa and incorporating movements from Afro-Cuban rumba has emerged as popular strategies for marking salsa's difference from white-washed Western Latin dance,[101] a strategy that counters erasures of blackness by the ballroom dance industry.

The casting of Vanessa Williams in the role of DanceSport champion may obscure the actual demographics of the sport; nonetheless, many factors designate DanceSport as a white practice. Although the term salsa may have been popularized through the marketing ploy of a single record company, the development and dissemination of the musical style and its accompanying dance style has been much less centralized than that of DanceSport. The birth of salsa has often been located in New York in the 1960s, although Cubans, Puerto Ricans, and numerous other Latino communities claim they were playing and dancing salsa long before Johnny Pacheo and Fania records popularized the term in 1967.[102] Salsa, a derivative of the Cuban *son* and mambo, is defined by its tendency to absorb elements from many different cultures and traditions. Rather than a single dance style or lexicon of steps, salsa might be best defined by the communities that coalesce around it. According to the Boricuan writer Mayra Santos Febres, salsa engenders a translocal community because the common local experiences of oppression and rebellion described in salsa lyrics and echoed in the movement cut across national boundaries. Though this translocal community shares a common spoken language in Spanish, it might be better defined by the values and experiences encompassed by salsa: skill at improvisation, mixed origins, polymetered rhythms that coexist and fuse, economic deprivation in *el barrio,* and feet that constantly shift in unpredictable patterns in response to the environment.[103]

As a symbol of pan-Latino identification for its Latino practitioners, salsa embraces the varied and hybrid racial identities that have fused to produce Latin American culture, including its African heritage. As salsa continues to gain popularity in white and Asian cultures, its hybrid racial identity starts to take on new meanings. Perhaps because it is transpiring within a global awareness of multiculturalism, the international salsa craze is being disseminated largely in opposition to ballroom social dance practices. Unlike the tango of the 1910s or the samba of the 1930s, which entered mainstream Western culture only after being filtered through white ballroom dancing masters, today's salsa students are obsessed with gaining access to the most revered salsa dancers and musicians.[104] Anyone who is dark-skinned and speaks Spanish generally qualifies as authentic to non-Latino salsa consumers. The mythical authentic salsero or salsera was never formally trained in salsa. He or she is a "natural" dancer. While it is true that social dance in Latin America has not, until recently, been taught in formal classes, it is a learned skill, acquired through a system of training involving years of observation and participation in a culture in which dance and music are often a part of everyday life.

The myth that salsa is a more authentic Latin dance form actually serves to reify the racial difference between "white" ballroom versions of Latin dancing and "colored" salsa practices. Although few people discuss this distinction in such overtly racial terms, less politically charged words tend to stand in for the unspoken racial difference. The differences are often condensed into two terms: *technique* and *sabor*.[105] The ballroom Latin dancer has technique derived from training and corporeal discipline. The salsa dancer has *sabor,* a word that could be poorly translated as flavor, fire, feeling, or soul—none of which capture the essence of *sabor,* that which provides the motivation for dancing. This distinction is also reflected in the terms studio dancer and street dancer. Salsa is usually referred to as a street dance, a name acquired because many of its early practitioners could not afford to dance on the polished sprung floors of the ballrooms and developed their dances literally on the street. Today, Latin dancers with little formal training but experience dancing in nightclubs and at private parties and family gatherings are still referred to by members of both the salsa and ballroom communities as street dancers. The difference between studio and street dancers may appear to be an issue of class, but it is greater than mere economics.

The fact that street dancers do not have formal dance training in structured classes does not mean that they have no training. Their training system relies rather on immersion in the culture. Failure to recognize this system as a form of training tends to reinforce destructive racial stereotypes. Someone who is formally trained in studio dancing appears, by some interpretations, to have not only the money to pay for lessons, but the moral restraint to appreciate strict codes of bodily control and emotional expression and the intellectual ability to understand its syntactical structures. Following this same line of reasoning, street dancing signals a community of people who not only cannot afford structured lessons, but whose emotional and sexual impulses cannot be contained by discipline and whose intellectual capacities are not sufficiently developed to grasp rules dictated by a dancing teacher. It is this moral and intellectual hierarchy implied in the distinction between studio and street Latin dancing that continues to sustain harmful racial stereotypes.

The myth that street salsa dancing has no technique is used as both an insult by the ballroom community and a marketing strategy by salsa dancers. Because it is less technical—that is to say, less strictly bound by rules and detailed muscular analysis—salsa dancing appears to be a more genuine dance experience. The absence of the strict structure dictated by official dancing organizations appears to allow salseros to respond more naturally both to the music and to their partners. Salsa dancing is uninhibited emotional expression, argue many of its proponents.[106] I counter that it is not the lack of technique in salsa social dance that enables people to feel a more poignant expressive experience. It is actually the specific technical structure of salsa dancing that creates space for more individual improvisation, creative expression, and *sabor*. So, although both ballroom Latin and salsa dancers tend to use the word technique to signal a specific kind of technique, one that has been theorized through the study of physiology and its written discourse, I use the term to describe the particular methods its practitioners utilize to produce any kind of movement, whether or not they can articulate their process.[107]

Ballroom Latin dancers maintain a consistent connection throughout the course of dancing so that every shift of weight is clearly communicated from one body to the other. They accomplish this tight connection by maintaining a stable frame in the arms and moving the rib cage and back within this frame. Salsa dancers maintain a looser connection through the hands, initiating leads by moving the arms or the entire body. Strong body-to-body connection through the hands is used only to initiate turns, not to coordinate each step. Though ballroom Latin dancers shun this loose connection because it inhibits faster exchanges of energy, it also enables more spontaneous improvisations. Perfect coordination of movement is not expected between salsa partners, so missteps become new steps rather than mistakes.

Aside from the possibilities it offers in individual improvisation for either partner, this difference in technique also requires a contrasting relationship between various muscles. In ballroom Latin, the major muscle groups in the stomach, back, pelvis, legs, and feet are always connected. Although they do not always move in the same direction at the same time, movement in any one area always affects the others. For example, shifting weight through the feet and bending one knee enables a rotation of the pelvis and subsequent movement across the ribs and back, which then produces a tiny pressure change in the man's hands on his partner's back, indicating to her the precise moment at which she should shift her weight. This strict interconnectedness of major muscle groups allows for the kind of speed in partnering dynamics that gives ballroom Latin its unique appeal. What it does not encourage, however, is the kind of polyrhythmic movement that is popular in salsa dancing. Because salsa music is based on many different rhythms interacting to produce its complex structure, dancers often mimic the instruments with different parts of their bodies. For example, they may move their feet in rhythm with the congas, thrust their rib cage forward in time to the *clave,* and shimmy their shoulders between hits of the cowbell. This disconnection of the muscle groups and their ability to initiate independent movements give salsa its particular style. This technique of polyrhythmic body articulation links salsa dancing most closely to those West African dance practices from which both the music and the movement draw much of their inspiration.[108] Thus, the defining characteristics of salsa and ballroom Latin are clearly linked to racialized movement practices—black West African dance practices, which foreground multiple points of articulation, and white Western concert dance traditions, particularly ballet, which privilege moving the pelvis and torso as a single unit. The failure to recognize African-derived dance techniques in salsa as acquired skill continues to perpetuate Eurocentric cultural biases.

The dichotomy between studio and street dancer can also reflect and reinforce other hierarchies of identity. This possibility was illustrated in an exchange I witnessed after a young female dancer performed two routines, a ballroom tango and a salsa. She danced the tango with another student also trained in ballroom technique, and their performance clearly reflected the ballroom priorities of elongated body lines, vertical posture, and precise footwork. She danced the salsa with a different partner, whose experience in salsa resulted in hunched torsos, internal focus, and unpredictable body positions. After the performance, the young woman's father commented on the difference between the two numbers, concluding that salsa was more of a "raw, uncultivated" dance form. When his daughter's salsa partner seemed to be offended, he tried to backtrack to imply that one was not better or worse, settling on the phrase "street dance" to describe salsa. In this case, race and ethnicity were not so much at issue, as both the father and the salsa partner were light-skinned Hispanics. There was, however, a class difference in evidence between the two men, as well as a different relationship to American citizenship and culture. As a Puerto Rican, the father had never endured the stigma of being an illegal immigrant—Puerto Ricans were granted U.S. citizenship in 1917. He held a high-status professional job and had successfully assimilated his family into American life. In contrast, the salsa dancer was a recent immigrant from Central America struggling with immigration issues and finances. The father's analysis of salsa as "raw, uncultivated, street" reflected his efforts to distinguish his own Latin identity (implicitly refined and cultured, like the ballroom dances) from that of the young salsero. Identifying them with his own higher-class position, the older man clearly preferred Latin dances in the ballroom style.

IDO *World Salsa Championships*

The connections and contentions between salsa and DanceSport Latin are heightened as they enter the same performance venues. Competitive salsa dancing has recently developed into a genre distinct from social salsa. Choreography featuring lifts, tricks, and flips sets these theatricalized salsa performances apart from their social counterparts. Because salsa competitions are rarely organized at a national level, drastic variations in rules and judging criteria encourage the preservation of regional differences. New York–style salsa, for example, is distinguished by its suave partnering, sophisticated poise, and commitment to the *clave* rhythm. Los Angeles dancers, on the other hand, are renowned for their speed, acrobatics, and attack. Several dance impresarios are currently organizing salsa competitions on national and international scales, forcing the variety of salsa styles into popular contention. On 14 September 2002 the International Dance Organization (IDO) hosted a competition called "The Official IDO 2002 World Salsa Championships" and held in conjunction with the Diamond DanceSport Championships. Despite attempts to draw in local crowds by advertising on Spanish television and radio stations, audience turnout was small, filling only six hundred of the four thousand seats at Disney's Wide World of Sports arena. The competition itself drew over forty entries from thirteen countries, primarily from Europe, Australia, and North America. Almost none of the dancers highly esteemed in the U.S. salsa community entered the contest, nor did anyone representing Puerto Rico or Cuba, the two countries most readily associated with salsa's origins. Only one couple from the Caribbean competed that day—Oslin Boekhoudt and Janice Kock from Aruba.

The competition was similar to that of DanceSport in many ways and was performed in the same venue before many of the same judges. The dancing differed from ballroom Latin primarily in the clarity of body lines and rhythms exhibited. DanceSport aesthetics dictate that limbs be fully outstretched at the end of each movement. Every position of an arm or leg must be suspended long enough for viewers to appreciate the picture before it blends into the next. Torso isolations and syncopations are likewise clearly articulated in DanceSport, each rhythm legible to the audience through focused presentation. For example, competitors might vibrate, pulse, or roll the pelvis, but they would not simultaneously attempt all three actions without clearly punctuating between changes in rhythm. The salsa competitors at this event seemed to be in perpetual motion, conveying a sense of excitement and wild abandon through their continual movement. Costumes and hair accentuated this picture—both more free-flowing and flamboyant than those typically seen in ballroom competition. None of the women had their hair glued in neat buns or twists; they chose instead to let their hair fly loose. Clothing, although just as finely tailored as that worn by DanceSport competitors, was also more outlandish. Fringe, hanging beads, and dangling fabric were liberally employed to extend and embellish the dancers' swinging and whirling bodies. Colors were even more vibrant than those seen in DanceSport, neon appearing more frequently and in more unusual combinations. Some skirts were a kaleidoscope of colors and prints, and several men wore fluorescent shoes and pants rather than the traditional black. Although lifts were prohibited, dancers were eager to outdo each other with daring tricks such as the neck drop, a move in which the lady falls straight back to the floor and is caught at her neck by the man's hand, leg, back, or foot before she hits the ground.

The dancers from Aruba were the only competitors who appeared to have neither choreography nor costume. Janice Kock was dressed in black cotton stretch pants and a simple blue shirt with flared sleeves, neither adorned with rhinestones or fringe. She was wearing dance sneakers instead of the spiked heels mandatory for female DanceSport competitors and commonly worn by salseras as well. Boekhoudt was dressed in simple black pants, sneakers to match Kock's, a blue print short-sleeved button-down shirt, and a bandana tied over his head. Neither his pants nor his shirt were tailored like those of the other men, whose body shapes were enhanced by fitted shirts and pants specifically designed to stay in place during a competition. Boekhoudt and Kock's dancing was smooth and easy—simple turns and steps taught in beginning level salsa classes. Her body rhythm was noticeably playful, and their dancing would have stood out as skilled in the context of a typical Latin nightclub. But surrounded by these well-trained dancers executing their moves with precision and control, they looked clearly out of place.

When the finalists were chosen, many were surprised to see that Boekhoudt and Kock had made the cut. The final round consisted of solos by each couple to a song of their choice (not a convention in DanceSport competition). Boekhoudt and Kock appeared starkly out of place in their casual clothes, her round belly hanging out from her open midriff in contrast to all the other well-cut athletes on the floor. But when the music began for their solo, no one could deny this young woman's passionate engagement with the music. It seemed that the drums possessed her as every part of her body started hammering out a different

2002 IDO Salsa World Champions Oslin Boekhoudt and Janice Kock. Salsation, Orlando, Florida, September 2002. Photo © 2002 by Jeff Davies, www.Propix.info.

rhythm to match the overlapping rhythms in the music. They barely did any turns or patterns requiring partnering skills, and their only dip was amateur and off-balance. But the response to their performance was astounding, and many in the audience rose to their feet for a standing ovation. When the final placements were called and Boekhoudt and Kock—the unknown, underdog couple from nowhere—were announced the winners, the building erupted into contentious uproar. Some spectators were thrilled at the result, while others screamed in disagreement. Boekhoudt and Kock didn't even know how to bow in the tradition of competitive dancers. Neither reserved nor gracious, they clasped their hands together and held them up in victory like sports heroes, their genuine surprise and naiveté refreshing to some and embarrassing to others.

Spectators exited the building engaged in heated debate. This couple had, after all, displayed few of the skills studio salsa students invested so much time and money trying to master. One Puerto Rican woman defended the winners ardently. "But that's what salsa is to me. That's what we grew up with. Rhythmical body movement." Although this couple displayed little speed, control, balance, partnering, and showmanship, that they had *sabor*—the undefinable heart and soul of Latin dance—and it was palpable throughout the stadium as they danced. Though many present were angry that dancers who demonstrated mastery over a wider variety of skills had been overlooked, they were simultaneously thrilled that a couple without the correct costume, body type, politics, and training had been able to walk away with the prize.

The judges' choice for first place had not seemed consistent with their selections for the finals, which had included two Italian couples, one Australian pair, and several American dancers. While the Italians and Australians had been dancing in a salsa style similar to that seen in Los Angeles, the four American couples had been dancing ballroom mambo with exactly the same technique and style as is practiced in DanceSport (and, in two cases, had performed exactly the same routine they had just executed in the ballroom competition the same evening). I would not classify their dancing as salsa because they performed something that was identifiable as a different form. They were not borrowing from ballroom mambo—they were dancing ballroom mambo under a different name. Their basic action was staccato and rebounding, not like the continuous rolling body action and weight shifts of salsa. Their movement patterns through space were at right angles, not in the circular shapes typical of salsa. Why were all these ballroom dancers selected for the final over salsa dancers who successfully combined social and theatrical styles? I turned to the competition rules in hopes of clarification. The rules stated:

Since Salsa around the world is danced in many styles, couples may dance any style of their choosing. In selecting the judges, the organizers chose instructors who have the ability to recognize quality dancing and will judge fairly and impartially without favoritism towards any particular beat, style, or regionalism. Judges will be looking for couples maintaining the character of Salsa both from its roots and as it is danced today in clubs around the world.[109]

These last words seemed crucial for explaining the inconsistency in the results. How were judges to evaluate whether salsa's character was maintained when one of its most defining characteristics *is* variation and difference? Salsa is danced in radically different ways throughout the world. Whose salsa was to be validated?

I interviewed Mark Midkiff, president of Salsation (the sponsoring organization), after the event in hopes of better understanding how this group of judges almost unanimously picked Boekhoudt and Kock as world salsa champions. Midkiff seemed pleased with the results. Given the enormous financial loss he was suffering after the event ($30,000 on that night alone, not to mention pre-event expenses), the publicity he would generate from the story of these poor kids from the Caribbean walking in without costumes or choreography to win a world championship might help make up the difference. His goal in assuming responsibility for organizing the event was to change the reputation of the IDO World Salsa Championships in the eyes of the salsa community. Previously integrated into a ballroom dance competition, with little participation from the Latino communities, this event had been regarded as a joke by salsa dancers—the ballroom dance industry's attempt to sanction and judge something it knew nothing about. Midkiff's motivation stemmed from an acute awareness of the industry's history of redefining dance forms for its own profit, stamping out other legitimate forms of Latin dance in favor of its own versions.

Though the competition results may have been a small step toward redress, they reproduce the racial stereotype that Latinos are primitive, untrained, and natural. These are also the very claims that have kept Latinos out of political and economic positions of power both globally and in the United States. To validate this version of salsa over others is to reinforce the stereotype that Latin is uneducated (they were uneducated in the movement vocabulary of competition dancing and the costume conventions), primitive (both in their movement and their dress), uncultured (movement is uncontained, uncontrolled, and even the bodies were uncontained), and natural (they had no choreography, they just danced what they felt). What about the skills that many salseros, some of Latino ethnic origin and others of varied national and ethnic backgrounds, demonstrated on the same night? Why was their version of Latin, which included but was not limited to moves that required control, education, and precision, not rewarded? Similar to the effect of minstrelsy for African Americans who still find themselves "cooning" for white audiences nearly a century after the actual practice of blackface has declined, the lasting legacy of brownface may be that

Latinos cannot escape performing the very caricatures from which they seek to be released.[110] I do not wish to deny Boekhoudt and Kock the glory they deserve for their world championship, but I also hope to caution against holding them up as icons of Latino victory. Their success is more likely to reinforce the difference between Latin Other and white ballroom dance than it is to bring about mutual understanding.

DECENTERING BALLROOM LATIN

The rapidly growing salsa dance industry—its power evident in the sheer volume of salsa classes, congresses, clubs, competitions, performance teams, Web sites, magazines, teaching videos, shoe manufacturers, and music producers worldwide—suggests that salsa may have already permanently decentered ballroom's version of Latin dance. I write these words in the heat of a national and international salsa dance craze, one that bears much in common with other social dance crazes that have preceded it, such as the rumba craze of the 1930s or the mambo craze of the 1950s. As salsa dancers adjust their moves to produce spectacular effects on competition stages and salsa teachers codify the steps, count the rhythms, and define the technique, salsa begins to lose some of its diversity, spontaneity, playfulness, and *sabor*. From one viewpoint, the new salsa industry may be autoexoticism at its best, Latinos packaging and selling, for each other as well as for the West and Asia, what people have come to expect from Latin dance. The image that equates Latin dance with wild abandon extends even to the mandate that female salsa dancers must have long, flowing hair. The allure of salsa for many Westerners and Asians is its suggestion of erotic sexuality. And yet in most Latin countries, where the Catholic church strongly influences social conduct, promiscuous sexual behavior is far less common than it is in the West. Some upper-class Latinos look down on the revealing clothing commonly worn at salsa clubs in the United States, pointing out that only the lower classes would dress like that in their own countries. While salsa clubs invariably have dress codes and valet parking, they usually coexist with metal detectors and security officers who frisk the men at the door, revealing how closely poverty and violence are chasing salseros as they scramble out of the barrio. And even though some salsa impresarios are marketing salsa as "color blind," including Los Angeles's own champion promoter Albert Torres, whose motto is "creating unity through salsa," its distance from the transformation Glamour promises is marked by racial as well as class difference.

I am hopeful that this particular historical moment, one in which Latinos and indeed all ethnic minorities have greater economic, political, and social power than ever before, will enable salsa to enjoy a different fate in American popular culture than other Latin dances. I hold out hope that there are ways to preserve some of salsa's unique qualities as it is incorporated into the white capitalist economic model so that it is not reduced to a footprint map in an Arthur Murray teaching manual. Many salsa teachers have already created models for teaching improvisation in formal class settings. Salsa's history of continually transforming itself in response to its environment, incorporating tricks from swing, hustle, and acrobatics when the environment calls for it, suggests that even in its codification there remains something about the embodied practice of salsa that resists commodification. Santos Febres writes:

> The salsa community is not a sedentary one: it never stays in one place for very long, and is often on the run. Salsa, not to mention salseros, cannot afford to get stale and formulaic. If they stop moving, improvising, and inventing new ways of carrying on, they become a target. If they stay put, they get towed away. The only way out of the conundrum is to keep moving, keep dancing, but this time to their own beat, their own clave.[111]

For Santos Febres, the salience of improvisation in salsa dancing serves as a metaphor for the skills that are necessary for survival in *el barrio*. So while Santos stops short of saying that Latinos learn these skills through their experience in dance clubs, she links values in dance to those of Latino culture in general. I hold out hope that salsa's popularity will help shift the center of the American social dance industry so that DanceSport and salsa are recognized as two of many interlocking cultural rhythms that commingle to produce the world's dance moves.

I have suggested that DanceSport is deeply entrenched in its racist history. But I am not convinced it is more or less pernicious than other American cultural practices that developed out of Western imperialism and colonialism. Despite her personal experience of racism, Maria Torres herself is remarkably upbeat about the changes she and others have inspired through their participation in DanceSport. Many DanceSport competitors have begun to study a broader range of Latin dance outside the ballroom industry; some have even changed their rhetoric to indicate that DanceSport is but one among many versions of Latin dance. The DanceSport establishment has begun to celebrate Maria Torres's contribution to DanceSport, albeit only after she received critical acclaim in other dance industries. Perhaps the greatest change will be enacted from pressures external to the DanceSport community. Alternative Latin dance communities and industries, particularly those of salsa and Argentine tango, are gaining greater popularity and recognition worldwide, forcing the ballroom industry to reexamine and redefine its own interpretation of Latin dancing.

My intent in drawing out these racial issues is not to condemn the practice of DanceSport, but rather to broaden the perspectives from which both its practitioners and its viewers understand its representations of Latinness. Brownface glamorizes racial difference, exaggerating its advantages, concealing its harmful effects, and masking far more than the white skin of its dancers. It obscures the racist history out of which this practice emerged as well as the ways in which race, gender, and class are often conflated in American discourse. Brownface provides enough cover for DanceSport's version of Latin sexy to remain classy. The brownface ritual is also one that negotiates the complex relations of class and nationality through a recognizable bodily discourse of race. It offers a model for assimilation into white Western culture. The Glamour Machine's powerful device of brownface recolors the history of Latin dancing, repainting the dark skin of its African roots and the racial politics in which it is implicated in a lighter, more palatable tone.

four

Exceeding the Limits of Competition:
Innovations in Theatrical Ballroom Dance

DanceSport suffers from identity confusion, simultaneously striving for recognition as art, entertainment, sport, and business. The four-pronged categorization causes strain within the industry as various factions lobby to foreground one aspect over the others. I have examined at length the effects of marketing ballroom dancing as business in America. However, the art-entertainment-sport triumvirate identified by the Dutch DanceSport coach Ruud Vermey merits further discussion. In his book *Latin: Thinking, Sensing and Doing in Latin American Dancing,* Vermey contends that art, entertainment, and sport have distinctly different objectives. The goal of an artistic project is to educate, inspire, or move an audience; the main focus of a show is to entertain; and the intent of a sports competition is to determine winners and losers. Not all three of these purposes can necessarily be pursued with equal success in a single instance of choreography. The ballroom dance industry as it is currently structured places much more value on show and sport than art because competitions and popular entertainment are its main performance venues. Vermey's work encourages dancers to explore the untapped artistic potential of DanceSport Latin and offers many practical tools for expanding both choreographic options and interpretations of basic steps. He advocates very few structural changes to the system itself. His only significant proposal is to substitute a collaborative, discussion-based judging system for the current biased method. His recommendations primarily suggest how to develop more artistry within the current frame of DanceSport competition. Vermey implies that by increasing artistic focus in competition, dancers will be more successful competitors.

Vermey's analysis is deeply rooted in choreology, a term coined by Rudolph Benesh in the 1950s and currently used to refer to the study of movement through the use of a movement notation system. Rudd Vermey applies theories developed by the movement theorists Rudolph van Laban and Irmgard Bartinieff (pioneers in movement analysis and dance notation) to DanceSport Latin. Instead of focusing on the narrative each of the Latin dances conveys, Vermey compares how they are distinguished by their differing attention to certain body parts, actions, use of space, rhythmic qualities, and dynamics in effort. In drawing attention away from *what* each dance conveys and noticing *how* the body communicates these messages, Vermey offers an alternative model for teaching and choreographing DanceSport Latin.

I will use the example of rumba to illustrate his methods. Ballroom rumba is traditionally considered to be a slow, sensuous dance of love. Choreographic decisions and styling choices are often made by enacting a particular narrative of love, one in which the woman entices the man, turns away from him, and then relinquishes her body to his embrace. Vermey does not ignore this thematic motivation but interrogates how it is accomplished through characteristic choices in each of the five categories (body, action, rhythm, space, and dynamics). Vermey argues, for example, that rumba is a dance built chiefly on stylized walking accentuating the hips (*body*). It foregrounds the *actions* of weight transfer merging into twisting. The *rhythmical phrasing* alternates between impact (accent on the end of a movement) and impulse (accent on the beginning of a movement), their continuous merging producing a seamless flow. *Spatial* patterns are not linear but focus on sliding, passing, and circling through a shared central space. The *dynamic* qualities that he finds most prominent in rumba are (based on Laban's categorization of effort) free, heavy, sustained, and flexible.[1] Vermey teaches dancers to examine each move in their choreography in order to decide which body part, action, rhythm, spatial orientation, and dynamic should be accentuated.

In addition to his choreological analysis, Vermey suggests many other routes for choreographic development in competitive ballroom dance. He calls attention to the underutilization of repetition, variation, phrasing, thematic development, and structural logic in DanceSport Latin routines. Although his brief ruminations about how each of these strategies might be applied to competition choreography do not offer the clear practical guidelines his choreological examinations produce, they do suggest many fertile routes for choreographic development. Slightly more sustained is Vermey's explication of nonverbal communication, particularly male and female courting behaviors, and its relationship to DanceSport choreography. Vermey applies theories of body language developed by the social psychologist Michael Argyle and the anthropologist Judith Lynne Hanna in order to analyze how movements in DanceSport Latin are coded as masculine and feminine. He concludes that many of the stylistic movements that characterize a "masculine" performance correspond to the body language identified by Argyle as dominant or hostile and by Hanna as stereotypical male courtship body language. Actions that are read as "feminine" in ballroom dance are likewise consistent with submissive, friendly, and stereotypically female physical postures and gestures. Although Vermey does not suggest alternative models for the portrayal of masculinity and femininity, he explicitly calls into question the appropriateness of performing this dominant/submissive dichotomy in the current sociopolitical context:

> To some, indeed many people, the portrayal of women as mere objects of sexual desire, thrown around by men, treated as men's pleasure is wholly distasteful today. . . . The portrayal of men also needs rethinking. . . . There are many different expressions of maleness which do not relate to aggression, power, and dominance. To preserve any self-respect, the Latin dance institution would do well to examine aspects of its functions which are insulting to male and female competitors and spectators alike.[2]

Although Vermey does not articulate how to rethink the masculine and feminine roles in Latin DanceSport, he challenges dancers and choreographers to be aware of their own role in perpetuating restrictive gender binaries.

The usefulness of Vermey's work for DanceSport competitors has been widely celebrated, and his theories are now taught worldwide by many of his disciples. Vermey continues to research and teach at his institute in the Netherlands, expanding and revising the theories presented in his published work. Though his paradigm continues to be generative for dancers pursuing championship competition titles, his inclination to develop these ideas to the full extent they suggest brings many competitors up against the limitations of the competition frame. For example, it may not be effective in competition choreography for a dancer to explore how far a body can be twisted or how long a rhythm can be sustained. As discussed in chapter 1, competitors are under tremendous pressure to display their skills in a very short time: the format of competition mandates particular directional changes, dynamic shifts, and recognizable body actions at predictable intervals. Moreover, DanceSport is still defined as stylized heterosexual courtship. New choreographic innovations are not practical in competition if they challenge this assumption too severely. For example, a twist stretched to the maximum possible for a human body may result in a shape so abstract that it doesn't appear to be referencing courtship. Those competitors who do push for redefinition of the level of abstraction acceptable in DanceSport performance meet mixed reviews, at times able to expand the boundaries and at other times chastised for their unconventional choreography.

Although Vermey is correct to a certain extent in assuming that judges will be impressed by the results of these artistic strategies, many coaches and competitors have questioned his apparent disregard for the competition frame in which the dancers he trains display their craft. In his crusade to encourage creativity in a form that has historically rewarded imitation of already proven techniques, Vermey may overstate his point. If, as he suggested at a seminar in New York, a dancer paints himself blue and stands on his head because that is how he feels rumba should be expressed, he is not going to win a DanceSport competition. Invested in the ostensible goal of winning, this creative competitor will likely be disappointed by his failure, not satisfied merely by realizing his own artistic vision. Though sport and entertainment may be complementary, sport and art often work at cross-purposes. Dancers are continuously struggling to find a resolution to the conflicts created by the uneasy union of sport and art in Dance-Sport, this very frustration a prime subject for film.

The inadequacy of the competition set-up for recognizing artistic developments was not merely represented in Baz Luhrmann's 1993 film *Strictly Ballroom;* the movie's very existence was one dancer's revenge on the ballroom dance industry. The film is based on a true story of a ballet dancer whose artistic innovations in ballroom dance competitions were ignored by the judges. Despite the creativity, skill, and popular appeal of his choreography, his radical departure from the conventions of the competition form was not received well by the establishment. Thirty years later he had his retribution with the release of the *Strictly Ballroom.* The fictionalized screen version goes like this.

The Australian Scott Hastings, who has been bred from birth to be a Dance-Sport champion, is gearing up for what all expect to be his year to win the Pan Pacific Grand Prix Amateur 5–Dance Latin American Championship. Much to his family's horror, Scott disregards the unwritten rules of competition and breaks out into his own "crowd-pleasing steps" during a preliminary competition. As a result of his offensive behavior, Scott's partner leaves him for the drunken champion, who has the judges in his pocket and spends his time in hot tubs with women instead of on the practice floor. The situation propels Scott's family into crisis, since the older generation was counting on his success to fulfill their own shattered championship dreams. His controlling mother whirls into overdrive in an attempt to ensure her son's success in competition irrespective of his own desires. She is enabled by her docile husband, who is lost in his own regrets of the past, unable to intercede on his son's behalf. Scott's preteen sister seems to be the only reasonable voice in the family, acting and speaking with a clarity and poise none of the adults can muster. When auditions for a new partner fail to turn up likely prospects, Scott finally agrees to give wallflower beginning student Fran a chance at training to become his new partner. They practice in secret, their shared investment in creativity rather than mastery of the preestablished form binding them together in a dance that seems destined to extend beyond the dance floor. When Fran's immigrant parents threaten to forbid her from going to the studio anymore, Scott must prove himself to her father, a flamenco virtuoso. It immediately becomes apparent that even Scott's own deviations from the ballroom version of paso doble pale in comparison to the Andalusian version, and Scott submits himself to the older man's tutelage. Meanwhile, Scott's family, frantic to find him a championship partner, eventually turns up a ringer right before the competition. Scott must finally choose between the wishes of his mother and the competition establishment or his new romantic love and creative innovation.

The film insightfully portrays many of the problems that plague the industry without wallowing in bitterness or cynicism. Of primary importance is the revelation that the rules of competition necessarily curtail artistic expression. But many of the secondary issues raised by the film are defining facets of the Dance-Sport industry—corruption of the judging system; perpetual entangling of performance of courtship with love off the dance floor; erasure of ethnic origins of the Latin dances in favor of white-washed versions; ballroom dance families' feelings of entitlement to championship titles; high melodrama; children who act like adults, adults who act like children; and disguise of the negative aspects of the industry for public performance of fairy-tale perfection. The conclusion of the film offers no resolution to any of these problems within the DanceSport industry. Its heroes triumph only by overthrowing the system, not by inspiring change within it. When Scott does finally opt to dance with Fran instead of the established champion, Tina Sparkle, he is disqualified. Their dance continues only when Scott's father leads the audience to create the music with their bodies, clapping out the rhythm and literally taking over the dance floor with the bodies of the populace. Not surprisingly, many DanceSport competitors disliked the film. It portrayed only the negative aspects of DanceSport and offered no solutions, short of abandoning the industry, to the multitude of problems it revealed.

Much of the DanceSport community was dismayed that the first feature film in which competitive ballroom dancing figured prominently portrayed so little of the pleasure competitive dancing brings to many of its participants, instead implying that anyone who does find satisfaction in DanceSport is neurotic, greedy, evil, self-centered, and unenlightened. To the nondancer, it read as an over-the-top parody, hyperbolic hyperbole. But many of those intimately connected to the DanceSport industry were unsettled by how close the film's semi-documentary frame came to capturing reality. "The costumes, they are so outrageous!" nondancing viewers squealed, delighting in what they take to be one of the most farcical aspects of the film. "But that's what we really wear," their ballroom dancing friends rather sheepishly pointed out, embarrassed that even the fashion needs little exaggeration to appear absurd when scrutinized under the camera's lens.

Though the onscreen hero's success may have obliquely intimated a future in which creativity was encouraged, the film hardly represented a realistic path for offscreen DanceSport mavericks. If Scott Hastings is to be looked to as an example for the DanceSport competitor who relinquishes his championship dreams in favor of authoring new artistic visions, even this fictional character's story suggests that one needs an elaborate support system in order to confront the competition establishment. Scott was able to garner the courage to dance "his way" only with the backing of a burgeoning love affair, familial support, a network of conscientious friends, and popular approval from spectators in the stands. The more practical model suggested by this film is not that of the character within the narrative, but that of the filmmakers. The choreography in *Strictly Ballroom* succeeds because it shifts the frame to that of a film about ballroom dance competitions, thus playing to a sympathetic movie audience, not a row of DanceSport judges. It is likewise in recontextualization—adapting DanceSport techniques and vocabulary to concert, film, or other theatrical venues—that I see the greatest possibilities for both new artistic innovation and destabilization of the Glamour Machine.

In concert or cabaret performances, representations of gender, race, sexuality, nationality, and class are no longer restricted to the narrow scope that defines the DanceSport competition performance. For example, Latin dance does not need to be characterized only by a narrative of erotic heterosexual courtship if it is not being judged against the expectations that delineate the competition performance. Both men and women can explore a greater range of aesthetics in their movement when not bound by their complementary roles in a dominant/submissive dyad. Outside of competition, new partnering combinations can be attempted, different body shapes foregrounded, new vocabulary inserted, and radical choreographic digression initiated. In the following pages, I will explicate choreography in which the dance techniques and physical skills developed in DanceSport competition are put to a different purpose, one that does not necessarily further the Glamour Machine. Some of these choreographers have been directly influenced by Vermey's teaching and scholarship, while others are independently exploring similar issues. In each case, I explore how the choreography of ballroom dances presented outside the frame of conventional competition challenges the Glamour Machine. Finally, I will return to the business of teaching and selling dance lessons to introduce two examples of programs that suggest alternatives to the classic studio model.

EXPANDING REPRESENTATION
OF GENDER AND SEXUALITY

Even within the DanceSport competition setting, the recent addition of a category called showdance, in which a couple performs a solo routine to music of their choice, has begun to encourage DanceSport competitors to push their choreography beyond that appropriate in traditional competition. Though still presented at DanceSport competitions and judged against some of the same technical standards, the couple's exclusive right to the floor, music, and audience for three minutes drastically opens up space for sustained thematic exploration and artistic development. Several couples have presented showdance routines that not only demonstrate an innovative integration of various vocabularies but actually re-envision identity, moving it beyond the restrictive prescriptions of traditional DanceSport.

Although showdance competition still mandates a male/female partnership, dancers explore through their choreography gender roles beyond those constructed by their corollary roles in ballroom dance aesthetic conventions. Although the representation of gender differs in the Latin and Standard categories (discussed in chapter 3), masculine and feminine in each is marked through contrasting roles. He initiates action and supports her body; she reacts to movement and relinquishes her weight to his strength. These roles mandate that she is showcased by him, touched by him (or herself), and supported by him, not vice versa. His weight is more often split between his two feet, his body expansive and stable in order to support her in vulnerable moves in which she balances on one leg. Except in kicks displaying her flexibility, she keeps her thighs together, performing a coy sexual modesty, in sharp contrast to his open legs, which advertise sexual availability. Many competitors are stretching the bounds of these demarcations of gender within competition—men performing turns and splits once reserved only for women and women enjoying the occasional initiation of an action. Fluid gender roles are more freely explored, however, in showdance and show routines.

Dima and Olga Sukachov's 1999 Ohio Star Ball showdance rumba successfully portrays a relationship in which masculine and feminine are established on like and equal terms. Although they do not entirely eliminate references to gender differences, they bring the two roles closer together than is typically seen in DanceSport. Costuming still marks them as different, her short skirt and high heels contrasting with his pants and flat shoes. However, the use of simple black costumes for both, with no extra glitter or rhinestones for her, draws their distinction closer to that typical in pedestrian life, not the cartoonish parody of gender often produced by DanceSport costumes. Their tight clothing, which still highlights a gendered sexuality, prevents them from looking androgynous or sexless. But their masculinity and femininity emanate from their straightforward identity as male and female, not through imitation of a mythical masculine or feminine. They dance the majority of their choreography side by side, performing nearly identical steps that further contribute to their portrayal of equal gender roles. When they do face each other and touch hands, they use only steps in which the male and female parts do not differ significantly, eschewing any dips or lines in which dimorphic body shapes are foregrounded. Their facial expressions are serious and unchanging, utilizing none of the baring of teeth and coquettish smiling that usually demarcate the male and female roles. They also eliminate all use of the arms except to establish occasional connection with each other, further reducing the points at which Latin technique differs in its expression of masculine and feminine.

The simplicity of their choreography and the starkness of its execution are startling, drawing attention to synchronicity in their leg, foot and body action and the harmony with which their separate bodies perform with singular purpose. One might have expected that by excising movement in which contrasting gender roles are highlighted, the dancers would no longer be recognizable as a couple, banished references to stereotypical courtship diminishing readability of their relationship. However, Dima and Olga Sukachov embody a different kind of partnership, one in which their bond is established not through teasing or flirting, but through common commitment to a shared vision.

The success of their performance, which offered a new interpretation of gender roles and possibly even a different model for how love can be portrayed in Latin dance, can be contrasted with less well developed efforts to challenge traditional gender roles. For example, Bill Sparks and Kimberly Mitchell's 1998 Ohio Star Ball showdance routine attempts to invert the dominant/submissive dichotomy. She enters leading him, as if he were either her dog or her sex slave, by collar and chain. After she makes him cower and beg for the privilege of dancing with her, they quickly return to a traditional cha cha in which the man leads and frames the lady. Other such attempts to reverse the power differential in ballroom partnerships seem to run up against similar obstacles. If the woman becomes dominant, how can the man possibly relate to her without becoming feminized, the label most feared by all male DanceSport competitors? Merely to reverse gender roles does little to change them; the inevitable return to traditional roles in experiments such as this one points to their impotence in actually shifting gender relations.

Another example of a showdance performance that effectively reenvisioned gender roles in Latin dance won the World South American Showdance Competition in 2001.[3] Dressed alike in black Lycra tops (hers cropped to reveal her taut belly), silver pants, and men's Latin shoes, the Slovenian competitors Sergej Milicija and Katja Klep integrate competition Latin with hip-hop body popping and locking. The effectiveness of their choreography is not in mere juxtaposition but in fusion that enables the combination of forms to enrich and enhance each other. Fan position, de rigueur in Latin routines (lady standing at a right angle to the man, her right leg extended toward him and her left hip rotated back to create internal twisting that foregrounds her leg, ankle, and hip), is appropriated by the hip-hop choreography, their joined hands becoming the point at which rapid isolations are passed from his body to hers. Their bodies seamlessly transition from one style to the next; the energetic connection between them alternately transmits ideas from DanceSport and breakdancing. Vocabulary is not the only concept borrowed from popular club dancing. Steps are executed in slow motion, fast-forward, retrograde, repetition, or stopped entirely, all in response to sudden shifts in the music. As if being spun by a trickster deejay, the music skips, breaks, repeats, and distorts. The dancers are never caught by his ruse, always offering a clever interpretation to what seem to be unexpected rifts in the track.

Milicija and Klep's performance suggests new possibilities both for the use of

DanceSport Latin in a performance not based on an oversexed love story and for revised gender roles in male-female partnerships. Like the Sukachovs, they dispense with the usually pretense of exaggerated passion and instead display calm facial expressions and understated gestures. However, Milicija and Klep's partnership is based not on stripping their routine to bare movement (as was the Sukachovs') but in developing another aesthetic vision. In contrast to Dima and Olga Sukachov's, Milicija and Klep's routine employs different moves for the man and woman. By aligning their choreography with hip-hop, a dance genre in which nearly all moves are executed similarly by men and women, each is able to select from a greater range of movement choices without violating gender norms. It is he who takes fifteen seconds to melt to the floor in a living rendition of Edvard Munch's *Scream* while she looked on, a refreshing reversal of roles of framer and framed.

Neither of the two performances I have identified as having effectively re-positioned masculine and feminine roles was specifically choreographed with gender at the center of its thematic investigation. In fact, precisely because each developed an artistic vision that did not foreground gender differences, new possibilities for masculine and feminine expression were unleashed. Although a targeted focus on gender in choreography could certainly generate diversity in gendered representation (and does for many choreographers of contemporary concert dance), some choreographies that specifically take on the gender binary required by ballroom dancing ironically reinscribe the traditional gender roles they critique. Such was the case in the exhibition *Tango Magic,* performed by Kenny and Marion Welsh and Stephen and Lindsey Hillier at the 1993 Ohio Star Ball. These performers try out on their bodies two myths of ballroom dancing—that the ideal couple moves as one person and that the ideal woman is a puppet manipulated by her male leader. Four dancers transform themselves into four couples—each one converting his or her own body into a male-female pair. From the waist down, each looked like a half man–half woman circus per-former. On the left leg, each wears a pant leg and flat shoe. On the right leg, each wears hose, a satin pump, and a skirt. The top half of each lady is repre-sented by a puppet held in each dancer's right arm. The gentleman's torso and head are represented by each performer's own. Thus, only one leg and one arm are sacrificed off the human body to designate woman, while the representation of man requires a human head and torso.

The choreography in this number reinforces the message of the costuming— that the woman's role in ballroom is primarily that of a leg and a painted face. The dancers, who for the most part do identical moves to produce the effect of a four-couple tango formation, primarily do the man's steps. The only times they do movements atypical for the male are when foregrounding the stocking-clad legs in kicks, rondes (circular low kicks), and eros lines (legs extended back-ward in an angled shape). Although the dancers embody the ideal of two bodies moving as one, they also expose the inadequacy of a single body for executing DanceSport choreography. Although it is an impressive routine, it does not display the speed, power, or dynamic changes produced by two bodies working in harmony. If we were to dispense with one person, however, it would clearly be the woman. Well, at least her head. Her legs seem to be a necessity for providing both power and aesthetic variation. One might conclude after watching this performance, however, that her torso and head (and presumably her brain) could just as easily be exchanged for a puppet.

Although this performance demonstrated that either a male or a female could manipulate that puppet equally well (the men and women execute the choreography with equivalent dexterity), it fails to offer an alternative beyond the binary so cleverly embodied. The exhibition is progressive in its transgression across many boundaries. Both men and women cross-dress and assume equal responsibility in the show. The gender roles themselves, however, remain entrenched in their traditional expression. Although *Tango Magic* does perform role reversal and even coexistence of two gender roles on one body, it does not suggest future possibilities for expanded gender roles, as does the choreography of Dima and Olga Sukachov or of Sergej Milicija and Katja Klep.

The showdance category helps to infuse DanceSport with fresh creative possibilities. However, multi-couple dance companies present even more expanded opportunities to explore the range of DanceSport's artistic potential. The work of Rudd Vermey's protégé Louis van Amstel, though he is certainly not the first or only competitor to adapt ballroom dance to stage, represents a current ongoing attempt to develop the choreographic possibilities suggested by Vermey's theories beyond the competition context.[4] After becoming world amateur Latin champion dancing for his home country of the Netherlands in 1994 and 1995, van Amstel immigrated to the United States, eventually capturing the United States Professional Latin Championships when he returned to competition in 2000. In 1997 van Amstel formed his first ballroom dance company, Van Dance Creations. Composed of twenty DanceSport champions scattered throughout the United States, the company convened for rehearsals at competitions around the country. Though such an arrangement allowed the participation of highly skilled dancers from many regions of the United States, it drastically limited the time and energy that could be invested in choreographic development. Infrequent practices were scheduled at midnight, after a long day of competition. Though the company's goal was to create a dance spectacular that brought ballroom to mainstream theatrical audiences in the spirit of shows such as *Riverdance* and *Forever Tango,* initial performances were at DanceSport competitions in front of other ballroom dance fanatics. This phase of the company's development culminated in the performance of *Ballati* at the California Open in Costa Mesa, California, on 13 and 14 February 1998. Shortly thereafter the company disbanded. It was eventually resuscitated under the name of Van Dance. Now based in New York, home to the nation's and possibly the world's most concentrated collection of highly skilled DanceSport competitors, van Amstel now relies more exclusively on dancers in the New York area, enabling more extended rehearsals and creative exploration. In 2002 van Amstel mounted a revised and expanded version of his earlier work in a performance titled *Latin Fusion* presented at New York's City Center on 22 and 23 June.

Both *Ballati* and *Latin Fusion* represent ambitious attempts to develop a viable stage form in which DanceSport is integrated with concepts and techniques from concert dance. The two shows are similar in format—a string of short numbers representing different DanceSport styles. Spotlighted individual couple presentations are intertwined with ensemble work, the majority of which consists of typical competition choreography performed by several couples in formation. Both programs fall short of presenting either a coherent or consistent vision, yet both shows exhibit moments in which innovative choreographic concepts articulate alternatives to the restrictive identities represented in traditional DanceSport performance.

Several of *Ballati*'s most generative sections are those in which the men dance without female partners. Released from their role as supporter and displayer of female beauty, they are able to unleash new directions for the representation of masculinity. In one of van Amstel's brief appearances during this show, he dances in a sultry entr'acte, which reads like a voyeuristic sojourn into his bedroom. His self-indulgent exploration of sensuality is refreshingly unconcerned with the audience, enrapt by the interplay between virtuosic muscular articulation and emotional expression. Clad only in jeans and his blond mane, van Amstel appears as bestial as he does vulnerable, expressing a masculinity simultaneously more aggressive and self-centered than that typical for men in Dance-Sport Latin. Later in the show, van Amstel joins three other male dancers, each of whom partners a pole shooting up from the floor. Not only does this brief section suggest partnership combinations besides those of man and woman, but it invokes an image of men who need not be paired with a woman in order to be sexy. While not necessarily homoerotic, the scene is at least autoerotic by virtue of the phallic poles with which the men dance. As in van Amstel's earlier vignette, this exclusively masculine space enables the men to explore both stronger and more sensual movement that does not risk overpowering or drawing attention away from a woman. Extracted from his role as one-half of a partnership, the male portrayed in these examples has greater freedom of movement.

Taking the male dancers out of the competition context seems to enable expressive possibilities not conveyed in competition, but the female dancers in this performance seem to suffer from the loss of the competition frame. After stripping the women of the high heels and dresses worn in DanceSport competition, van Amstel seems unsure of how to develop solo choreography for the women in his company that does not reproduce the traditional feminine role.

Although outfitted with running pants and jazz sneakers, which should enable a greater range of motion, the women reproduce the narrowly defined Latin aesthetic. Thighs and ankles are modestly rotated inward, hips and legs are foregrounded, and arms extend as if to showcase diamonds on the fingertips and the bosom from which they emerge. Experts at receiving momentum and completing movement phrases initiated by a partner, the female dancers appear weaker without either the physical power of or the visual comparison to the corollary masculine role.

Such an imbalance in expanding gender roles is no longer evident, however, in a later version of this work performed in *Latin Fusion.* The show's penultimate section, "Box Cha Cha," successfully articulates alternative partnering possibilities and new gender roles for both sexes. The poles utilized in van Amstel's earlier choreography are replaced with an extensive industrial scaffold that covers the stage throughout the duration. The interlocking grids of metal create visual variation in space and provide ample opportunity for dancers to partner inanimate objects. Some of the choreography is executed in new spatial orientations as several dancers hang and swing from the scaffold as if it were a playground toy. Each strip of metal becomes a potential partner that dancers can use to execute basic Latin steps with speed and power equivalent to that generated with a human partner. Dancers check and rebound off the cage and each other as they exchange flesh for steel with ease. The substitution of object for human does not devalue the live dancers but actually helps to establish their identity as individuals who can thrive without a partner. Since ballroom dancers' unique skills are in partnering, extended solo choreography does not showcase their strengths. However, van Amstel's tactic of transferring these partnering skills to a new kind of partnership helps to produce an image of accomplished dancers who are no longer merely one-half of a whole. Both men and women can stand alone as complete artistic agents.

Although human-human partnerships are primarily male-female, men and women no longer seem dependent on one another for their identity. Both men and women are dressed in brightly colored work overalls and dance sneakers and often execute identical choreography. Their dancing, however, is hardly asexual or androgynous. The tops of the overalls drop open, revealing brightly colored Latin dresses for the women and shirts for the men. The combination of the workmen's pants and the jeweled fabric on each body mirrors the coexistence of traditional and unconventional throughout the routine. There is even a brief solo in which van Amstel partners another man in the cast (Martin van Buren), their combined strength and magnetism producing one of the most breathtaking moments in the entire show. The choreography suggests neither abandoning the sexual gendering of traditional DanceSport nor remaining constrained by its limits. The fluid exchange back and forth between different kinds of partnering, some gendered and some not, suggests a world in which DanceSport's past is folded into a future in which identity, gender, and even sexual orientation are less narrowly defined. Like the unisex duet (Sukachovs) and the choreography of the body-popping Latin couple (Milicija and Klep), "Box Cha Cha" effectively models new gender roles and relationships for the ballroom Latin partnership.

THE GENERATIVE POWER OF HUMOR

Like most sporting events, dance competitions maintain an earnest focus on the tension between the potential winners and losers that seems to preclude space for humor. Ballroom dance exhibition and even showdance competition, however, create space in which experimentation with humor, although rarely utilized, becomes possible. The DanceSport judge and coach Wendy Johnson often uses comedy as a basis for her work. Her choreography provides me the opportunity to theorize why humor is so rarely invoked in ballroom performances.

A stubborn piece of toilet paper hardly seems like the winning ingredient to turn a traditional waltz routine into a showstopper, and yet it helped Nick Cotton and Maria Hansen win the showdance competition at the Ohio Star Ball in 1997. In their waltz routine, choreographed by Johnson and Michael Babineau, Cotton attempts to dispose of a piece of toilet paper (which is stuck successively to his shoe, his hand, his partner's back, and his partner's hair) without letting Hansen notice that anything is amiss in their blissful romance. The cleverness of this performance is not merely the joke itself, for many a three-year-old has exercised scatological humor, but the context in which the dancers frame their slapstick. Reminiscent of a Marx Brothers sketch, this ruse's success is in the layering of who is doing the duping and who is being duped. It takes the audience a few moments to realize that the toilet paper is *supposed* to be stuck to Cotton's shoe (i.e., is part of the performance and not a grooming oversight), and we are exposed as the first to be duped. Most of the audience members laugh at the joke that has been played on us rather than harboring resentment, especially because this revelation allows us to trade in our anxiety about their public embarrassment for an emotionally supportive role in Cotton's enterprise to hide this evidence of his humanity from Hansen. The audience can then enjoy the illusion that we are in on something she isn't. It is no longer we but Hansen who becomes the duped. Of course, we are simultaneously aware that she really is in on the joke, for she has obviously practiced to precision when to turn her head to play to maximum effect the tension between the location of that stubborn piece of tissue and her line of vision.

To continue imagining that Hansen is the one being duped allows us enough distance from a situation with which we can all identify that we can enter safely into the realm of fantasy. Through willing suspension of disbelief, spectators are able to mediate their own anxieties. What performer hasn't feared appearing onstage with some embarrassing evidence of human frailty, whether it be an open zipper or a dress that falls off (as in the Japanese and American versions of the film *Shall We Dance?*). Hansen's uninterrupted state of blissful romance, in spite of the entire audience's literally laughing in her face, highlights the difficulty and absurdity of the situation all DanceSport competitors face—projecting the illusion of a particular emotional state (romance, passion, sexual desire, etc.) that is often directly counter to what one is feeling under the given external circumstances (fear, anger, anxiety, etc.).

But there is yet another layer to this joke, one that exposes a social anxiety that extends beyond the ballroom. Cotton is performing a double identity—presenting one image of himself to his lady (suave, debonair gentleman whose role is to showcase her beauty) and an entirely different one to the public (comedian). The man's role in this number, and indeed on the competition floor, is to fool the lady into believing that his attention is focused exclusively on her, or at least to fool the audience into thinking he is fooling her. If his task is to convince her she is the center of his world, her job is to convince him he is successful, as Hansen does well by strategically averting her gaze while Cotton grasps at the offending tissue. Highlighting the artificiality of this relationship, one that is enacted every time a couple steps onto the competition floor, introduces a self-reflexivity into the dance partnership that opens up possibilities for alternative constructions of this relationship.

Cotton and Hansen's routine pokes fun at both the public roles mandated in DanceSport and the tension produced by competition. The parody enables a critique that is nonthreatening in its lighthearted approach, the transformation of a piece of toilet paper into the crown jewel at one of the most prestigious dance competitions in the United States, exempting its embedded social critique from earnest criticism. In calling attention to the pretence required to create DanceSport's "gentleman" and "lady," this piece begins to expose the smoke and mirrors behind Glamorous production. By foregrounding that which is usually hidden, ignored, and disguised in DanceSport—ordinary human error—DanceSport superstars are recast as mortals with mundane bodily functions. Cotton and Hansen's failure to embody the ideal waltzing couple actually undermines the Glamour Machine's contention that such a romanticized identity is possible and desirable. By making the failure entertaining and therefore more successful than the ideal itself (this routine did, after all, win the showdance competition), Cotton and Hansen offer an alternative to the Glamorous Dance-Sport image.

The success of humor in this particular routine suggests it may be a rich avenue for future choreography that challenges the Glamour Machine. Several theorists of laughter, particularly that associated with the carnivalesque, have noted the generative power of laughter to encourage transgression and invite social change. In Mikhail Bakhtin's much-cited work on carnival, he writes that festive folk laughter "means the defeat of power, of earthly kings, of the earthly upper classes, of all that oppresses and restricts."[5] Although a Dance-Sport competition is not the medieval carnival upon which Bakhtin's analysis is based, this particular routine does have many carnivalesque qualities, including inversion and unusual juxtaposition of high and low. The normal social order is momentarily thrown into a state of flux when a piece of toilet paper becomes the complement to a high-fashion ensemble and defecation becomes the focus of a white-tie affair. I suspect the progressive energy inspired by humor partially explains why it has been ignored by ballroom choreography. The lack of humor in ballroom performances may be due, at least in part, to a resistance to change. It is not a conscious choice or a deliberate thwarting of progress, but the effect of performance generated within an industry that relies on commodification for its economic survival. Formulas for generating laughter cannot be sold in charts like dance steps. Degrees of turn are not easily translated into comedic outcome. However, the difficulty of selling humor in dance should be weighed against the generative potential produced by laughter. Even in an industry that relies heavily on the appeal of nostalgia, classic movement quickly becomes stale if it does not continue to evolve. For those wishing to introduce new artistic or creative possibilities or to inspire any kind of change in ballroom dancing, humor should be considered as potentially one of the most powerful and underutilized tools in the choreographic arsenal.

LIFE VERSUS GLAMOUR: REDRAWING THE CURTAIN

DanceSport reinforces restrictive categories of identity on two levels: through representation in its choreography and through human interactions determined by the industry structure. So far, I have discussed ways in which representation of identity might be reimagined through innovative choreography that reflects a greater range of gendered or sexualized character types. As agents of the Glamour Machine that reproduce unequal and often repressive identity positions, however, the social interactions produced through the DanceSport industry's structure are equally potent. Theatrical ballroom dance may threaten the power of the Glamour Machine not only because the representation of identity in performance can be redefined, but also because the stage venue produces a greater distance between performers and their audience. DanceSport Glamour relies on the proximity of subjects from drastically different social positions and their continued fascination with each other. By clearly separating audience from performer, the concert performance of ballroom dancing no longer tantalizes and tortures participants through simultaneous proximity and distance. It is not that individuals from different backgrounds cannot be invited to join the same performing group, but that the theatrical system does not freeze them in positions of unequal power. Increasing the distance between performance and life helps to clarify the difference between the portrayal of intimacy and actual intimacy. Glamour thrives on the conflation of performance of intimacy with intimacy freely exchanged between peers. Performers on a stage that is clearly demarcated by a proscenium arch and a velvet curtain are confident of when the performance begins and ends. They are able to take off their characters with the makeup after the curtain call and less likely to be strained by the perpetual performance of Glamour endemic in the DanceSport industry. The very existence of a ballroom dance company as an alternative space in which to perform DanceSport is in itself a major challenge to the Glamour Machine. The experiences of the Wayne Foster ballroom dancers illustrate this point.

The DanceSport competitors Curtis Collins and Natalie Mavor choreographed group ballroom dance numbers for Wayne Foster Entertainment between 1999 and 2001.[6] Appearing as a specialty dance act during four-hour entertainment interactive spectacles at $300-a-plate dinner dances, these numbers were expected to reproduce stereotypical ballroom and Latin images for popular consumption. Although the representation of identity in the choreography did little to suggest alternative social structures, the very existence of this outlet for many Los Angeles–based ballroom dancers offered them an alternative to DanceSport Glamour. Ballroom dancing was only a single element in a much larger spectacle. A sixteen-piece band, six vocalists, a dozen jazz dancers, a stilt-walker, noisemakers, party favors, stage lights, tambourines, sailor hats for the audience to wear during their "In the Navy" number, and a white grand piano at center stage all contributed to an atmosphere of revelry. The stages were often constructed on site in outdoor tents, but there was always a backstage where the chaos of warm-ups, costume changes, makeup bags, and candy bar wrappers was hidden from the audience.

This clear separation of viewers and performers in space did not, however, produce a similar dichotomy in class position. The relative class position of audience members and dancers was never relevant. The insignificance of relative class status in this example is in stark contrast to the ballroom competition, where the professional dancing with his amateur partner never forgets that he is a hired personal servant. Although the audience members at a Wayne Foster event may have been of a higher social class than many of the performers, the limited interaction at a personal level between the two groups never encouraged these comparisons. Often performers were literally confined to the kitchen until the moment their bodies were required on stage. Ironically, this physical location in a space associated with service did not heighten tensions of social inequality. Instead, the clear separation of on- and offstage buffered these dancers, if only temporarily, from the perpetual performance of Glamour the life of a DanceSport celebrity demands.

The actions of a few dancers at industrial shows are in themselves hardly a threat to the contemporary structure of the ballroom dance industry. However, the different social relations in evidence in this example suggest that an industry that more clearly separated social and theatrical iterations of ballroom dancing would no longer be one in which Glamour determined social hierarchies. The Wayne Foster dancers step in and out of their temporary role as objects of desire with little trepidation or remorse, able to drop their performance personas the moment they pass the curtain that demarcates backstage. In contrast, the current competition structure, particularly the American system of pro-am, necessitates continual performances of one's position, denying professional dancers any time offstage. They do not merely represent particular gender, class, racial, and sexual identities for a one-hour show. Rather, DanceSport professionals consciously perform these identities all day, every day, as they teach, rehearse, socialize, or appear in public in full view of students, teachers, or judges.[7] Amateurs in turn mimic these self-conscious performances of identity in hopes of becoming more Glamorous themselves. Because so much of the current ballroom industry relies on perpetual public performance of identity, identity positions are reified, and participants tend to lose a sense of agency outside the expectations of the roles into which they have been cast. Continual conflation of performance and life tends to cause discomfort, anxiety, and even disgust for those caught at this interstice.

One possible means of alleviating this tension is by shifting the focus of performance-based ballroom dancing from competition to performance. While the few ballroom dance companies that have attempted to bring DanceSport to concert stages over the past twenty years have rarely provided full-time employment for dancers, they have offered professional ballroom dancers a respite from their role in perpetuating cycles of desire and consumption. Many of the DanceSport industry's most insidious effects are produced by the structure of competition. In addition to the performance of status required by the proximity of producers and consumers of Glamour, competition pits dancers against each other, at times ravaging their self-confidence and sense of self-worth in its cutthroat division of human beings into winners and losers. In contrast, the camaraderie and creative exchange enabled by a group endeavor can be an intoxicating pleasure for dancers accustomed to competition. Most DanceSport competitors who have performed in a ballroom dance company recall the experience as one of the most rewarding in their dance careers, the cooperation engendering community and growth.

The very formation of a ballroom dance company does to a certain extent threaten to destabilize the current structure of DanceSport, yet one company made a critique of the industry the explicit subject of its performance. The Company of Choice, a dance company based in California, presented *Against Line of Dance* in Costa Mesa, California, on 9 January 2000. This production attempted to combine theater and dance in a narrative performance that employs DanceSport vocabulary to critique the ballroom dance industry. Echoing one of the major themes portrayed in *Strictly Ballroom,* the show brought into question the restrictions on individual creativity produced by competition structure. The competition format and its many rules that stifle creative expression might be their most obvious target, but the performers took on the industry as a larger system.

The tension between the dancers and the DanceSport establishment is set up in the first scene through two parallel monologues performed by the main character, the Girl (Mary Pinizzotto), and her nemesis, the Judge Narrator (Grover Raupp-Montano). The Girl represents the DanceSport competitor, and the Judge, dressed in English legal robe and wig, represents the DanceSport establishment (his English attire a nod to the English domination of DanceSport). The Girl laments that she is trapped in a system that denies self-expression. The Judge pontificates on the importance of competitors' adherence to the rules, particularly the unwritten expectations of conduct and deportment in social situations. The show follows her search to find herself within this restrictive industry.

The first dance number dramatizes the conflict. Set at a cocktail party at which several judges evaluate proper behavior, heterosexually paired dancers enter the scene holding up translucent plastic masks. These blur but do not obscure the faces of the dancers, underscoring the blurring of the public and private personas of DanceSport competitors. Most dancers become so accustomed to wearing the symbolic mask that they lose sight of any distinction between the self and a public performance of it. The choreography highlights the strain of holding up one's "mask" at all times: the plastic masks are not attached to the costumes but are instead held to the face with one hand at all times. In one section of the piece, dancers sustain a pose as they slowly walk back and forth on a two-dimensional plane. This technique further underscores the message that these two-dimensional people are trapped in their postures like figures on an Egyptian vase. Toward the end of the scene, the inebriated dancers drop their masks. A firm reprimand by the judges reminds them to regain their masked personas before scurrying offstage.

The second dance number features dancers in hospital scrubs and masks, an oblique reference to the sickly state of the DanceSport industry. The surgical garb and absence of physical touch in the second scene symbolizes the impersonal side of ballroom dancing. The "clinical" movement is ironically the most beautiful and creatively expressive of the show. Each dancer faces a different alignment and performs basic rumba steps solo, without a partner. Like the scaffold choreography in *Latin Fusion,* the separation of the dancers while they perform basic Latin figures helps to establish their legitimacy as individual artists, not just complementary halves of a heterosexual pair. The movement is deliciously slow, the dancers' energy so measured and tightly bound that they appear to be moving through water. The pace and simplicity of the choreography, a direct contrast to that seen in competition, enables viewers to appreciate the shapes created by the steps and the negative space they frame. Later in the number, the dancers pair up to execute the same basic moves in heterosexual partnerships, but the couples refrain from touching each other. Virtual energy between the partners becomes palpable, appearing to extend their physical bodies. At moments reminiscent of the Sukachovs' stripped-down rumba showdance, the simplicity of the choreography suggests an alternative to the definition of rumba as love story. In this scene, rumba does not represent a romantic interaction between a heterosexual couple; it becomes instead an exhibition of specific techniques of walking and turning that foreground long leg lines and rolling hip action.

The show's overall narrative is less clearly developed than these early numbers. If the Girl's search to find herself is the central conflict of the drama, its resolution is less than satisfying. After being wheeled away on a gurney at the end of act 1, the Girl is committed to an insane asylum in act 2. In the last scene, she pulls herself off the bed by a colored streamer that descends from the ceiling, strips herself of a few costume pieces that have been piled on her, and struts off dismissively. According to Pinizzotto (who played the Girl), her final actions were intended to symbolize recognition that she did not need all those costumes and colors to be herself—"she had it all along."[8] I suspect a conflation between the Girl's individual soul-searching and the show's broader social commentary on the dance industry contributed to the unconvincing resolution. If the Girl's situation is a metaphor for the relationship between the dancers and the industry, her departure represents the dancers' walking out as well. But where would they go? Certainly they would not abandon their jobs to perform in underfunded artistic experiments such as this, at least not if they wanted to eat too. I don't think that the choreographers are quite willing to suggest a rejection of the system *tout court,* at least not until they have a viable alternative for earning their living.

The character of the Girl may not have been convincing in her discovery of new choreographic expression within the narrative frame, but the real-life choreographers—Tsha Marie, Andrew Winnett, Desmond James, and Mary Pinizzotto—present choreography that departs radically from DanceSport. Ironically, this innovative choreography is performed not by the Girl (who is, after all, looking for it), but by the rest of the cast. The Girl's bursts of movement are performed in typical DanceSport style while the chorus dancers, who ostensibly represent the repressed masses, embody innovative and creative ideas. Overall, the show is a very brave and stimulating experiment and suggests exciting possibilities for development. Several of its weaknesses may stem from ambiguity on the part of the choreographers about the critique they are making. Given the hospital references, they are quite obviously suggesting that something is very sickly wrong with the industry. However, they seem uncertain exactly what should change. If they want more room for self-expression, how should competition change to enable it? If they are critiquing professional dancers' loss of personal autonomy, how could the industry be reshaped to allow them more freedom in their social lives? Do they want people to just walk out on it all like the Girl? Because most of the dancers who performed in this show are still competing in the DanceSport circuit, their answer has largely been to struggle for resolution within the system.

Although the show's creators offer few practical answers to many of the questions they raise, the performance itself attempts to open up dialogue among dancers about the very problems that are so often disguised by the Glamour Machine. The choreography in both the mask scene and the clinical section is an answer to the competition structure's tendency to repress creativity. These dancers create an alternative venue for the presentation of innovative ballroom dance choreography, sidestepping the formidable challenge of revamping the competition format. The creators are less successful in resolving the other major theme underlying the story—that of maintaining a personal sense of self in the midst of intense pressures to perform a caricature of oneself that conforms to industry expectations. This second issue is primarily an effect of the Glamour Machine, each player compelled to perform his or her role in Glamour in order to reap its pleasures. The tendency of Glamour to dictate individual behavior is unlikely to be believably resolved in performance unless an audience outside of contemporary DanceSport practitioners is cultivated. This particular performance was given to a group of ballroom dance students at the culmination of their own pro-am showcase. Many of the dancers in the show stepped off the stage to perform their Glamorous selves to their students moments later. There seemed to be little awareness in the audience that the critique was of their own relationships with their teachers. Since DanceSport teachers are so adept at holding their own masks up when not onstage, most students did not recognize their own role in the tension represented. Despite its shortcomings, this effort to dramatize some of Glamour's well-guarded woes offers a point of resistance at which some dance lovers are attempting to shift the structure of DanceSport practice.

AN ANTIDOTE TO GLAMOUR?

Many of the performances I have discussed engage with one or more of the criticisms I make of the American ballroom dance industry. Of the problematic representations of identity so often prescribed in DanceSport performance, gender is most frequently addressed in theatrical choreography. Almost every show I describe calls attention to the repressive gender roles, and several of them actually pioneer a new model for gender representation in DanceSport Latin. Though few performances specifically critique the compulsory heterosexuality implicit in DanceSport and even fewer articulate a homosexual love story, performances in which ballroom dancing is framed as something more than representation of love and sex allow possibilities for multiple sexual preferences to occupy the world they create. For example, Louis van Amstel's choreography in "Box Cha Cha" suggests a world in which sex (and not necessarily monogamous sex between a man and a woman) is only one of several themes that give Latin dance meaning. Likewise, much of the choreography in *Against Line of Dance* uses Latin vocabulary to convey messages that are not based in romantic love or sexual intrigue.

Although both of these performances in which Latin is constructed as more than an embodiment of sexual desire may on one level help to expand Western stereotypes of Latin culture, almost no theatrical staging of DanceSport actively tries to redress cultural appropriation of Latin dances by the white dance industry. In fact, this was a major failing of van Amstel's *Latin Fusion*. The group choreography included movements borrowed from jazz, hip-hop, and modern dance yet virtually no Latin beyond that appropriated by DanceSport. There was no Brazilian samba or Afro-Cuban rumba performed in the show, nor were there any Brazilian or Cuban dancers. The cast was composed exclusively of DanceSport competitors residing in the United States and the Netherlands, all of whom displayed the skills they developed as ballroom dance competitors. Though some musical selections were unconventional and ballroom dances were combined in atypical ways (e.g., a tango/paso doble medley), such choices hardly comprise a cutting-edge fusion of Latin dance.

In order to more conscientiously engage with Latin dance beyond its narrow representation in DanceSport, choreographers must seriously study Latin dance forms being practiced in Latin America and invite a range of artists to collaborate on equal terms. The efforts of some DanceSport competitors to borrow steps and rhythms from Latin dance practices outside the ballroom industry usually result in further colonization of the forms. A cue might be taken from the salsa dance industry, which enriches its own tradition of Latin fusion by inviting Afro-Cuban rumba artists to perform and give classes beside the salsa dancers at congresses. Because experts from various Latin cultures and traditions are presented as equals at salsa events, students learn to understand their own practice as only one of many vibrant and interactive Latin dance communities. Dance events sponsored by ballroom dancers rarely include instruction or performance of Latin dance that has not been validated by the DanceSport competition system. Although pressures from Latin dance industries external to the ballroom system (salsa and tango in particular) are helping to recontextualize ballroom's version of Latin dance, theatrical collaboration across Latin dance genres represents another major opportunity for redressing Western cultural imperialism.

Even more than stereotypes of race or gender, representations of class, classiness, and elevated class position may be the most defining features of ballroom dancing. DanceSport appears to promise its participants class transformation, but it simultaneously reinforces hierarchical social structures that sustain gross inequalities of economic and social order. As long as DanceSport competitions are only marketed to the fiscal elite, mass popularity is unlikely to enable substantial numbers of dancers to enter a higher socioeconomic stratum. Adaptation of DanceSport to concert stages suggests a possible antidote to the Glamour Machine not only because restrictive representations of identity can be redefined, but also because the clear separation of audience and practitioner shifts Glamour's power. Stage shows, though not necessarily less dependent on fantasies of transformation, contain and delineate the space of Glamorous desire, releasing producers and consumers of Glamour to live the majority of their lives outside its sphere of influence.

As for the pedagogy and business of DanceSport: I recognize that the types of artistic experiments I have described are possible only alongside economic and education models that support them. Almost every false promise and negative effect of DanceSport Glamour can be linked to how the Glamour Machine separates people from their money. The u.s. ballroom dance industry is currently based on high-end sales to a small customer base, rather than low-priced sales to a larger consumer base. Catering to the dance addict rather than the dance dilettante has proved so much more profitable that it has emerged as nearly the only ballroom dance business model. Dance addicts are not born; they are cultivated by the Glamour Machine. The system exploits human needs and vulnerabilities created by other social failings and persuades its followers that continued financial investment in acquiring Glamour capital will someday pay off. But if an alternative economic model for teaching ballroom dance were viable, then the power of Glamour might be deflated. Below, I describe two recent programs in which an unconventional approach to teaching and funding ballroom dance is being tested. Both the high school ballroom dance program at St. Cloud High School and the performing arts collaborative Pharcyde Dance Center focus on teaching children in group class settings, rather than the common model of teaching adults in high-priced private lessons. Both enable students to learn dance techniques without requiring outrageous financial investment, and both forge alliances among participants by emphasizing their similar social status rather than through highlighting and sustaining difference. It is no coincidence that I have identified youth programs as potential sites of departure from Glamour; it is always easier to start reforms with the next generation than with those already indoctrinated in the current system.

I have not chosen to write about the two most successful models for teaching youth ballroom dancing in these United States—those in the New York/New Jersey area which cater to Eastern European immigrants, and those in Utah and Idaho supported by the Church of Latter-day Saints. Both the Eastern European and Mormon cultures value DanceSport, resulting in cultural messages that teach boys as well as girls that learning dance is acceptable, even desirable. This difference gives these groups a significant advantage over those that must fight the deeply entrenched American belief that dance is not masculine. I chose not to focus on the Mormon or Eastern European programs partly because they may be difficult to reproduce in more heterogeneous American communities, but also because they feed more directly into the contemporary industry of Glamour. Both produce championship dancers who become agents of Glamour. Perhaps it is because St. Cloud and Pharcyde are newer programs and have not yet been co-opted by the Glamour Machine that I see them as particularly hopeful points of departure from it.

St. Cloud High School Dance Techniques

The Paradise Ballroom, located next to a bull pasture in rural central Florida, is a distant nexus on the web of Glamour agents. Although the studio's founder and owner, Patty Holden, worked for Fred Astaire Studios for many years and competed in DanceSport, she has never run her studio like the ones in which she was trained. Most of her students only attend group classes; few take private lessons or enter competition. They are not pressured into spending more time or money than their lifestyles allow, and few take their hobby to the level of obsession. Most students have never even seen DanceSport; outings to the monthly USABDA dance in nearby Orlando constitute the full extent of their dance-related travel. Holden's studio is not a viable business model for others to emulate: it rarely breaks even and does not supply Holden with her primary income. However, it was into this low-key social ballroom dance environment that Nancy Barber, a dean at the local public high school, entered as a new student in December of 1998. Barber enjoyed dancing so much that she soon began to envision bringing ballroom dancing into her high school. Within three months, she had approached the principal with a proposal to start a ballroom dance program. Although Barber had no previous dance training, the strength of her record as a teacher convinced the administrator to support her plan. By the following fall, Nancy Barber began teaching her first classes of Dance Techniques at St. Cloud High School.

Ballroom dance has been a tremendously successful program at St. Cloud High School, drawing students from many different social groups and maintaining high enrollment over four years. The students regularly perform at local events and school assemblies, impressing the community with their waltzing grace and acrobatic swing tricks. Parents and teachers anecdotally report that students' participation in this dance class improves self-esteem, social skills, and performance in academic classes. Though there is no statistical data supporting these stories, my own interactions with these children as a guest teacher and choreographer over the past three years has convinced me that dance brings positive value to their lives. I have witnessed changes in body carriage and confidence, listened to their tales of social success as a result of dance skills, and watched many of them grow into mature, well-adjusted young adults.

The town of St. Cloud is a small, predominantly white, working-class community of people who are not very cosmopolitan in their experiences or tastes.[9] It hardly seemed like the right fit for a ballroom dance program, but the composition of the town works for the classes in two ways. First of all, ballroom dance signifies for many in this community a higher class than their own, and taking ballroom dance lessons suggests self-improvement. Whereas kids in a wealthier community might dismiss ballroom dance because it is associated with the generation of their parents or grandparents, the youth of St. Cloud have embraced ballroom dance as "cool" owing partly to its distance from their own cultural background. Furthermore, the limited income of many of these families keeps ballroom dance a healthy sidebar to the more important foci of family and work in this community. The students' newfound passion for dance does not distract them from the other central activities of teenage life. But this may be as much a credit to their teacher as to their parents. Few of these kids participate in competition, which is not to suggest that a high school program that focused on competitive ballroom dancing could not have the same effects. However, perhaps it is easier to foster a healthy level of investment in dance without the pressure of competition and the potential of pitting the students against one another. Barber's students learn social ballroom dance, social etiquette, and some performance skills. They do not covet rhinestones or better tanning creams and have modest aspirations for their own dancing. Their distance from Glamour's center has allowed them to escape its propaganda.

The program has limitations. The students acquire fewer technical skills in dance than those in other programs, owing in part to the group class format, which prohibits the individualized attention essential for learning advanced partnering skills. Although Barber's own dance training is limited, what she lacks in dance knowledge she more than compensates for in her enthusiasm and remarkable rapport with students. Her students are respectful, responsible, and considerate, cooperation and tolerance for difference being one of her most successful lessons. Barber does not explicitly teach her students to question the gender or racial assumptions on which ballroom dancing is based, although many of the girls do learn to lead as well as follow because of a gender disparity in enrollment. Such a practice helps to redress the dangers of teaching the roles of leader and follower as mutually exclusive and predetermined by sex. If students learn that movement is gendered—that males initiate and females react—they may internalize and extend these lessons outside the dance studio, thus limiting their range of behavior in other situations. A counter-argument suggests that by teaching the techniques for producing masculine and feminine movement as agreed upon by Western aesthetics, students learn valuable tools for negotiating the gendered world in which they live. I believe that students should learn both how to fulfill their expected gender roles and how to counter them. They should be prepared to inhabit the world as it is currently gendered and the world they may help to refashion. In my ideal ballroom program, all students would learn both roles. I must admit, however, from my own personal experience teaching many classes in which I asked all students of both sexes to learn to lead and follow, such an ideal is rarely practical. Most students' resistance to divorcing the roles from gender is high, for they recognize that others will read gender into their performance. For example, few teenage boys are willing to dance with each other in public when the movement genre has historically referenced courtship. The stakes are too high and anxiety about homosexuality too acute. However, even Barber's use of the terms "leader" and "follower" instead of "gentleman" and "lady" are important steps toward denaturalizing the gender roles in ballroom dance.

Overall, the program provides great value to the students, teacher, and community without sustaining vast inequalities among or between them. Barber earns a salary, and all the kids at the school have equal access to dance education. This model suggests that other high school ballroom dance programs would likewise enrich a community. The St. Cloud program might not have been so successful without Barber's previously established reputation and relationships in the community or the support of Patty Holden at the Paradise Ballroom, where students can practice at the dances and classes for reduced rates. The example of St. Cloud demonstrates that the commitment of one or two individuals in a single community can have an enormous impact. I hope that the effect will extend far beyond St. Could, and that this model will inspire others to pioneer similar initiatives in their own school systems.

Pharcyde Dance Center

Alexis is a seven-year-old African American girl with a keen mind, astonishing focus, and ferocious hip action. Holding herself up so that the top of her head is level with her teacher's pelvic girdle, Alexis proudly demonstrates a hip twist and alemana for the class. While attentions wander in other parts of the room, Alexis carefully draws her right foot in to meet her left and drives her hip back as she settles her weight into the floor in an astounding display of precision and control. This is her last day of class during a 2004 summer dance intensive at Pharcyde Dance Center in Jacksonville, Florida, where she takes ballroom-style Latin, ballet, jazz, hip-hop, and creative movement on a daily basis. Alexis is a remarkable child in many respects. She has extraordinary talent and intelligence and exhibits more motivation and discipline than most students of any age. Given that one is hard-pressed to find even one African American at an American DanceSport competition, her mere presence in a DanceSport class is noteworthy. But Alexis has landed at an unusual place. The unique priorities and structures of Pharcyde Dance Center draw children from diverse ethnic and socioeconomic backgrounds into DanceSport through a model that suggests alternative possibilities to those reproduced by the Glamour Machine.

Pharcyde's directors, Leslie Peck and Isaiah Meders, met while working in a ballroom dance studio in 1998. Dissatisfied with the sales tactics they were required to employ and frustrated that actual skill in dance was one of the lowest priorities for teachers and students alike in this environment, they began discussing strategies for teaching ballroom dance in a way that had more ethical integrity and personal satisfaction than their current jobs allowed. Five years of experimentation and re-envisioning have led them to the point where they seem to have laid the foundation for a successful program. Pharcyde is a nonprofit, child-focused, multidisciplinary dance education center that also supports a professional ballroom dance company and outreach programs in local schools.

Of central significance is the configuration of Pharcyde as a nonprofit entity. Not only does this status allow them to apply for grants and solicit tax-deductible donations, it also shapes the very philosophy of their practice. Instead of focusing on maximizing profits as the dance-as-businesses model requires, Pharcyde maintains a vision of providing a service to the community—educating, uplifting, and improving society through dance. Because most for-profit ballroom dance studios sell dance lessons by aligning them with personal benefits such as increased confidence and social skills, it may not seem a radical idea. However, what sets Pharcyde apart is its focus on community. Rather than improving only the lives of those who can afford to pay thousands of dollars for the benefits of dance, Pharcyde attempts to reach out to the entire community by offering inexpensive group classes, volunteering in the schools, performing at charity events, offering scholarships, and holding fundraisers for students.

In addition to teaching classes at their own facility, Pharcyde teachers offer regular salsa and Latin classes in local elementary, middle, and high schools. Many of their classes service inner-city schools with little or no arts funding. The Pharcyde programs introduce dance to children who might otherwise never get any experience in the performing arts. These classes are currently taught on a volunteer basis, although Pharcyde is hoping to secure a grant that would fund these weekly classes. If successful, they would be able to employ dance company members to teach dance in the public schools. Currently, company turnover is high: most members have to work nine-to-five jobs and often cannot handle the strain of late-night practices on top of a day job. By creating fulfilling job opportunities in their organization, Meders and Peck hope to be able to keep young talented dancers in their professional company.

Pharcyde has recently partnered with a ballet school in order to create a multidisciplinary dance center. All students are encouraged to take several courses of study, choosing from among ballroom, Latin, ballet, jazz, hip-hop, tap, and modern. Cross-training in multiple dance techniques improves students' skills in their chosen area of focus and opens their minds to multiple ways of thinking and moving. Other attempts to integrate performing arts and ballroom dance have met with limited success. The Pharcyde merger seems more likely to succeed because the teachers actually believe in the value of all the forms of dance offered at the school. Ballroom and performing arts dance students often view each other with skepticism and derision because they are ignorant about each others' forms, a viewpoint usually perpetuated by the teachers. At Pharcyde, however, the teachers really believe in the merger. Peck has a bachelor's degree in dance and maintains strong ties with her background in performing arts. The director of Pharcyde's ballet department, Linda Jenkins, is open-minded about the value of ballroom classes for her ballet students. She has been impressed with their positive effects on students and particularly swayed by the positive changes she saw in her own nine-year-old son after he began ballroom classes.

Unlike the students at St. Cloud, the kids at Pharcyde are trained for competition. They learn little about social dancing but instead focus on competition-style International Latin. The syllabus and teaching techniques used are primarily adopted from those presented by guest coaches from the Russian studios in New York. Although competition may eventually drive some of these children to obsessive focus on victory over personal growth and development, so far Peck and Meders appear to have maintained a healthy emotional environment for their students. Relationships are fostered among peers, and the system is not dependent on sustaining gross inequalities among its participants.

Pharcyde is still in its infancy and has not yet proved that a nonprofit model that relies on grants and private donations is economically viable. Currently, Pharcyde continues to teach adults in addition to its youth program. It supports much of the outreach and scholarship programming through pro-am private lessons, meaning that it still depends on DanceSport Glamour for its economic base. So although neither the Pharcyde program nor that at St. Cloud High School has entirely escaped all the dangers inherent in DanceSport Glamour, they do suggest possibilities for teaching ballroom dancing in environments that are more psychologically and socially healthy for the participants and the communities in which they are situated.

POINTS OF DEPARTURE

I realize that my condemnation of the Glamour Machine may appear to some readers as overstated and foolish as the antidance treatises of the nineteenth century seem to us today. Much like the reformed dancing master who calms his guilty conscience by preaching against the moral abomination of indulging in the fleshly pleasure of dance he has only recently renounced, I too might be accused of dwelling on the less than admirable facets of the dance industry that shamefully intoxicated me. I hope that readers can look beyond the biases wrought by my own penance for having succumbed to the temptations of

Glamour and my frustration at not having been more successful as a competitor. DanceSport fans may be indignant that I have focused so much attention on the negative aspects of the industry, but my intent is not to bring it down. On the contrary, I hope that by drawing critical attention to the history of ballroom dance as social practice, artistic activity, and business enterprise, I will increase its status as a subject worthy of serious consideration. I hope that readers will also recognize the ambivalence even in my criticisms, where, in the words of Janice Ross writing about the reformed dancing master penning his admonition, "the pleasure of doing is revisited in the pleasure of retelling."[10] My anti-Glamour crusade is equal parts love and hate.

I cannot judge fairly for any individual participant whether the personal and social damages effected by DanceSport Glamour eclipse its positive effects. My analysis is not easily translated into a mathematical sum of gains and losses, nor do I have a solution to the many problems I have identified. Instead, I offer two points of departure for readers to consider in their own engagement with the Glamour Machine. The first is a challenge for DanceSport enthusiasts to envision and build a different system. I hope to inspire a critical mass of dancers to create a new or alternative future for DanceSport, one that is not dependent on the gross inequality and social distance of its participants. To do so, we must imagine and enact new teaching models that do not reinforce class hierarchies, taking our cue from successful performing arts schools that have pioneered outreach and scholarship programs for the economically underprivileged. We should strive to create performance opportunities beyond those of competition to expand the creative possibilities open to dancers and help to maintain a clearer distinction between social and performance genres of partner dance. We will need to examine the mutually exclusive gender roles and compulsory heterosexuality reproduced by DanceSport in order to challenge their sexist and heterosexist effects. We should be more vigilant about questioning the racist history upon which DanceSport is built and fight to counteract the negative racial stereotypes it reproduces. Finally, we will have to create new institutional and economic models that support these visions.

Dance scholars can also contribute to this project. The better we understand the specific events and circumstances that enabled the Glamour Machine to garner such power, the greater our chances of intervening in its course. I hope that my work, which fleshes out the historical and contemporary principles by which the system is structured, will suggest ways to reshape its future. I anticipate that scholars will continue to generate new models for researching the history of social and improvisational dance, increasing awareness that artifacts may be found on the bodies of practitioners rather than in archives. More scholarship rigorously considering the histories of various Latin dance traditions in their specificity, examining the points at which they cross and are altered as a result of their meeting, could significantly shift the discourse.

My second suggestion turns the critique away from DanceSport and focuses instead on the larger cultural systems propelling people into its bewitching grasp. We should question what DanceSport Glamour tells us about contemporary American culture, both its fundamental character and its deep failings. In this endeavor, scholars of dance studies could make a major contribution by continuing to broaden their field of study. While dance scholars have been immersed in the indispensable task of building a canon of literature about the non-profit art world, for-profit dance studios and competition circuits have been reshaping America's next generations of dancers. It is no coincidence that three reality television shows (ABC's *Dancing with the Stars*, FOX's *So You Think You Can Dance?*, and TLC's *Ballroom Bootcamp*) structured around dance competition were runaway hits in 2005. Competition is the American *modus operandi*, and dance is no exception. Serious students of dance are learning their craft through competitions ranging from ballet and hip-hop to Native American fancy dance and South Asian *kathak*. Yet there is virtually no serious scholarship on dance competitions. Nor has there been significant critical inquiry into the institutional and economic structures of dance as industry. While there have been some notable exceptions, such as Lynn Garafola, who gives equal weight to "art," "enterprise," and "audience" in her book on the Ballets Russes, very few academic projects draw attention to the intersection of art and business. It is time danceomanes conquered their queasiness about discussing the indelicate subject of money and launched critical investigations into dance commerce.

DanceSport addicts are by no means the only people suffering from some form of Glamour addiction. Readers will see many similarities between the DanceSport industry I describe and analogous phenomena organized around ice skating, cheerleading, gymnastics, dance team, beauty pageants, and martial arts. Beyond the obvious parallels with other competitively-based physical practices, DanceSport is symptomatic of a much broader social condition. America is obsessed with Glamour. The ubiquitous appeal of Glamour was explained eloquently by cultural critic Virginia Postrel, who writes,

> Glamour is not just beauty or luxury. It is not a style but an effect, a quality that depends on the play of imagination. Its power is not sensation but inspiration. War can be glamorous; so can police work or garage entrepreneurship or laboratory science. Their glamour includes the risks but omits the tedium, the sore feet, the dirt, the accounting. Glamour is never boring. Its grace makes the difficult seem achievable, available to all. Its mystery invites identification without the distracting or deflating details of intimate knowledge: You could be like this, it suggests. You could have this life. Through its grace and mystery, glamour transports us from the world of compromises, constraints, and disappointments.[11]

Despite common knowledge that Glamour's perfect world is an impossible fantasy, Glamour serves an important function in society, instilling hope in people striving for its unattainable ideals. Postrel writes, "yet for all their empirical failings, cultural ideals supply essential purpose and meaning. They keep societies from falling into cynicism or despair."[12]

On the one hand, Glamour's persistent appeal reveals America's fundamental optimism for a better future. The power of Glamour, however, as the prevailing expression of this optimism, is an ominous portent. While Postrel identifies positive value in Glamour, she also concedes that it can be fantastically destructive, recognizing that the same mechanisms of Glamour present in Hollywood films of the 1930s also enabled the rise of the Nazi Party. Glamour's terrible danger is its one-sided view of the world, its ability to blind its adherents to an unpleasant odor or genocide with equal finesse. I believe that the success of Glamour in entertainment, commerce, and politics signals our culture's inability to maintain a sense of optimism when faced with the kinds of violence, danger, pain, and loss that define human existence. Ill-equipped to reconcile the inequalities and adversities of life with faith in its possibilities for transformation, many people choose to escape to the alternate reality of Glamour. While we are distracted in the thralls of its seductions, we forfeit vital opportunities to reshape the ordinary world we leave behind. To break the cycle of addiction, we must learn to sustain aspirations and dreams even after the beguiling veneer of Glamour has been shattered.

Notes

NOTES TO INTRODUCTION

1. Both the professional and the amateur international governing bodies for competitive ballroom dancing changed their names to reflect the updated reconceptualization. The International Council of Amateur Dancers (ICAD) became the International DanceSport Federation (IDSF) in 1989. The International Council of Ballroom Dancing (ICBD), the umbrella organization for professional ballroom dance organizations, became the World Dance & Dance Sport Council (WD&DSC) in 1991. For a history of the quest to acquire Olympic status for ballroom dance, see Daniel Long, "Qualifying for Olympic Status: The Process and Implications for Competitive Ballroom Dance" (master's thesis, Brigham Young University, 1999).

2. Although DanceSport is now an official Olympic sport, it may never actually be granted space on the Olympic schedule. It has been denied inclusion in the 2008 Olympics.

3. My use of the term machine draws on Michel Foucault's conceptualization of power as a decentered conglomeration of forces: "Power has its principle not so much in a person as in a certain concerted distribution of bodies, surfaces, lights, gazes; in an arrangement whose internal mechanism produce the relation in which individuals are caught." Michel Foucault, *Discipline and Punish: The Birth of the Prison,* trans. Alan Sheridan (1977; New York: Vintage Books, 1995), 202. The concept of a machine to describe large cultural systems has been used by several other theorists, including Antonio Benitez Rojo, who describes the trafficking in slaves that created the New World Caribbean as a "machine of machines . . . a conjunction of machines coupled together." Rojo, *The Repeating Island: The Caribbean and the Postmodern Perspective,* trans. James Maraniss (Durham, NC: Duke University Press, 1992), 6. Rojo's use of the term invokes interlocking processes, rooted in disparate locations, that converged to enable the plantation system. While certainly not as mammoth or pernicious, the Glamour Machine too is a decentralized system that relies on and sustains unequal power dynamics.

4. Peter Bailey, "Parasexuality and Glamour: The Victorian Barmaid as Cultural Prototype," *Gender and History* 2.2 (1990): 163.

5. See Ann Wagner, *Adversaries of Dance: From the Puritans to the Present* (Urbana: University of Illinois Press, 1997); T. A. Faulkner, *From the Ball-room to Hell* (Chicago: Church Press, 1894); Janice Ross, *Moving Lessons: Margaret H'Doubler and the Beginning of Dance in American Education* (Madison: University of Wisconsin Press, 2000).

6. See Linda J. Tomko, *Dancing Class: Gender, Ethnicity, and Social Divides in American Dance, 1890–1920* (Bloomington: Indiana University Press, 1997); Julie Malnig, "Two-stepping to Glory," *Moving History/Dancing Cultures: A Dance History Reader,* ed. Ann Dils and Ann Cooper Albright (Middletown, CT: Wesleyan University Press, 2001), 271–287; and Ross, *Moving Lessons.*

7. See Bailey, "Parasexuality and Glamour"; Linda Mizejewski, *Ziegfeld Girl: Image and Icon in Culture and Cinema* (Durham, NC: Duke University Press, 1997); and Stephen Gundle, "Mapping the Origins of Glamour: Giovanni Boldini, Paris and the Belle Epoque," *Journal of European Studies* 23.3 (September 1999): 269–298.

8. Mizejewski, *Ziegfeld Girl,* 11.

9. Pierre Bourdieu, *Distinction: A Social Critique of the Judgment of Taste,* trans. Richard Nice (Cambridge, MA: Harvard University Press, 1984).

10. For a critique of Bourdieu, see, e.g., Dorinne Kondo, who laments that the "lived nature of the classificatory struggle never sufficiently emerges from the totalizing grid of classification." *About Face: Performing Race in Fashion and Theatre* (New York: Routledge, 1997), 111.

11. Bourdieu, 6.

12. For a discussion and critique of polysemy in cultural studies, see Don Slater, *Consumer Culture and Modernity* (Cambridge: Polity Press, 1997), 166–177.

13. My own background—an upper-middle-class family and a postgraduate education leading to a professional DanceSport career—illustrates an obvious exception to this generalization.

14. Rule 2.1.16 of the USA DanceSport Rulebook 2002–2003, United States Amateur Ballroom Dancers Association. It is significant to note that it is not the governing body for the DanceSport professionals that regulates disputes about amateur and professional status. The governing body for amateur competitors chooses whom to allow into its ranks. The distinction between amateur and professional competitors evolved to protect amateur competitors from competition with highly skilled professionals, not to segregate the professionals into an elite league of their own.

15. Patricia Penny counters that it is actually a misperception that most ballroom dancers in Britain are working class, hypothesizing that commentaries on television and the media have contributed to this stereotype. The 112 dancers she surveys are distributed across social classes. "Dancing at the Interface of the Social and the Theatrical: Focus on the Participatory Patterns of Contemporary Competition Ballroom Dancers in Britain," *Dance Research: The Journal of the Society for Dance Research* 17.1 (1999): 58.

16. There are a few innovative exceptions to this generalization, mostly centered in Russian immigrant communities. For example, the Kaiser Dance Academy in Brooklyn, New York, has hundreds of (Russian) children enrolled in group classes, this volume helping to support training and travel for the studio's top amateur competitors. Rising Stars Dance Academy in Saddlebrook, New Jersey, featured in a National Public Radio story on youth immigrant ballroom dance communities, is another such studio. Nancy Solomon, "Immigrant Dancers," National Public Radio, 27 June 2002.

17. Bourdieu, 190.

18. Malnig, "Two-stepping to Glory."

19. John J. MacAloon, "Olympic Games and the Theory of Spectacle in Modern Societies," *Rite, Drama, Festival, Spectacle: Rehearsals toward a Theory of Cultural Performance,* ed. John J. MacAloon (Philadelphia: Institute for the Study of Human Issues, 1984), 257.

20. There are in fact several sexual liaisons across class lines portrayed in this film, including the relationship of the working-class Johnny with the wealthy, older Vivian, and that of the Princeton waiter Robbie with the working-class dancer Penny. Baby's transgression is more disruptive of the established social order because she publicly admits to it rather than keeping her affair (as the others do) behind closed doors.

21. Ann Cooper Albright, *Choreographing Difference: The Body and Identity in Contemporary Dance* (Hanover, NH: Wesleyan University Press, 1997), 3.

22. Throughout the text, I use the terms "Western" and "non-Western" to distinguish between dominant Euro-American cultural values and those traditionally considered foreign from this majority position. I recognize that continued use of language that situates the West at its center may on some levels reinscribe the global hierarchies I seek to disrupt. I choose to use this imperfect vocabulary, however, because these are the terms in which the discourse I critique has been forged, both in the academy and in the media. I also concede that my choice of terminology historically based on an East-West geographical division may seem inappropriate given that I write specifically about Latin America (which is, of course, in the Western hemisphere) as a non-Western trope. While many people might contend that the classification of nations as Western or non-Western is now largely an economic division, "Western" nations being those with significant industrial wealth and power irrespective of their location on a map, I suggest that the concept of "Western" evokes more than national origin. The West is an ideological position of power, and Western culture is the dominant culture in global consciousness. I hope that through my use of the terms Western and non-Western I can make visible the structures of cultural domination and subordination I critique. For a discussion of use of the terms Western and non-Western, see Georgina Born and David Hesmondhalgh, "Introduction: On Difference, Representation, and Appropriation in Music," *Western Music and Its Others: Difference, Representation, and Appropriation in Music,* ed. Georgina Born and David Hesmondhalgh (Berkeley: University of California Press, 2000), 47.

23. Marta Savigliano, *Tango and the Political Economy of Passion* (Boulder, CO: Westview Press, 1994), 2.

24. Ibid., 30–32.

25. Cynthia J. Novack, *Sharing the Dance: Contact Improvisation and American Culture* (Madison: University of Wisconsin Press, 1990); Sally Ann Ness, *Body, Movement, and Culture: Kinesthetic and Visual Symbolism in a Philippine Community* (Philadelphia: University of Pennsylvania Press, 1992).

26. For a discussion of ballroom dance competitions as a site for anthropological fieldwork, see Jonathan S. Marion, "'Where' Is 'There': Towards a Translocal Anthropology," *Anthropology News* (May 2005): 18–19.

27. For an analysis of how church support enables the success of the ballroom dance program at Brigham Young University, see Amy Cristine Farhood, "The Mormon Church and the Gold Bar: A Look at Conservative Religion and Ballroom Dance at Brigham Young University," in *Dancing in the Millennium: An International Conference, Washington, DC, 19–23 July, 2000,* comp. Juliette Crone-Willis (2000), 162–167.

NOTES TO CHAPTER I

1. Judith Butler, *Gender Trouble: Feminism and the Subversion of Identity* (New York: Routledge, 1999).

2. The United States Amateur Ballroom Dancers Association (USABDA) is the governing body for amateur DanceSport competitions in the United States. In 2005 the organization changed its name to USA Dance.

3. The National Dance Council of America (NDCA) is the governing body of professional and pro-am DanceSport competition in the United States. Competitions are owned and operated by individual organizers but sanctioned and regulated by the NDCA. Fred Astaire and Arthur Murray both run competitions open to their own studios and students only. NDCA-sanctioned competitions are open to all students and studios, provided they pay yearly NDCA membership fees, and tend to have higher levels of dancing than the franchise-sponsored events.

4. More commonly, people categorize the difference between American and International Style Latin by the timing of the knee action: dancers land onto a straight knee in International Style and onto a bent knee in American Style. Competitive American Style dancers have gradually quickened the timing of the leg action so that many now land on a straight leg, making this distinction almost meaningless.

5. For more on the gendered leader-follower binary see Juliet McMains, "Tradition and Transgression: Gender Roles in Ballroom Dance" (bachelor's thesis, Harvard University, 1994).

6. I realize that using the concept of race as if it were a categorical definitive runs the risk of reifying the very category I find problematic. For example, Noel Ignatiev and John Garvey argue in *Race Traitor* (New York: Routledge, 1996) that the category of race itself is the cause of racism. I believe, however, that the concept is still useful when interrogating how institutions and ideologies draw upon racial stereotyping in order to sustain discrimination. In other words, in order to diffuse the power of race to create categories and hierarchies, we must continue to expose how this socially constructed concept functions as if it were a natural fact. When I use terms such as white, Asian, black, African American, and Latino, I do so with awareness that these are fluid categories constructed by racist ideologies.

7. While actual conspiracy to fix the results of a DanceSport competition is certainly rare, if it ever does occur, the suspicion of fraud is rampant when judges' marks differ from public opinion. Such misgivings speak more to the range of opinion as to what constitutes good dancing than it does to any intentional deception on the part of judges or organizers. The public tendency to mistrust the impartiality of judges was in evidence during the first season of the television show *Dancing with*

the Stars, when audience favorite John O'Hurley was overtaken by Kelly Monaco in the final episode. Accusations that the results were rigged were so persistent that ABC was pressured into sponsoring a rematch.

8. Scrutineering refers to the practice of calculating final placements from the judges' raw marks based on an extensive set of rules. Rule 11 addresses determining final results in the case of a tie.

9. The audience-performance relationship appears to be more similar to that in pre-1850 American theater than to that of today. Theatergoers of the early nineteenth century expected the social performance in the audience to be of as much consequence as that onstage. The house was well lit, and spectators socialized throughout the three-to-four-hour duration of the performance. According to the scholar Robert Allen, the transformation of theater from a social space for people of many different classes to one that catered to the bourgeois resulted in changes that brought audience behavior much closer to that expected in modern theaters. After 1860 the now primarily bourgeois audiences sat sedately in the dark throughout the duration of the show, content to focus on the stage rather than each other for their entertainment. Robert Allen, *Horrible Prettiness: Burlesque and American Culture* (Chapel Hill: University of North Carolina Press, 1991), 72–73. I believe that, as in pre-1850s theater, the disparate class makeup of the audience at a DanceSport competition contributes to the significance of performative behavior by spectators.

10. The ultimate achievement as a DanceSport professional is to be in such high demand as a coach of competitive couples (both amateur and professional) that one never has to dance pro-am. This is a luxury only a very few teachers can afford.

11. John Feinstein, "The Wednesday Waltz," *Golf Magazine* 38.7 (1996): 22. Although this article makes no mention of dance, the author uses waltz in his title as a metaphor for the careful maneuvering (through conversation and physical movement) required by the players in pro-am games. If pro-am in any sport is primarily about achieving balance and harmony in relationships as suggested by the waltz metaphor, then DanceSport pro-am is doubly difficult, because the waltz must be perfected both figuratively and literally.

12. Susan Bordo, *Unbearable Weight: Feminism, Western Culture, and the Body* (Berkeley: University of California Press, 1993).

13. Ibid., 171–174.

14. Amy L. Best, *Prom Night: Youth, Schools, and Popular Culture* (New York: Routledge, 2000), 35. Best argues that prom night is equaled only by the wedding night in its singular centrality to the construction of feminine identity for American women.

15. Mikhail Bakhtin, *Rabelais and His World,* trans. Helen Iswolsky (Bloomington: Indiana University Press, 1984); Peter Stallybrass and Allon White, *The Politics and Poetics of Transgression* (Ithaca, NY: Cornell University Press, 1986); and Julia Kristeva, *Powers of Horror: An Essay on Abjection,* trans. Leon S. Roudiez (New York: Columbia University Press, 1982).

16. Mary Russo, *The Female Grotesque: Risk, Excess and Modernity* (New York: Routledge, 1995), 53.

17. Ibid., 40.

18. Ballroom dance studios can be grouped into two broad categories: those in which the teachers are employees of the studio and those in which independent teachers rent space from the studio, each setting his or her own rates, promotions, and schedules. Studios that hire employees to teach may be either franchises of a national chain or independently owned. This generates a point of confusion because the term independent is often used to describe all studios that are not part of a national chain, whether or not their teachers are employees or renting space to run their own businesses. In this particular example, the studio I describe hires no employees, and the teachers pay a floor fee for shared use of the space.

19. This practice has been dramatized in several ballroom dance films. The 1936 film *Swingtime,* starring Fred Astaire and Gingers Rogers, includes a scene in which the dance studio receptionist explains that students are given a complementary free lesson to evaluate their aptitude for dancing. She then slips up to reveal that the "evaluation" is only a ploy to assure students of their talent so that they are more willing to invest in a dance course. In the 2002 Hong Kong film *Dance of a Dream,* a potential student is assured of her natural ability based only on her posture and the shape of her legs. The teacher woos her with fantastical tales of her imminent rise to dancing stardom before she even steps on the dance floor.

20. Tom Chapman, *Teaching Ballroom: The Business* (Leawood, KS: Leathers, 2002), 31.

21. Selling ballroom dance lessons by aligning them with increased popularity has a long history in the American ballroom dance industry. Advertisements for Arthur Murray's mail-order dance lesson usually hinged on such a promise. Advertisements in *Popular Mechanics* in 1923–1924 began with headlines such as "Why Good Dancers Are Popular," "No More Wallflowers: You Can Now Learn to Be a Popular Dancer in One Evening," and "Why Miss Half the Fun in Life? BE POPULAR—Learn to dance *well.*" A 1937 newspaper advertisement for a free Arthur Murray Dance book with the submission of labels from Fleishmann's yeast (marketed to cure acne) boasts, "Don't Miss this OPPORTUNITY! START NOW to Clear up Your Skin! Learn the New Dance Steps! WIN POPULARITY!" (author's personal collection, original source unidentified.)

22. Although this studio system is not the only model operating in the United States, it is the most common. Less expensive dance courses are offered through nonprofit community centers, church groups, or universities.

23. I'd like to thank my student Devon Lockwood for so clearly articulating to me this threefold expectation.

24. Quoted here are the English subtitles of the Cantonese dialogue.

25. Edward T. Hall pioneered studies of distance in personal interactions, demonstrating that proximity to others can be interpreted differently by individuals from diverse cultures or by those bringing divergent expectations to the interaction. *The Silent Language* (Garden City, NY: Doubleday, 1959).

26. Virginia Postrel, "A Golden World," *Glamour: Fashion, Industrial Design, Architecture,* ed. Joseph Rosa (New Haven, CT: San Francisco Museum of Modern Art in association with Yale University Press, 2004), 28–29.

27. I am not suggesting that all ballroom dance teachers practice escapist denial in every situation. Some are politically active in forums that are removed from the ballroom

dance industry and may choose to turn a blind eye only when their business is at stake.

28. See Jane Kuenz, "Working at the Rat," for discussion of Disney's control over employees and corporate cover-up. Project on Disney, *Inside the Mouse: Work and Play at Disney World* (Durham, NC: Duke University Press, 1995), 110–162.

29. Raymond Williams, *Problems in Materialism and Culture* (Trowbridge: Redwood Burn, 1980), 189.

30. Stuart Ewen, *All Consuming Images: The Politics of Style in Contemporary Culture* (Basic Books, 1999), 247.

31. Sara Thornton, *Club Cultures: Music, Media, and Subcultural Capital* (Hanover, NH: Wesleyan University Press, 1996), 91.

32. Ewen similarly comments on the disconnect between the actual and perceived power of movie stars, 100.

33. Glenn D. Walters, *The Addiction Concept: Working Hypothesis or Self-fulfilling Prophesy?* (Boston: Allyn & Bacon, 1999), 1.

34. Ibid., 10.

35. I am not the only dance scholar to note the tendency of referring to compulsive dance practice as an addiction. Marta Savigliano writes, "In the milongas of contemporary Buenos Aires, tango is referred to as a drug, and the practice of tango as an addiction. . . . After being hooked up, obsessed, irresistibly drawn to cross, again and again, the border from the everyday world into the tango world, risking family ties, breaking friendships, failing work engagements, ignoring coups d'etat and other social and moral obligations, the milongueros and milongueras feel compelled to explain, to identify a cause and invest it with insurmountable power." *Angora Matta: Fatal Acts of North-South Translation* (Middletown, CT: Wesleyan University Press, 2003), 160–161.

36. The most extreme manifestation of this phenomenon was illustrated by the fourteen-times-undefeated world Latin Champion who reentered DanceSport competition a year after her retirement. Returning to the dance floor with a much younger and inexperienced partner, she could not even make the top forty-eight at major competitions. Unable to withstand public criticism unleashed upon her, she abandoned her comeback after a few competitions.

37. Jean Baudrillard is most often credited for developing the idea that "the real" has been eclipsed by a system of signs that refer only back to each other. *For a Critique of the Political Economy of the Sign* (St. Louis, MO: Telos, 1981). For an excellent secondary source, see Don Slater, *Consumer Culture and Modernity* (Cambridge: Polity Press, 1997). See also Stuart Ewen for critique of "the dominance of surface over substance," 271.

38. Guy Debord, *Society of the Spectacle* (Detroit, MI: Black & Red, 1983).

NOTES TO CHAPTER 2

1. My definition of social dance is specific to partnered social dance forms as they are distinguished from DanceSport. I choose the term social dance, rather than popular or vernacular, because this is the term used by its practitioners. For other definitions

of social and vernacular dance, see Robert P. Crease, "Divine Frivolity: Movement and Vernacular Dance," *Dancing in the Millennium: An International Conference, 19–23 July, 2000,* comp. Juliette Crone-Willis (2000), 110–114, and Barbara Cohen-Stratyner, "Social Dance: Contexts and Definitions," *Dance Research Journal* 33.2 (2001): 121–123.

2. In her book on gay club culture, Fiona Buckland makes a similar statement: "'Improvised social dancing' is a verb, rather than a noun, an activity rather than an object of knowledge." *Impossible Dance: Club Culture and Queer World-making* (Middletown, CT: Wesleyan University Press, 2002), 7. She makes this point, however, in order to draw a distinction between the club dancing about which she writes and more organized forms of social dancing such as tango or lindy hop. I am actually aligning these same forms—tango and lindy hop—with the active dancing from which Buckland distances them. I do this in order to distinguish tango and lindy hop from the even more highly ritualized social dance practices of the ballroom. In other words, tango and lindy hop (and I will add salsa) are for Buckland the examples of static dance objects, whereas for me they are examples of living dance practices. These three categories of social dance—ballroom, swing/tango/salsa, and club dance—are on a continuum with regard to degree of freedom in improvisational choices. Ballroom dance is the most tightly structured, with the least room for improvisation by the practitioners; club dancing is the least circumscribed, with the most room for personal variation. Buckland and I are consistent in choosing to stress the present progressive form of the verb "to dance" when calling attention to a more improvisational practice, despite the fact that we actually name the same practices by opposite terms.

3. Full-page images of these and dozens of other Western dance manuals of the period can be seen at *American Memory: An American Ballroom Companion,* Library of Congress, http://memory.loc.gov/ammem/dihtml/dihome.html.

4. G. Hepburn Wilson, "Danse moderne à la Parisienne," *The Spirit of the Dance: Fellowship,* 1.2 (1914): 2. According to Kathryn Murray, Wilson was the first dancing teacher to offer private rather than group classes. Kathryn Murray with Betty Hannah Hoffman, *My Husband, Arthur Murray* (New York: Simon & Schuster, 1960), 42. Given the profitability of private lessons, his promotion of individuality in dance may have been as much a part of his marketing scheme as a response to the general trend toward individual style.

5. Julie Malnig, "Two-stepping to Glory: Social Dance and the Rhetoric of Social Mobility," *Moving History/Dancing Cultures: A Dance History Reader,* ed. Ann Dils and Ann Cooper Albright (Middletown, CT: Wesleyan University Press, 2001), 283.

6. The dance star Irene Castle is often credited with propelling radical reform in women's dress and hairstyles (the "Castle Bob" was emulated throughout the country). Her influence is dramatized in the 1939 RKO film *The Story of Irene and Vernon Castle.* For another account of her impact on fashion see Ann A. Kilbridge and A. Algoso, *The Complete Book on Disco and Ballroom Dancing* (Los Alamitos, CA: Hwong, 1979).

7. Susan C. Cook, "Talking Machines and Moving Bodies: Marketing Dance Music before World War I," *Dancing in the Millennium: An International Conference, Proceedings, Washington, 19–23 July, 2000,* comp. Juliette Crone-Willis (2000), 75–78.

8. Edward A. Myers uses these terms writing about his experience as an Arthur Murray dance teacher in 1979–1980. "Ballroom Dance as a Commodity: An Anthropological Viewpoint," *Journal for the Anthropological Study of Human Movement*, 3.2 (1984): 74–83.

9. Julie Malnig chronicles the careers of many of these couples in her extensive history of noted dance exhibition teams. *Dancing till Dawn: A Century of Exhibition Ballroom Dancing* (New York: New York University Press, 1992).

10. Linda J. Tomko, *Dancing Class: Gender, Ethnicity, and Social Divides in American Dance, 1890–1920* (Bloomington: Indiana University Press, 1997), 27.

11. Danielle Anne Robinson, "Race in Motion: Reconstructing the Practice, Profession, and Politics of Social Dancing, New York City, 1900–1930" (Ph.D. diss., University of California, Riverside, 2004). In her genealogy of improvisation, Susan Foster points out the debt improvisational dance owes to African American cultural practices, particularly jazz music. Susan Leigh Foster, *Dances That Describe Themselves: The Improvised Choreography of Richard Bull* (Middletown, CT: Wesleyan University Press, 2002), 19–68. For discussion of characteristics of African-based dance, see Robert Farris Thompson, *African Art in Motion: Icon and Act in the Collection of Katherine Coryton White* (Los Angeles: University of California Press, 1974); Marshall Stearns and Jean Stearns, *Jazz Dance: The Story of American Vernacular Dance* (New York: Da Capo Press, 1994); and Jacqui Malone, *Steppin' on the Blues: The Visible Rhythms of African American Dance* (Urbana, IL: University of Chicago Press, 1996).

12. Robinson, "Race in Motion," 171.

13. See Allen Dodworth, *Dancing and Its Relations to Education and Social Life* (New York: Harper & Brothers, 1885), and Rosetta O'Neill, "The Dodworth Family and Ballroom Dancing in New York," *Chronicles of the American Dance*, ed. Paul Magriel (New York: Henry Holt, 1948), 81–100.

14. Some of these treatises can be found in Ann Wagner, *Adversaries of Dance: From the Puritans to the Present* (Urbana: University of Illinois Press, 1997), and Maureen Needham, ed., *I See America Dancing: Selected Readings, 1685–2000* (Urbana: University of Illinois Press, 2002).

15. Irene Castle, *Castles in the Air* (New York: Da Capo Press, 1980), 86–87.

16. Susan C. Cook, "Tango Lizards and Girlish Men: Performing Masculinity on the Social Dance Floor," *Proceedings Society of Dance History Scholars, Reflecting our Past; Reflecting our Future, Barnard College, New York City, 19–22 June 1997*, comp. Linda J. Tomko (1997), 41–55.

17. Vernon Castle and Irene Castle, *Modern Dancing* (New York: Harper & Brothers, 1914), 18.

18. Ibid., 20.

19. History of Arthur Murray International, http://www.dancetonight.com/amihistory.html (accessed 4 March 2006).

20. For some histories of swing, see Craig Hutchinson, *Swing Dancer* (Falls Church, VA: Potomac Swing Dance Club, 1998); Normal Miller with Evette Jensen, *Swingin' at the Savoy: The Memoir of a Jazz Dancer* (Philadelphia: Temple University Press, 1996); Stearns and Stearns, *Jazz Dance*; Lewis A. Erenberg, *Swingin' the Dream: Big Band Jazz and the Rebirth of American Culture* (Chicago: University of Chi-

cago Press, 1998); and Sonny Watson, *Sonny Watson's StreetSwing.com* http://www.streetswing.com/homepage.htm (accessed 7 February 2006).

21. Arthur Murray, *The Modern Dances* (New York: Arthur Murray School of Dancing, 1925), 7.

22. Stuart Ross, "I Taught for Arthur Murray: High Pressure Ballyhoo Has Turned Ballroom Dancing into a Multi-million Dollar Business," *Dance Magazine,* August 1946: 29.

23. Arthur Murray teachers, managers, and studio owners Richard Wilbur, Chuck Pistole, Marge Bennati, and Pat Traymore all recalled the impact the introduction of the medal system had in enabling teachers to sell larger dance courses.

24. Ross, 11.

25. Fred Astaire home page, http://www.fredastaire.com (accessed 13 August 2000).

26. Arthur Murray International home page, http://www.arthurmurray.com (accessed 13 August 2000).

27. Danielle Robinson recounts the efforts of these American dance organizations to mobilize a unified front in her unpublished manuscript, "Qualifying Essay," 21 December 2000, Department of Dance, University of California, Riverside, 69–70.

28. The participants named at these early meetings were the teachers of the oldest generation of ballroom dance teachers alive today, many of whom personally confirm that little has changed in the standard ballroom technique since the 1930s, although all admit that the Latin has developed dramatically from its early iterations in the 1950s.

29. Phillip J. S. Richardson, *A History of English Ballroom Dancing, 1910–1945: The Story of the Development of the Modern English Style* (London: Herbert Jenkins, 1946), 42.

30. Richardson writes: "Just as in the big world there had been a struggle against despotic autocracy so in the dancing world had there been a revolt against the autocracy of the Victorian dancing master and the formal dances of the last generation. Unfortunately just as in the big world the struggle for liberty had on occasions gone to extremes and in places developed into bolshevism, so in the ballroom there had been a tendency towards an artistic bolshevism. I therefore warned my listeners that this new spirit of the dance would end in chaos if fundamental technique be entirely jettisoned. This bolshevism would be greater than it is but for the good taste which is innate in so many." Richardson, 42.

31. Ibid., 58.

32. Ibid., 75.

33. Ibid., 78.

34. Ibid., 44.

35. Ibid., 62.

36. Ibid., 97.

37. "Palais" refers to the new dance halls that opened up in England beginning in 1919 that catered to the modern dances rather than old-time sequence dancing.

38. Richardson, 90.

39. Ibid.

40. Ibid., 143.

41. In her biography of Arthur Murray, the dancer's wife, Kathryn Murray, recalls that the front of every Arthur Murray studio was besieged by limousines chauffeuring society's wealthiest and most influential men and women to their regular dance lessons. Murray, *My Husband, Arthur Murray.*

42. Whereas Silvester stresses the importance of learning dancing from a qualified teacher, Murray's books include detailed drawings and instructions about how long to practice each movement before moving on to the next step.

43. Victor Silvester, *Theory and Technique of Ballroom Dancing* (London: Herbert Jenkins, 1936), 12.

44. Victor Silvester, *Modern Ballroom Dancing* (London: Herbert Jenkins, 1948), 9.

45. Silvester, *Theory and Technique,* 12.

46. Frank Regan, personal interview, 10 November 2001.

47. Skippy Blair, personal interview, 24 May 2002.

48. Craig Hutchinson locates each of these forms geographically and temporally in his history *Swing Dancer.*

49. *Palladium: Where Mambo Was King,* prod. Kevin Kaufman and Bobby Sanabria, dir. Kevin Kaufman, Bravo, 2002.

50. Bill Irvine and Bobbie Irvine, *The Dancing Years* (London: W. H. Allen, 1970), 154.

51. Irvine and Irvine, 154.

52. Richard Wilbur, an Arthur Murray franchise owner through the period of decline in the 1960s, suggests another possible reason for the drastic shift in studio enrollment. Negative publicity involving fraud, illegal marketing practices, and exploitative sales strategies in the ballroom dance business hit its peak in the mid-1960s. Several studios were closed down as state and federal agencies began to regulate ballroom dance business with unprecedented concern. Richard Wilbur recalls that he had to hire a lobbyist to ensure that the state of Florida didn't pass such restrictive laws that running a ballroom dance studio became impossible (Richard Wilbur, personal interview, 2 June 2003). Although negative publicity certainly may have contributed to the decline in studio activity, it is also likely that an already waning public interest in dance lessons led studio owners to increase sales pressures, eventually contributing to the legal debacles that marred the industry's reputation.

53. The ballroom dance industry's turn away from improvisation in the 1960s, particularly when compared to contemporaneous endorsement of improvisation by concert dancers, further supports my hypothesis that DanceSport Glamour sustains hierarchical inequalities. Writing specifically about the improvisational choreography of 1960s modern dancers such as Richard Bull, the dance scholar Susan Foster links improvisation with other democratic and social egalitarian values being promoted at the time:

> Improvisation served repeatedly as a site where difference could be acknowledged and accepted. Implemented in diverse artistic contexts, improvisation broke through standardized social regimens by revealing deeply embedded assumptions about status and protocol, unmasking organizations of power and assisting in the instantiation of an alternative, more

egalitarian model of social relations. Improvisation also embraced a vision of democracy as an egalitarian, collective struggle to acknowledge difference—racial, gendered, sexual, and class-based—even if it did not always articulate a means for reckoning with, or sorting through these differences. (Foster, *Dances That Describe Themselves*, 64)

The rejection of improvisation by the ballroom dance industry at the same historical moment modern dance companies were embracing it reflects the radically divergent political positions in which they were situated. Many modern dancers identified with leftward-leaning ideologies, envisioning through their dancing a new social order in which differences of gender, race, class, and sexuality did not map directly to social, economic, and political inequalities. The continued suppression of improvisation by the ballroom dance industry suggests that it was aligned with more conservative political agendas that sought to sustain hierarchical social distinctions.

54. Edward Myers's anthropological analysis of Arthur Murray studios in the early 1980s is consistent with this view that competitive and social dancing exist on a single continuum: "Finally, besides learning to dance socially students may be encouraged by staff to learn choreographed routines. These offer the excitement of competition and exhibition which are considered to be expressions of the highest levels of achievement in social dancing." Myers, "Ballroom Dance as a Commodity," 81.

55. See, for example, NBC broadcasts of DanceSport Championships in 1998, in which footage of social dance is interspersed with competition.

56. Notable exceptions to this generalization include studios in the New York metropolitan area that cater to Russian children and youth programs in Utah. Both these areas have large communities of children who are drawn into the sport by peers who are already DanceSport competitors.

57. Organizations such as USA Dance (formerly USABDA) represent both social and competition dancers. As of 1 January 2006, 23 percent of the organization's 20,326 members were DanceSport athletes and 74 percent were recreational dancers (personal communication with Gerald Bonmer, membership director). Although DanceSport competitors are a minority of the membership, they are the major focus of the organization, which sponsors its top athletes to represent the United States at international competitions. A 1991 press release declares, "Our goal is to have a membership consisting of 40% DanceSport athletes and 60% recreational dancers who support DanceSport participation in the Olympics." As this statement demonstrates, support from social dancers is absolutely essential to the success of DanceSport competitors.

58. The president of the Russian DanceSport Federation, Leonid Pletnov, offered his own theory of why DanceSport is so popular in Russia. During a personal conversation, he suggested that because open embrace of aristocratic culture and individual competition were suppressed for so long under Communist rule, new social freedoms have enabled reactionary embrace of these same values. DanceSport combines much of what was forbidden during stricter regimes, including performance

of extreme class difference in the reference to elite culture and intense personal competition.

59. Growth of the American DanceSport industry has also been aided by the Mormon church, which endorses ballroom dancing as a healthy activity to promote youth courtship. Brigham Young University (financially supported by the church) houses a ballroom dance program that enrolls five thousand students each semester. Though encouraging courtship may be at least partial motivation for their promotion of ballroom dancing, it is DanceSport, not social dancing, that is at the center of most Utah programs. For description of the Mormon church's support of ballroom dancing at BYU, see Amy Cristine Farhood, "The Mormon Church and the Gold Bar: A Look at Conservative Religion and Ballroom Dance at Brigham Young University," *Dancing in the Millennium: An International Conference, 19–23 July, 2000*, comp. Juliette Crone-Willis (2000), 162–167.

60. Though not quite as popular in the United States as salsa and West Coast swing, Argentine tango also shares with these social dances many of the structures that invite improvisation and creativity, encouraging social dancers to interpret the timing of each step differently, according to how they hear the music. Several other swing communities, including lindy hop and shag, could also be included on this list of improvisation-centered social partner dance forms.

61. Susan Leigh Foster, *Reading Dancing: Bodies and Subjects in Contemporary American Dance* (Berkeley: University of California Press, 1986), 179.

62. Eve Babitz, *Two by Two: Tango, Two-step, and the L.A. Night* (New York: Simon & Schuster, 1999) 89.

63. MIT's ballroom dance club has been drawing two hundred people to its weekly ballroom dance classes for over twenty-five years. The popularity of ballroom dance at one of the nation's most prestigious technical universities supports a commonly held belief that engineers, who are well trained in reading charts and applying formulas, are drawn to ballroom dance precisely because it encourages solving each movement problem through application of established rules.

64. My argument is consistent with that of Stephen Gundle, who contends that the modern use of the term "glamour" was fundamentally linked to "the transition from a slow-moving, rigidly hierarchical type of society in which the aristocracy determined what was new, beautiful and desirable to a capitalist order in which money was king. Social barriers were by no means broken down, but . . . there was much more movement of every type and greater proximity of people of differing origins." I suggest that, like the glamour of late-nineteenth-century Europe, the Glamour of ballroom dance is dependent on the convergence of people from different social backgrounds and at least the possibility of shifts in social status. Gundle, "Mapping the Origins of Glamour: Giovanni Boldini, Paris and the Belle Epoque," *Journal of European Studies* 23.3 (September 1999): 273.

65. Malnig, "Two-stepping to Glory," 284.

66. The economist Juliet Schor argues in her book *The Overspent American: Upscaling, Downshifting, and the New Consumer* (New York: Basic Books, 1998) that recent changes in social structures, compounded by identification with characters on television, have put Americans in contact with a greater range of income brackets

than ever before, commonly resulting in desire for consumer goods outside one's income range. Although Schor does not explore effects beyond the economic, I believe that the desire she identifies operates at many levels, leading many people to believe that they can effect a complete change of social class status.

NOTES TO CHAPTER 3

1. Before the Industrial Revolution, pale skin was a sign of upper-class leisure, representing an individual's exemption from the toils of outdoor labor.

2. The Latin dances are not the first to have been reinterpreted by the French to represent another nation's character. In their examination of nineteenth-century ballet, Lisa Arkin and Marian Smith reveal that French ballet dancers relied as heavily on stereotype as they did on actual study of the technique to portray dances from Italy, Spain, Poland, Egypt, and Russia: "A certain repertory of markers, then, was sufficient to function emblematically, reinforcing the spectators' sense that they were somehow gaining access to the essence of a culture or nation. . . . So character dance was not truly expected to reproduce authentic folk dance in the modern-day ethnographic sense, but instead was distilled, its salient features thereby thrown into high relief." Lisa C. Arkin and Marian Smith, "National Dance in the Romantic Ballet," *Rethinking the Sylph: New Perspectives on the Romantic Ballet*, ed. Lynn Garafola (Hanover, NH: Wesleyan University Press, 1997), 36.

3. Marta Savigliano, *Tango and the Political Economy of Passion* (Boulder, CO: Westview Press, 1994) 125.

4. Ibid., 119.

5. Most dancers I interviewed who knew Pierre personally could not recall a surname. Because he was known personally and professionally as Pierre and published his technique book under his given name only, several historians have incorrectly assumed that Pierre's surname was Lavelle (an understandable error, because his name so often accompanies that of Doris Lavelle). Irene Evans, a close friend of Doris Lavelle, reveals Pierre's full name in *A Concise History of Latin American Dancing in the UK* (United Kingdom Alliance of Professional Teachers of Dancing, 1992). In the words of Bill Irvine, "The Latin American was promoted by Pierre and Lavelle. That's the end of the story. They promoted Latin in every possible way. They were the grandfathers and grandmother of Latin American dancing in our country. Two people. And they made it a point—they traveled to the Caribbean and they studied what they were seeing, picked up this and picked up that and brought it all back to England." Bill Irvine, personal interview, 10 September 1999.

6. Pierre, *Latin and American Dances for Students and Teachers* (London, 1948).

7. Ibid., 71.

8. Frank Regan, personal interview, 10 November 2001.

9. Fernando Ortiz defines transculturation as "the process of transition from one culture to another. . . . This does not consist merely in acquiring another culture . . . but the process also necessarily involves the loss or uprooting of a previous culture. . . . In addition it carries the idea of the consequent creation of new cultural phenomena . . . The result of every union of cultures is similar to that of the repro-

ductive process between individuals: the offspring always has something of both parents but is always different from each of them." *Cuban Counterpoint: Tobacco and Sugar* (New York: A. A. Knopf, 1947), 102–3.

10. In an article written for the *Dancing Times* (the same English periodical that convened the conferences at which the ballroom dances were standardized in the 1920s), Eduardo Leigh describes the various styles of Cuban rumba and finally concludes, "I had great difficulty in balancing the reality of *rumba* in Cuba and the polished, somewhat bloodless (although elegant) concoction we acknowledge in Europe. They're simply different dances!" "The Rumba Trail," *Dancing Times* (January 1997): 343. The American dancer Riba Brandis is similarly baffled when she attempts to compare Cuban and ballroom versions of rumba: "It seems the English speaking visitors to Cuba got the name wrong. Perhaps they confused the term rumba with the danzon, the beguine or the bolero." "Differences in Latin Style Dancing: Authentic Latin vs. American Social Latin vs. International Competition Latin," *Dancing USA,* October–November 1998: 9.

11. Because ballroom styles of rumba have experienced much greater international exposure, not only has this aspect of Cuban culture been misrepresented for decades, but many Cuban rumba artists are still struggling in the shadow of ballroom rumba's more prominent legacy. It is difficult for Cuban rumba dancers in the United States to earn a living teaching or performing their craft because so few people know what it is, assuming that rumba is what they learned at Arthur Murray's.

12. Isabelle Leymarie, "De la rumba brava à la rumba de salon," *Danses latines: Le désir des continents*, ed. Élisabeth Dorier-Apprill (Paris: Éditions Autrement, 2001).

13. Robin Moore, "The Commercial Rumba in Afrocuban Arts as International Popular Culture," *Latin American Music Review* 16.2 (1995): 165–198; Moore, *Nationalizing Blackness: Afrocubanismo and Artistic Revolution in Havana, 1920–1940* (Pittsburgh: University of Pittsburgh Press, 1997).

14. In a personal communication, the dance scholar Yvonne Daniel suggested to me that codification of the American ballroom style of rumba led to a change in spelling—Americans referring to "rhumba" in contrast to the Cuban "rumba." Evidence from ballroom dance manuals does not, however, support this interpretation. Ballroom dancers have, from the 1930s to the present day, used both spellings, with no identifiable pattern for choice of one over the other. I agree with Daniel's sentiment that had the "h" been used more consistently in the American Style, it would have helped to maintain the distinction between Afro-Cuban rumba and the new ballroom invention in America.

15. For more on traditional Afro-Cuban rumba, see Larry Crook, "A Musical Analysis of the Cuban Rumba," *Latin American Music Review* 3.1 (1982): 92–123; Yvonne Daniel, "Cuban Dance: An Orchard of Caribbean Creativity," *Caribbean Dance From Abakuá To Zouk: How Movement Shapes Identity,* ed. Susanna Sloat (Gainesville: University Press of Florida, 2002) 23–55; Daniel, *Rumba: Dance and Social Change in Contemporary Cuba* (Bloomington: Indiana University Press, 1995); Daniel, "Rumba Then and Now: *Quindembo,*" *The Social And Popular Dance Reader,* ed. Julie Malnig (University of Illinois Press, forthcoming); Isabelle Leymarie, *Cuban Fire: The Story of Salsa and Latin Jazz* (London: Continuum, 2002); and Moore,

Nationalizing Blackness. I would like to thank Yvonne Daniel for her generous dialogue with me about the relationship between different styles of rumba.

16. Moore, *Nationalizing Blackness,* 170.

17. Ibid., 57.

18. The musicologist Isabelle Leymarie writes that in the early 1920s, the American record companies Victor and Columbia "spread the *danzón,* the *son,* the *guaracha,* and the bolero abroad, labeling almost everything 'rumba.'" *Cuban Fire,* 49. The music historian John Storm Roberts identifies Don Azpiazú's popular song "The Peanut Vendor," the musical composition regarded as heralding in the 1930s rumba craze in Europe and America, as a type of *son.* He further argues that "virtually all of the pieces known to the U.S. as rumbas were in fact something else . . . the majority were sones." *The Latin Tinge: The Impact of Latin American Music on the United States,* 2nd ed. (New York: Oxford University Press, 1999), 77. Xavier Cugat himself, the Cuban-raised musician whose Latin American dance band became an institution at New York's Waldorf-Astoria Hotel, used the term rumba as a generic catch-all for many Cuban musical styles. He writes in his autobiography that "the rumba, or course is actually the name for more than one dance. The son and danzón are both rumbas." *Rumba Is My Life* (New York: Didier, 1948), 197.

19. Moore, *Nationalizing Blackness,* 180.

20. I am grateful to the staff at the Cinémathèque de la Danse in Paris for allowing me to view a compilation of dance scenes from these films (*Les rumberas*), starring dancers including Amalia Aguilar, Rosa Carmina, and Ninón Sevilla. See also Mayra Martínez, "Rumberas en México," *Revolución y cultura* 11 (November 1989): 40–45.

21. Many dance manuals identify the American rumba as the Cuban *son,* including that written by the 1930s Latin dance film stars Veloz and Yolanda ([Frank] Veloz and Yolanda [Veloz], with Willard Hall, *Tango and Rumba: The Dances of Today and Tomorrow* [New York: Harper & Brothers, 1938]). Other manuals asserting that the American rumba is actually the Cuban *son* include Richard M. Stephenson and Joseph Iaccarino, *The Complete Book of Ballroom Dancing* (New York: Doubleday, 1980); and Peter Buckman, *Let's Dance: Social, Ballroom and Folk Dancing* (New York: Paddington Press, 1978). Even historians of Cuban music conclude that the ballroom rumba grew out of the Cuban *son.* See Leymarie, "De la rumba brava à la rumba de salon," 95.

22. American Rumba Committee, *The American Rumba* (New York: Rudor, 1943), 8.

23. Ibid.

24. Arthur Murray, *How to Become a Good Dancer* (New York: Simon & Schuster, 1947), 137.

25. Their names are not spelled consistently in the sources. In her book, Evans identifies this couple as "Pepe and Suzy Riviera," 10. In her book, Doris Lavelle names Pierre's Cuban teacher as "Pepe Rivera." Lavelle, *Latin and American Dances* (London: Sir Isaac Pitman & Sons, 1965), 1.

26. There is evidence that English dance teachers were aware that this simplified counting system failed to capture the complex syncopated *clave* rhythm that characterized Cuban music and dance but they adopted the system for simplicity in teaching.

See, for example, the various systems for counting rumba rhythms Frank Borrows offers in his technique book *Theory and Technique of Latin-American Dancing* (London: Frederick Muller, 1961), 12–15.

27. Evans, 12.

28. Borrows, 3–4. This theory that Cuban rumba taught in Europe is based on mambo is repeated by Marc Martin in the "Rumba" section of his book *Viens danser: La samba, la rumba, le cha cha cha* (Vitry-sur-Seine: Éditions Aguer, 1996), 2.

29. This description of Cuban mambo dancing is based on the instruction I received from numerous Cuban dance teachers and scholars in Havana in December 2005. See also Daniel, "Rumba Then and Now."

30. For the story of Enrique Jorrin's invention of cha cha chá, see Isabelle Leymarie, "Mambo et cha-cha-cha," *Danses latines: Le désir des continents,* ed. Élisabeth Dorier-Apprill (Paris: Éditions Autrement, 2001), 111; Max Salazar, *Mambo Kingdom: Latin Music in New York* (New York: Schirmer Trade Books, 2002), 181; and Lise Waxer, "Of Mambo Kings and Songs of Love: Dance Music in Havana and New York from the 1930s to the 1950s," *Latin American Music Review,* 15.2 (Autumn–Winter 1994): 139–176.

31. Kathryn Murray writes in her biography of Arthur Murray, "Another dance that gave him pause was the cha-cha-cha. At first we taught it by counting out 'one-two-cha-cha-cha.' This worked in practice but was impossible to diagram; it looked like five beats to a measure. Arthur retired into his office with the problem and after two hours emerged with a solution. He changed the name of the dance to cha-cha and the count to one-two-three-cha-cha. The two 'cha-chas' are said very quickly, making one beat, or a total of four beats to the measure." Kathryn Murray with Betty Hannah Hoffman, *My Husband, Arthur Murray* (New York: Simon & Schuster, 1960), 9.

32. Quoted in Evans, 11.

33. Ibid., 15. Martin also asserts that ballroom-style paso doble was "born" in Spain but "developed" in France. *Viens danser.*

34. According to Bill Irvine, Josephine Bradley wrote the English jive syllabus after inviting American GIs to her studio to demonstrate swing. Bill Irvine, personal interview, 10 September 1999.

35. Philip J. S. Richardson, *A History of English Ballroom Dancing, 1910–45: The Story of the Development of the Modern English Style* (London: Herbert Jenkins, 1946), 114.

36. Ibid., 93.

37. Arthur Murray, *How to Become a Good Dancer* (New York: Simon & Schuster, 1942), 175.

38. According to Sam Sodano, United States Latin DanceSport champion in the 1960s and 1970s, Walter Laird single-handedly convinced the entire ballroom community that Latin dance should be executed by straightening the knee before transferring weight onto the leg. "I give Walter Laird credit, the most credit in the world, because he had the whole world, and they're still doing it, straighten their legs before you put your weight on it. This was him. He convinced the whole world that this is the way to do a rumba walk." Sodano recalls his reaction upon first seeing the American dancers Bobby Medeiros and Sharon Hawkins employ this new tech-

nique after studying in England. "Why are you doing that, it looks like an ostrich? Why are you doing that kind of leg action?" Compared to the relaxed knee action they had used prior to their English training, Sodano believed the new action looked stiff and awkward, inhibiting the continuous rolling action of the hips. Sam Sodano, personal interview, 17 May 2003.

39. Felix Chavez, personal interview, 6 May 1998.

40. Frank Regan, personal interview, 10 November 2001.

41. Sam Sodano recalled virtually the identical story in a personal interview, 17 May 2003.

42. Enio Cordoba, personal interview, 22 March 2001. This sentiment is also portrayed in the film *Strictly Ballroom,* in which the head of the Australia Dancing Federation forbids new steps from being danced in competition so that his own instructional videotapes retain their elite, expert status.

43. In 2006 the members of the WD&DSC included Australia, Austria, Barbados, Belgium, Bulgaria, Canada, China, Chinese Taipei, Croatia, Czech Republic, Denmark, Estonia, Finland, France, Georgia, Germany, Great Britain, Greece, Hong Kong, Hungary, Iceland, Indonesia, Ireland, Israel, Italy, Japan, Latvia, Lebanon, Lithuania, Malaysia, Malta, Moldova, Monaco, the Netherlands, New Zealand, Norway, Philippines, Poland, Portugal, Russia, Scotland, Serbia and Montenegro, Singapore, Slovakia, Slovenia, South Africa, South Korea, Spain, Sweden, Switzerland, Thailand, Ukraine, United States, and seven nonvoting introductory members, including Mexico. WD&DSC, http://www.wddsc.com/dancesport/dscommittee/index 03a.htm (accessed 8 February 2006).

44. Neil Clover, "The Importance of Ballroom Dance," *Dancing USA,* January–February 1992: 19.

45. For the cardinal work on performativity, see Judith Butler, *Bodies That Matter: On the Discursive Limits of "Sex"* (New York: Routledge, 1993).

46. Ellen J. Gainor, "'A World without Collisions': Ballroom Dance in Athol Fugard's *'Master Harold'. . . and the Boys," Bodies of the Text: Dance as Theory, Literature as Dance,* ed. Ellen W. Goellner and Jacqueline Shea Murphy (New Brunswick, NJ: Rutgers University Press, 1995), 127–128.

47. I choose to use the word "Latino," rather than "Hispanic," to refer to people of Latin American descent because Latino is often regarded as a more inclusive term, encompassing not just those from Spanish ancestry but those of African, indigenous, and mixed ancestry. Because I write primarily about DanceSport in the United States, I use the term "Latino," rather than "Latin American," which is more commonly used outside the United States. Many of the points I make about Latinos living in the United States are analogous to the experiences of Latin Americans living in other countries.

48. For literature on historically changing scientific, legal, and social definitions of race see Kimberle Crenshaw et al., eds., *Critical Race Theory: The Key Writings That Formed the Movement* (New York: New Press, 1996); Richard Delgado and Jean Stefancic, eds., *Critical Race Theory: The Cutting Edge* (Philadelphia: Temple University Press, 1999); Paul Gilroy, *Against Race: Imaging Political Culture Beyond the Color Line* (Cambridge, MA: Belknap Press of Harvard University Press, 2000); Ian

F. Haney López, *White by Law: The Legal Construction of Race* (New York: New York University Press, 1996); Mari J. Matsuda, *Where is Your Body? And Other Essays on Race, Gender and the Law* (Boston: Beacon Press, 1996); and Michael Omi and Howard Winant, *Racial Formation in the United States from the 1960s to the 1990s* (New York: Routledge, 1994).

49. The opening of Robyn Wiegman's chapter "Visual Modernity" begins with just such an example from Nella Larsen's *Passing*. Weigman, *American Anatomies: Theorizing Race and Gender* (Durham, NC: Duke University Press, 1995), 21.

50. Some American television programs that feature DanceSport have started to separate the two categories, producing one program that is just Latin and another for the Standard competition.

51. For theories of the Other, see Homi K. Bhabha, "The Other Question: Difference, Discrimination and the Discourse of Colonialism," *Out There: Marginalization and Contemporary Cultures,* ed. Russell Ferguson et al. (New York: New Museum of Contemporary Art; Cambridge, MA: MIT Press, 1990), 71–87; and Edward Said, *Orientalism* (New York: Vintage Books, 1978).

52. I chose the imperfect term "nonwhite" over alternatives such as "people of color" because I wish to emphasize that white is a color (racial position) and to foreground that it is one's relationship to whiteness that is most important for access to power. See Richard Dyer, *White* (New York: Routledge, 1997), for a discussion of terminology.

53. Even those Latin DanceSport competitors who identify their own ethnic heritage as Latin American are performing an identity position that differs from that performed by Latin American salseros.

54. Dyer, 49.

55. Sometimes all-female competitions are held when there are not enough male partners and the women dance with each other in preparation for dancing with a male partner. This practice and its interpretation as the female partner being a poor stand-in for a "real" (i.e., male partner) is illustrated in the film *Strictly Ballroom*. The main character Scott tells his hopeful partner Fran, "You've been dancing with a woman for two years. You've never even had a partner." On the other end of the spectrum, there are some same-sex dance competitions held in Europe that encourage representation of homosexual courtship.

56. NCDA Rules and Regulations, January 2006, 3. While certainly not the first or only gender bender causing commotion, I entered several college and USABDA sponsored competitions dancing with another woman in 1993–1994. Despite disapproval by several judges and viewers, we often scored quite well, winning several events over mixed-sex couples. One judge commented that he could not mark us well because he felt uncomfortable telling a biological male that I was a better man than he, assuming that one's mastery of the male role on the dance floor was directly correlated to masculinity off the dance floor.

57. International DanceSport Federation home page, http://www.idsf.net (accessed 3 March 2006).

58. My examination of gender as it emerges out of raced discourse is inspired by the work of Wiegman in *American Anatomies*. Challenging many earlier feminist as-

sumptions, Wiegman suggests that, historically, social identity was based on racial difference before gender became a significant category of difference. In other words, gender emerged as a significant axis by which individuals measured their relationship to the social only after the landscape of racial divisions had been mapped.

59. The following comparison is between the International Style Latin and Standard. American Style Rhythm is not significantly different from the International Latin on any of the points raised in this analysis of raced gender categories; however, American Style Smooth dancing allows the couple to break out of closed hold. The American Style Smooth dancers share some of the restraint of International Style Standard dancers but exhibit more of the freedom seen in Latin dancing. Their location on this map would be in between the Latin and Standard couple, the woman more independent and the man more visually prominent than in Standard, but certainly more conservative than the Latin man and woman.

60. Savigliano, *Tango,* 69–71.

61. George Lipsitz writes about the political struggle, "Wilson's speeches and statements in support of his own campaign on behalf of Proposition 187 made special and nearly obsessive mention of the relatively small number of Mexican immigrant women who give birth to children in California hospitals, taking advantage of stereotypes of Mexicans as sexually unrestrained—as if forming families is an illicit activity, as if childbirth is an unnatural and perverse practice of the poor, as if anyone would be better off if expectant mothers and their children were denied prenatal care or childbirth under safe conditions." *The Possessive Investment in Whiteness: How White People Profit from Identity Politics* (Philadelphia: Temple University Press, 1998), 51.

62. Charles Ramírez Berg, *Latino Images in Film: Stereotypes, Subversion, and Resistance* (Austin: University of Texas Press, 2002), 76.

64. Nanette Kutner, "Valentino's Own Version of the Tango," *Dance Lover's Magazine* 3.5 (1925): 22–23, quoted in Gaylyn Studlar, "Valentino, 'Optic Intoxication,' and Dance Madness," *Screening the Male: Exploring Masculinities in Hollywood Cinema,* ed. Steven Cohan and Ina Rae Hark (London: Routledge, 1993), 32.

64. Lorine Pruette, "Should Men Be Protected?" *Nation* 125 (1927): 200–201, quoted in Studlar, 27.

65. Studlar, 27.

66. Savigliano, *Tango,* 40–53. See, for example, her account of El Cívico and La Moreira.

67. Alicia Arrizón, *Latina Performance* (Bloomington: Indiana University Press, 1999), addresses analogous strategies in which Latina performance artists fight Latino/ Latina homophobia through performance.

68. Although there are almost no same-sex competitions in the United States, there are more opportunities for same-sex couples to compete together in Europe. See Eric Marx, "In the Ballroom, a Redefinition of a 'Couple,'" *New York Times,* 14 July 2004. The Gay Games, hosted in Chicago in July 2006, offers several well-attended same-sex DanceSport events.

69. Hazel Fletcher, personal interview, 9 September 1999.

70. See, for example, Pierre Bourdieu, *Distinction: A Social Critique of the Judgment of Taste,* trans. Richard Nice (Cambridge, MA: Harvard University Press, 1984), 190–193.

71. Linda Mizejewski, *Ziegfeld Girl: Image and Icon in Culture and Cinema* (Durham, NC: Duke University Press, 1997), 10–11.

72. DanceSport is a popular sport for children in Eastern Europe. One reading of Eastern European immigrant participation in American DanceSport suggests that it reconnects them to their ethnic and cultural heritage. For entire communities of immigrants who have seen their children represent the United States at world championships, DanceSport becomes not only a symbol for assimilation but a vehicle through which they gain acceptance into American society.

73. Although I recognize that authenticity is a constructed concept, it is the trope by which these dancers strive to differentiate themselves from ballroom Latin dancers.

74. Eric Lott, *Love and Theft: Blackface Minstrelsy and the American Working Class* (New York: Oxford University Press, 1993), 6.

75. Dyer, 49.

76. This reaction is dramatized in the 1998 film *Dance with Me* when Cheyenne's character, having just arrived from Cuba to an American ballroom dance studio says, "That's cha cha chá? I never seen a Latin dance that looked like that."

77. The scholar Jane Desmond suggests that use of dark body paint to increase the sexual potency of a dance performance is hardly a recent phenomenon. Desmond points out that the modern dance pioneer Ruth St. Denis used body paint in her 1906 portrayal of a Hindu goddess in *Radha*. Desmond argues that the paint enabled St. Denis to benefit from stereotypes of Eastern women as sexually available without forfeiting her own white privilege, resulting in a performance that was both sexually charged and respectable enough to be well received by middle-class white audiences. Desmond, "Dancing Out the Difference: Cultural Imperialism and Ruth St. Denis's *Radha* of 1906," *Moving History/Dancing Cultures: A Dance History Reader,* ed. Ann Dils and Ann Cooper Albright (Middletown, CT: Wesleyan University Press, 2001), 265–266.

78. Similar to the contemporary use of brownface masks, the use of physical masks to project sexual desire onto others was also noted by Peter Stallybrass and Allon White in their work on eighteenth-century carnival. "A sort of refined mimicry sets into the salons and ballroom of Europe in which the imagery, masks and costumes of the popular carnival are being (literally) put on by the aristocracy and the bourgeoisie in order to simultaneously express and conceal their sexual desire and the pleasures of the body." Peter Stallybrass and Allon White, *The Politics and Poetics of Transgression* (Ithaca, NY: Cornell University Press, 1986), 103.

79. This class analysis is only relevant in the American context. Pro-am competition has been, until very recently, a uniquely American phenomenon. There is little class distinction between amateur and professional dancers in most European countries.

80. Celeste Frazer Delgado, "Exploding the Exotic: Re-thinking Performance at the End of Civilization," paper presented at the University of California, Riverside, 11 May 1999.

81. Several other authors have noted this failure to recognize African-based contributions to American culture. See Brenda Dixon Gottschild, "Some Thoughts on Choreographing History," *Meaning in Motion: New Cultural Studies of Dance,* ed. Jane C. Desmond (Durham, NC: Duke University Press, 1997), 167–177; and Michele Wallace, "Modernism, Postmodernism and the Problem of the Visual in Afro-

American Culture," *Out There: Marginalization and Contemporary Cultures,* ed. Russell Ferguson et al. (New York: New Museum of Contemporary Art; Cambridge, MA: MIT Press, 1990), 39–49.

82. There are several histories written about each of these dances and their trajectories out of the barrios and into mainstream and upper-class culture. For example, see Vernon W. Boggs, ed., *Salsiology: Afro-Cuban Music and the Evolution of Salsa in New York* (New York: Greenwood Press, 1992); Daniel, *Rumba;* Savigliano, *Tango;* and Hermano Vianna, *The Mystery of Samba: Popular Music and National Identity in Brazil,* trans. and ed. John Charles Chasteen (Chapel Hill: University of North Carolina Press, 1999).

83. Susan Leigh Foster's work on the history of ballet suggests that the impetus to organize the body into straight lines in the Latin dances may have also been an attempt to neutralize its disruptive potential. She argues that developments in ballet technique during the nineteenth century disciplined the body into geometrical shapes and mathematical structures. She writes of this new Pythagoreanized ballet body: "The body largely did what it was told. It did not initiate or carry on a discourse, and ballet did not cultivate impulses. Sporadic rambunctious initiatives on the body's part such as those manifest in the can can or the tango could only be interpreted as licentious and lacking in all aesthetic values." Foster, *Choreography and Narrative: Ballet's Staging of Story and Desire* (Bloomington: Indiana University Press, 1996), 258. This shift allowed ballet to move to a higher position in the rational world of European culture. A similar geometry of the body in the ballroom Latin dances helped them to move from their position in lower-class and nonwhite popular culture in Latin America to prominence in higher-class white European and American society.

84. I have made these generalizations on the basis of several years of observation and practice of ballroom Latin, salsa, Argentine tango, Brazilian samba, lindy hop, and Afro-Cuban rumba. Conversations (both verbal and physical) with Cheryl Bush, Alexandra Gisher, Jesús Morales, Gloria Otero, Christian Perry, and Anna Scott were particularly useful in clarifying these distinctions.

85. Richard C. Green, "Doin' da Butt: Performance, Race, and Black Bodies," Dancing in the Millennium Conference, Washington, DC, 22 July 2000.

86. This alignment is consistent with other Western dance techniques, such as ballet and modern. The aesthetic of the vanishing buttocks was used throughout much of the twentieth century as justification for excluding black dancers from ballet companies. See Brenda Dixon Gottschild, *The Black Dancing Body: A Geography from Coon to Cool* (New York: Palgrave MacMillan, 2003). A 1995 dance piece, *Batty Moves,* choreographed by Jawole Zollar for Urban Bush Women, capitalizes on this tension between requirements in ballet and modern to hide the butt and celebration of the butt in African dance and African diasporic dance and movement practices. Ananya Chatterjea writes: "Zollar choreographed *Batty Moves* because she felt strongly that in Euro-American modes of training, specifically ballet and modern idioms, dancers' buttocks were drained of movement, poetry, and passion. . . . The piece . . . is inspired by movements of the butt: several of the movements are initiated with or end with the butt, whereas others transform traditional movements from the modern dance vocabulary by substituting the erect spine and aligned pel-

vis for more curved lines of the back." *Butting Out: Reading Resistive Choreographies through Works by Jawole Willa Jo Zollar and Chandralekha* (Middletown, CT: Wesleyan University Press, 2004), 182.

87. Savigliano, *Tango,* 149–153.

88. See, for example, their first appearance in Hollywood films in the 1937 Marx Brothers film, *A Day at the Races.*

89. Arthur Murray, *How to Become a Good Dancer: With Dance Secrets by Kathryn Murray* (New York: Simon & Schuster, 1959), 219.

90. Victor Silvester and Philip J. S. Richardson, *The Art of the Ballroom* (London: Herbert Jenkins, 1936), 32.

91. Ibid., 37.

92. Demographics in South Africa, where DanceSport is popular in the black and white populations, suggest the most significant departure from the American situation. Thanks to the South African dance historian Roger Wiblin for confirmation of this trend.

93. "*Dance with Me:* The Movie," *Dance Beat,* ed. 0898 (1998), 22.

94. Particular thanks to the DanceSport competitors Charleton Alicia, Dedelle Barbanti, Jorge Geronimo, Maria Torres, and Daniel Vasco for sharing their ideas on this subject with me.

95. Maria Torres, personal interview, 23 August 2001.

96. Thanks to the DanceSport coach and judge Victor Kanevsky for suggesting that the language "too street" probably meant, for the judges who used it, that her footwork was imprecise.

97. Jennifer Robertson argues that the dramatization of Japanese empire through shows in which revue actors played Chinese and Indonesian colonized citizens "portrayed the proper way—that is the 'Japanese' way—to look and sound Chinese and Indonesian." *Takarazuka: Sexual Politics and Popular Culture in Modern Japan* (Berkeley: University of California Press, 1998), 97.

98. Very few members of the cast were Cuban. Los Angeles's substantial Hispanic population is predominantly of Mexican and Central American origin. Casting choices were not apparently based on whether the dancers looked Cuban, but on whether they fit some visual image of "Latin." One dancer of mixed Salvadorian and American heritage was told that he was dismissed from the audition because he looked too white for the Latin parts and too Latin for the white parts (personal communication).

99. Rafael is pictured dancing Cuban rumba, Los Angeles–style salsa, and Cuban *casino rueda* at different points during the film.

100. Eddie Torres, interviewed by Diane Duggan, 30 August 2001, transcript, New York Public Library Dance Research Collection.

101. The casting of Vanessa Williams, an African American, in the role of DanceSport champion may obscure the actual demographics of the sport, but DanceSport has very few black participants. White dancers from a variety of countries and ethnicities (particularly Eastern Europe), Asians (and Asian Americans), and a growing number of Latinos constitute the competitors and audience at any DanceSport event.

102. For histories of salsa music, see Jorge Duany, "Popular Music in Puerto Rico: To-

ward an Anthropology of *Salsa*," *Latin American Music Review* 5.2 (1984): 186–216; Boggs, *Salsiology;* Peter Manuel, "Puerto Rican Music and Cultural Identity: Creative Appropriation of Cuban Sources from Danza to Salsa," *Ethnomusicology* 38.2 (1994): 249–280; Leonardo Padura Fuentes, *Faces of Salsa: A Spoken History of the Music,* trans. Stephen J. Clark (Washington, DC: Smithsonian Books, 2003); and Lise Waxer, ed., *Situating Salsa: Global Markets and Local Meanings in Latin Popular Music* (New York: Routledge, 2002);

103. Mayra Santos Febres, "Salsa as Translocation," *Everynight Life: Culture and Dance in Latin/o America,* ed. Celeste Frazer Delgado and Jose Esteban Muñoz (Durham, NC: Duke University Press, 1997), 175–188. For analysis of how embodied identities are created through salsa dance, see Patria Román-Velázquez, *The Making of Latin London: Salsa Music, Place, and Identity* (Aldershot, England: Ashgate, 1999).

104. Many ballroom studios and white salsa teachers are also cashing in on salsa mania. Some teach ballroom mambo and call it salsa, while others have studied salsa as it is practiced in contemporary nightclubs and teach techniques that depart from ballroom forms.

105. I am grateful to Jesús Morales for directing me to the significance of *sabor* for salsa dancers.

106. This logic, however, is in direct opposition to many Western concert dance traditions, which operate under the premise that physical discipline of the body is the means through which artistic expression is possible. For example, Martha Graham, one of the greatest modern dance luminaries of all time, was adamant that physical discipline through mastery of a particular movement technique was the key to emotional, spiritual, and artistic expression. See Martha Graham, "Martha Graham Speaks," *Dance Observer* 30.4 (April 1963): 53–55; Susan Leigh Foster, *Reading Dancing: Bodies and Subjects in Contemporary American Dance* (Berkeley: University of California Press, 1986). But as many subsequent experimental dance forms (such as those spawned by the 1960s Judson Church performance of postmodern dance) have demonstrated, fewer technical rules can also lead to a greater range of choices in personal expression. Likewise, in social dance, technical structure can both enable and inhibit expression, depending on how it is applied.

107. My use of the word technique to describe all movement practices rather than just those with well-articulated pedagogical models is indebted to an early work of Marcel Mauss, "Body Techniques," trans. Ben Brewer, *Sociology and Psychology: Essays* (London: Routledge, 1979), 97–123, and subsequent development of his ideas by dance scholars such as Susan Leigh Foster, "Dancing Bodies," *Meaning in Motion: New Cultural Studies of Dance,* ed. Jane C. Desmond (Durham, NC: Duke University Press, 1997), 235–257; and Cynthia Novack, *Sharing the Dance: Contact Improvisation and American Culture* (Madison: University of Wisconsin Press, 1990);.

108. The dance scholar Yvonne Daniel identifies the African character of a dance in the same terms: "The emphasis on moving hips permits the torso to divide its movement potential, and to create separate visual rhythms, polyrhythms between the upper and lower torso. The 'divided' torso of son is African as opposed to European dance of the period, which generally used the entire torso as a stabilizer for arm and leg movement." Daniel, "Cuban Dance," 43. For discussion of character-

istics of West African dance, which include body segmentation and polyrhythmic movement, see Brenda Dixon Gottschild, *Digging the Africanist Presence in American Performance: Dance and Other Contexts* (Westport, CT: Greenwood Press, 1996); Jacqui Malone, *Steppin' on the Blues: The Visible Rhythms of African American Dance* (Urbana, IL: University of Chicago Press, 1996); Anna Beatrice Scott, "Spectacle and Dancing Bodies That Matter: Or If It Don't Fit, Don't Force It," *Meaning in Motion,* ed. Jane C. Desmond (Durham, NC: Duke University Press, 1997), 259–268: and Robert Farris Thompson, *African Art in Motion: Icon and Act in the Collection of Katherine Coryton White* (Los Angeles: University of California Press, 1974).

109. Salsation home page, http://www.salsationonline.com (accessed 16 September 2002).

110. The persistence of minstrel stereotypes in contemporary popular culture, particularly as they are assumed by African Americans, was portrayed with chilling force in Spike Lee's film *Bamboozled.* See also Cynthia Lucia, ed., "Race, Media and Money: A Critical Symposium on Spike Lee's *Bamboozled,*" *Cineaste* 24.2 (2001): 10–17.

111. Santos Febres, 186.

NOTES TO CHAPTER 4

1. Ruud Vermey, *Latin: Thinking, Sensing and Doing in Latin American Dancing* (Munich: Kastell Verlag, 1994), 122.

2. Ibid., 99.

3. "South American" is a true misnomer: neither South American dancing nor South American competitors are included in the event. This recent addition to DanceSport world championship titles is for competitors who compete in DanceSport Latin, standard competitors vying for the title of "Classic Showdance Champion."

4. The most widely recognized ballroom dance company was Pierre Dulaine and Yvonne Marceau's American Ballroom Theatre, based out of New York, in the 1980s. There have also been companies convened by Frank Regan (American Dance Montage), Wilson Burns and Margaret Barrera (Ballroom Dancesport Theatre of Southwest Florida), and Peter Maxwell (Peter Maxwell's Ballroom Theatre). The DanceSport patron Marguerite Hanlon and the choreographer John Ford have also produced a number of "dance dramas" in which they act out a well-known story through ballroom dance and pantomime. Hanlon and Ford also produced a ballroom dance medley featuring many top DanceSport competitors called *Ballroom Fever,* staged for television and performed live at Madison Square Garden in 1999. The most substantial recent attempt to bring theatrical ballroom to mainstream theatre audiences was the mounting of the thirty-dancer ballroom spectacle *Burn the Floor* in the late 1990s.

5. Mikhail Bakhtin, *Rabelais and His World,* trans. Helen Iswolsky (Bloomington: Indiana University Press, 1984), 92.

6. I danced in the group from summer of 2000 to summer of 2001. This analysis is based on my experience as well as that of my colleagues.

7. Though some might argue that all identity is performative as described by Judith Butler, I contend that performance of identity in the ballroom industry is much more extreme than that in ordinary life and is determined by a much narrower set of expectations and linked more consciously to pursuit of status and money.

8. Telephone interview with Mary Pinizzotto, 15 January 2000.

9. The 2000 Census data reports St. Cloud is a town of 20,000 whose population is 85 percent white and 14 percent Hispanic with a median household income of $36,000.

10. Janice Ross, *Moving Lessons: Margaret H'Doubler and the Beginning of Dance in American Education* (Madison: University of Wisconsin Press, 2000), 40.

11. Virginia Postrel, "A Golden World," *Glamour: Fashion, Industrial Design, Architecture,* ed. Joseph Rosa (New Haven, CT: San Francisco Museum of Modern Art in association with Yale University Press, 2004), 24.

12. Ibid., 31.

References

INTERVIEWS

Blair, Skippy. Personal interview. 24 May 2002.

Chavez, Felix. Personal interview. 6 May 1998.

Cordoba, Enio. Personal interview. 22 March 2001.

Fletcher, Hazel. Personal interview. 9 September 1999.

Irvine, Bill. Personal interview. 10 September 1999.

Lee, Lorna. Personal interview. 10 September 1999.

Midkiff, Mark. Telephone interview. 18 September 2002.

Pinizzotto, Mary. Telephone interview. 15 January 2000.

Regan, Frank. Personal interview. 10 November 2001.

Sodano, Sam. Personal interview, 17 May 2003.

Torres, Maria. Telephone interview. 23 August 2001.

Wilbur, Richard. Personal interview. 2 June 2003.

Numerous other individuals in the DanceSport community participated in formal and informal interviews throughout the many years of this research project. All interviews were conducted by the author.

BIBLIOGRAPHY

Albright, Ann Cooper. *Choreographing Difference: The Body and Identity in Contemporary Dance.* Hanover, NH: Wesleyan University Press, 1997.

Allen, Robert C. *Horrible Prettiness: Burlesque and American Culture.* Chapel Hill: University of North Carolina Press, 1991.

American Memory: An American Ballroom Companion. Library of Congress, Washington. http://memory.loc.gov/ammem/dihtml/dihome.html, accessed 7 February 2006.

American Rumba Committee. *The American Rumba.* New York: Rudor, 1943.

Arkin, Lisa C., and Marian Smith. "National Dance in the Romantic Ballet." *Rethinking the Sylph: New Perspectives on the Romantic Ballet.* Ed. Lynn Garafola. Hanover, NH: Wesleyan University Press, 1997. 11–68.

Arthur Murray International home page. http://www.arthurmurray.com, accessed 13 August 2006.

Arthur Murray International History. http://www.dancetonight.com/amihistory.html, accessed 4 March 2006.

Arrizón, Alicia. *Latina Performance: Traversing the Stage.* Bloomington: Indiana University Press, 1999.

Astaire, Fred. *Steps in Time.* New York: Da Capo Press, 1979.

Babitz, Eve. *Two by Two: Tango, Two-step, and the L.A. Night.* New York: Simon & Schuster, 1999.

Bailey, Peter. "Parasexuality and Glamour: The Victorian Barmaid as Cultural Prototype." *Gender and History* 2.2 (1990): 148–72.

Bakhtin, Mikhail. *Rabelais and His World.* Trans. Helen Iswolsky. Bloomington: Indiana University Press, 1984.

Ball-room Dancing without a Master and Complete Guide to the Etiquette, Toilet, Dress and Management of the Ball-room; with all the Principal Dances in Popular Use. New York: Hurst, 1872.

Banes, Sally. *Writing Dancing in the Age of Postmodernism.* Hanover, NH: Wesleyan University Press, 1994.

Baudrillard, Jean. *For a Critique of the Political Economy of the Sign.* St. Louis, MO: Telos, 1981.

Benitez Rojo, Antonio. *The Repeating Island: The Caribbean and the Postmodern Perspective (Post-Contemporary Intervention*s). Trans. James Maraniss. Durham, NC: Duke University Press, 1992.

Best, Amy L. *Prom Night: Youth, Schools, and Popular Culture.* New York: Routledge, 2000.

Bhabha, Homi K. "The Other Question: Difference, Discrimination and the Discourse of Colonialism." *Out There: Marginalization and Contemporary Cultures.* Ed. Russell Ferguson, Martha Gever, Trinh T. Minh-ha, and Cornel West. New York: New Museum of Contemporary Art; Cambridge, MA: MIT Press, 1990. 71–87.

Boggs, Vernon W., ed. *Salsiology: Afro-Cuban Music and the Evolution of Salsa in New York City.* New York: Greenwood Press, 1992.

Bordo, Susan. *Unbearable Weight: Feminism, Western Culture, and the Body.* Berkeley: University of California Press, 1993.

Born, Georgina, and David Hesmondhalgh. "Introduction: On Difference, Representation, and Appropriation in Music." *Western Music and Its Others: Difference, Representation, and Appropriation in Music.* Ed. Georgina Born and David Hesmondhalgh. Berkeley: University of California Press, 2000. 1–58.

Borrows, Frank. *Theory and Technique of Latin-American Dancing.* London: Frederick Muller, 1964.

Bourdieu, Pierre. *Distinction: A Social Critique of the Judgment of Taste.* Trans. Richard Nice. Cambridge, MA: Harvard University Press, 1984.

Brandis, Riba. "Differences in Latin Style Dancing: Authentic Latin vs. American Social Latin vs. International Competition Latin." *Dancing USA,* October–November 1998: 9.

Browning, Barbara. *Samba: Resistance in Motion.* Bloomington: Indiana University Press, 1995.

Buckland, Fiona. *Impossible Dance: Club Culture and Queer World-making.* Middletown, CT: Wesleyan University Press, 2002.

Buckman, Peter. *Let's Dance: Social, Ballroom and Folk Dancing.* New York: Paddington Press, 1978.

Butler, Judith. *Bodies That Matter: On the Discursive Limits of "Sex."* New York: Routledge, 1993.

———. *Gender Trouble: Feminism and the Subversion of Identity.* New York: Routledge, 1999.

Castle, Irene. *Castles in the Air.* New York: Da Capo Press, 1980.

Castle, Vernon, and Irene Castle. *Modern Dancing.* New York: Harper & Brothers, 1914.

Chapman, Tom. *Teaching Ballroom: The Business.* Leawood, KS: Leathers, 2002.

Chatterjea, Ananya. *Butting Out: Reading Resistive Choreographies through Works by Jawole Willa Jo Zollar and Chandralekha.* Middletown, CT: Wesleyan University Press, 2004.

Clark, Christine and James O'Donnell, eds. *Becoming and Unbecoming White: Owning and Disowning a Racial Identity.* Westport, CT: Bergin & Garvey, 1999.

Clover, Neil. "The Importance of Ballroom Dance." *Dancing USA,* January–February 1992: 19.

Cohen-Stratyner, Barbara. "Social Dance: Contexts and Definitions." *Dance Research Journal* 33.2 (2001): 121–123.

Collins, Patricia Hill. *Fighting Words: Black Women and the Search for Truth.* Minneapolis: University of Minnesota Press, 1998.

Cook, Susan C. "Talking Machines and Moving Bodies: Marketing Dance Music before World War I." *Dancing in the Millennium: An International Conference, Proceedings, Washington, DC, 19–23 July, 2000.* Comp. Juliette Crone-Willis, 2000. 75–78.

———. "Tango Lizards and Girlish Men: Performing Masculinity on the Social Dance Floor." *Proceedings Society of Dance History Scholars, Reflecting our Past; Reflecting our Future, Barnard College, New York City, 19–22 June 1997.* Comp. Linda J. Tomko, 1997. 41–55.

Craik, Jennifer. *The Face of Fashion: Cultural Studies in Fashion.* New York: Routledge, 1994.

Crease, Robert P. "Divine Frivolity: Movement and Vernacular Dance." *Dancing in the Millennium: An International Conference, Washington, DC, 19–23 July, 2000.* Comp. Juliette Crone-Willis, 2000. 110–114.

Crenshaw, Kimberle, Neil Gotanda, Garry Peller, and Kendall Thomas, eds. *Critical Race Theory: The Key Writings That Formed the Movement.* New York: New Press, 1996.

Crook, Larry. "A Musical Analysis of the Cuban Rumba." *Latin American Music Review* 3.1 (1982): 92–123.

Cugat, Xavier. *Rumba Is My Life.* New York: Didier, 1948.

"Dance with Me: The Movie." *Dance Beat,* ed. 0898, 1998.

Daniel, Yvonne. "Cuban Dance: An Orchard of Caribbean Creativity." *Caribbean Dance from Abakuá To Zouk: How Movement Shapes Identity.* Ed. Susanna Sloat. Gainesville: University Press of Florida, 2002. 23–55.

———. "Rumba Then and Now: *Quindembo.*" *The Social And Popular Dance Reader.* Ed. Julie Malnig. University of Illinois Press, forthcoming.

———. *Rumba: Dance and Social Change in Contemporary Cuba.* Bloomington: Indiana University Press, 1995.

Debord, Guy. *Society of the Spectacle*. Detroit, MI: Black & Red, 1983.

Delgado, Richard, and Jean Stefancic, eds. *Critical Race Theory: The Cutting Edge*. Philadelphia: Temple University Press, 1999.

———. *Critical White Studies: Looking behind the Mirror*. Philadelphia: Temple University Press, 1997.

Desmond, Jane. "Dancing Out the Difference: Cultural Imperialism and Ruth St. Denis's *Radha* of 1906." *Moving History/Dancing Cultures: A Dance History Reader*. Ed. Ann Dils and Ann Cooper Albright. Middletown, CT: Wesleyan University Press, 2001. 256–270.

Desmond, Jane C. "Embodying Difference: Issues in Dance and Cultural Studies." *Meaning in Motion: New Cultural Studies of Dance*. Ed. Jane C. Desmond. Durham, NC: Duke University Press, 1997. 29–54.

Dixon Gottschild, Brenda. *The Black Dancing Body: A Geography from Coon to Cool*. New York: Palgrave MacMillan, 2003.

———. *Digging the Africanist Presence in American Performance: Dance and Other Contexts*. Westport, CT: Greenwood Press, 1996.

———. "Some Thoughts on Choreographing History." *Meaning in Motion: New Cultural Studies of Dance*. Ed. Jane C. Desmond. Durham, NC: Duke University Press, 1997. 167–177.

———. *Waltzing in the Dark: African American Vaudeville and Race Politics in the Swing Era*. New York: Palgrave, 2000.

Dodworth, Allen. *Dancing and Its Relations to Education and Social Life*. New York: Harper & Brothers, 1885.

Duany, Jorge. "Popular Music in Puerto Rico: Toward an Anthropology of *Salsa*." *Latin American Music Review* 5.2 (1984): 186–216.

Dyer, Richard. *White*. New York: Routledge, 1997.

Erenberg, Lewis A. *Swingin' the Dream: Big Band Jazz and the Rebirth of American Culture*. Chicago: University of Chicago Press, 1998.

Evans, Irene. *A Concise History of Latin American Dancing in the UK*. United Kingdom Alliance of Professional Teachers of Dancing, 1992.

Ewen, Stuart. *All Consuming Images: The Politics of Style in Contemporary Culture*. Basic Books, 1999.

Farhood, Amy Cristine. "The Mormon Church and the Gold Bar: A Look at Conservative Religion and Ballroom Dance at Brigham Young University." *Dancing in the Millennium: An International Conference, Washington, DC, 19–23 July, 2000*. Comp. Juliette Crone-Willis, 2000. 162–167.

Faulkner, T. A. *From the Ball-room to Hell*. Chicago: Church Press, 1894.

Feinstein, John. "The Wednesday Waltz." *Golf Magazine* 38.7 (1996): 20–23.

Fiske, John, and John Hartley. "Dance as Light Entertainment." *Parallel Lines: Media Representations of Dance*. Ed. Stephanie Jordan and David Allen. London: John Libby, 1993. 37–50.

Foster, Susan Leigh. *Choreography and Narrative: Ballet's Staging of Story and Desire*. Bloomington: Indiana University Press, 1996.

———. *Dances That Describe Themselves: The Improvised Choreography of Richard Bull*. Middletown, CT: Wesleyan University Press, 2002.

———. "Dancing Bodies." *Meaning in Motion: New Cultural Studies of Dance.* Ed. Jane C. Desmond. Durham, NC: Duke University Press, 1997. 235–257.

———. *Reading Dancing: Bodies and Subjects in Contemporary American Dance.* Berkeley: University of California Press, 1986.

Foster, Susan Leigh, ed. *Choreographing History.* Bloomington: Indiana University Press, 1995.

Foucault, Michel. *The Archeology of Knowledge and the Discourse on Language.* Trans. A. M. Sheridan Smith. New York: Pantheon Books, 1972.

———. *Discipline and Punish: The Birth of the Prison.* Trans. Alan Sheridan. 1977. New York: Vintage Books, 1995.

———. *The Order of Things: An Archaeology of the Human Sciences.* 1970. New York: Vintage Books, 1994.

Frankenburg, Ruth, ed. *Displacing Whiteness: Essays in Social and Cultural Criticism.* Durham, NC: Duke University Press, 1997.

Frazer Delgado, Celeste. "Exploding the Exotic: Re-thinking Performance at the End of Civilization." Paper presented at the University of California, Riverside, 11 May 1999.

Frazer Delgado, Celeste, and Jose Esteban Muñoz. "Rebellions of Everynight Life." *Everynight Life: Culture and Dance in Latin/o America.* Ed. Celeste Frazer Delgado and Jose Esteban Muñoz. Durham, NC: Duke University Press, 1997. 9–32.

Fred Astaire Dance Studios home page. http://fredastaire.com/, accessed 13 August 2000.

Fusco, Coco. *English Is Broken Here: Notes on Cultural Confusion in the Americas.* New York: New Press, 1995.

Fuss, Diana. *Essentially Speaking: Feminsim, Nature and Difference.* New York: Routledge, 1989.

Gainor, Ellen J. "'A World without Collisions': Ballroom Dance in Athol Fugard's *'Master Harold'*... *and the Boys.*" *Bodies of the Text: Dance as Theory, Literature as Dance.* Ed. Ellen W. Goellner and Jacqueline Shea Murphy. New Brunswick, NJ: Rutgers University Press, 1995. 125–138.

Garafola, Lynn. *Diaghilev's Ballets Russes.* New York: Oxford University Press, 1989.

Gilroy, Paul. *Against Race: Imaging Political Culture beyond the Color Line.* Cambridge, MA: Belknap Press of Harvard University Press, 2000.

Graham, Martha. "Martha Graham Speaks." *Dance Observer* 30.4 (1963): 53–55.

Green, Richard C. "Doin' da Butt: Performance, Race, and Black Bodies." Dancing in the Millennium Conference, Washington, DC, 22 July 2000.

Gundle, Stephen. "Mapping the Origins of Glamour: Giovanni Boldini, Paris and the Belle Epoque." *Journal of European Studies* 23.3 (September 1999): 269–298.

Hall, Edward T. *The Silent Language.* Garden City, NY: Doubleday, 1959.

Hall, Stuart. "For Allon White: Metaphors of Transformation." *Carnival, Hysteria and Writing: Collected Essays and Autobiography.* Ed. Allon White. Oxford: Oxford University Press, 1993. 1–25.

Haney López, Ian F. *White by Law: The Legal Construction of Race.* New York: New York University Press, 1996.

Hopkins, J. S. *The Tango and Other Up-to-date Dances.* Chicago: Saalfield, 1914.

Howe, Elias. *Complete Ball-room Hand Book.* Boston: Ditson, 1858.

Hutchinson, Craig. *Swing Dancer.* Falls Church, VA: Potomac Swing Dance Club, 1998.

Ignatiev, Noel, and John Garvey, eds. *Race Traitor.* New York: Routledge, 1996.

International DanceSport Federation home page. http://www.idsf.net/index.tpl, accessed 3 March 2006.

Irvine, Bill, and Bobbie Irvine. *The Dancing Years.* London: W. H. Allen, 1970.

Jameson, Fredric. *Postmodernism, or, The Cultural Logic of Late Capitalism.* Durham, NC: Duke University Press, 1991.

Kilbridge, Ann A., and A. Algoso. *The Complete Book on Disco and Ballroom Dancing.* Los Alamitos, CA: Hwong, 1979.

Kincheloe, Joe L., Shirley R. Steinberg, Nelson M. Rodriguez, and Ronald E. Chennault, eds. *White Reign: Deploying Whiteness in America.* New York: St. Martin's Press, 1998.

Kondo, Dorinne. *About Face: Performing Race in Fashion and Theatre.* New York: Routledge, 1997.

Kristeva, Julia. *Powers of Horror: An Essay on Abjection.* Trans. Leon S. Roudiez. New York: Columbia University Press, 1982.

Laird, Walter. *Technique of Latin Dancing.* London: International Dance Teachers' Association, 1964.

———. *The Technique of Latin American Dancing.* London: International Dance Teachers' Association, 1983.

Lavelle, Doris. *Latin and American Dances.* London: Sir Isaac Pitman & Sons, 1965.

Leigh, Eduardo. "The Rumba Trail." *Dancing Times* (January 1997): 340–343.

Leymarie, Isabelle. *Cuban Fire: The Story of Salsa and Latin Jazz.* London: Continuum, 2002.

———. "De la rumba brava à la rumba de salon." *Danses latines: Le désir des continents.* Ed. Élisabeth Dorier-Apprill. Paris: Éditions Autrement, 2001. 94–103.

———. "Mambo et cha-cha-cha." *Danses latines: Le désir des continents.* Ed. Élisabeth Dorier-Apprill. Paris: Éditions Autrement, 2001. 102–121.

Lipsitz, George. *The Possessive Investment in Whiteness: How White People Profit from Identity Politics.* Philadelphia: Temple University Press, 1998.

———. *Dangerous Crossroads: Popular Music, Postmodernism, and the Poetics of Place.* New York: Verso, 1994.

Long, Daniel. "Qualifying for Olympic Status: The Process and Implications for Competitive Ballroom Dance." Master's thesis, Brigham Young University, 1999.

Lott, Eric. *Love and Theft: Blackface Minstrelsy and the American Working Class.* New York: Oxford University Press, 1993.

Lowe, Lisa. *Immigrant Acts: On Asian American Cultural Politics.* Durham, NC: Duke University Press, 1996.

Lucia, Cynthia, ed. "Race, Media and Money: A Critical Symposium on Spike Lee's *Bamboozled.*" *Cineaste* 26.2 (2001): 10–17.

MacAloon, John J. "Olympic Games and the Theory of Spectacle in Modern Societies." *Rite, Drama, Festival, Spectacle: Rehearsals toward a Theory of Cultural Performance.* Ed. John J. MacAloon. Philadelphia: Institute for the Study of Human Issues, 1984.

Malnig, Julie. *Dancing till Dawn: A Century of Exhibition Ballroom Dancing.* New York: New York University Press, 1992.

———. "Two-stepping to Glory: Social Dance and the Rhetoric of Social Mobility." *Moving History/Dancing Cultures: A Dance History Reader.* Ed. Ann Dils and Ann Cooper Albright. Middletown, CT: Wesleyan University Press, 2001. 271–287.

Malone, Jacqui. *Steppin' on the Blues: The Visible Rhythms of African American Dance.* Urbana, IL: University of Chicago Press, 1996.

Manuel, Peter. "Puerto Rican Music and Cultural Identity: Creative Appropriation of Cuban Sources from Danza to Salsa." *Ethnomusicology* 38.2 (1994): 249–280.

———. "The Soul of the Barrio: Thirty Years of Salsa." *NACLA Report on the Americas* 28.2 (1994): 22–29.

Marion, Jonathan S. "'Where' Is 'There'? Towards a Translocal Anthropology." *Anthropology News* (May 2005): 18–19.

Martin, Marc. *Viens danser: La samba, la rumba, le cha cha cha.* Vitry-sur-Seine: Éditions Aguer, 1996.

Martínez, Mayra. "Rumberas en México." *Revolución y cultura* 11 (November 1989): 40–45.

Marx, Eric. "In the Ballroom, a Redefinition of a 'Couple.'" *New York Times,* 14 July 2004.

Matsuda, Mari J. *Where Is Your Body? And Other Essays on Race, Gender and the Law* Boston: Beacon Press, 1996.

Mauss, Marcel. "Body Techniques." Trans. Ben Brewer. *Sociology and Psychology*: *Essays.* London: Routledge, 1979. 97–123.

McMains, Juliet. "Brownface: Representations of Latin-ness in Dancesport." *Dance Research Journal* 33.2 (2001): 54–71.

———. "Dancing Latin/Latin Dancing: Salsa and DanceSport." *The Social and Popular Dance Reader.* Ed. Julie Malnig. University of Illinois Press, forthcoming.

———. "Tradition and Transgression: Gender Roles in Ballroom Dance." Bachelor's thesis, Harvard University, 1994.

Miller, Norma, with Evette Jensen. *Swingin' at the Savoy: The Memoir of a Jazz Dancer.* Philadelphia: Temple University Press, 1996.

Mizejewski, Linda. *Ziegfeld Girl: Image and Icon in Culture and Cinema.* Durham, NC: Duke University Press, 1997.

Moore, Robin D. "The Commercial Rumba in Afrocuban Arts as International Popular Culture." *Latin American Music Review* 16.2 (1995): 165–198.

———. *Nationalizing Blackness: Afrocubanismo and Artistic Revolution in Havana, 1920–1940.* Pittsburgh: University of Pittsburgh Press, 1997.

Morris, Gay, ed. *Moving Words: Re-writing Dance.* New York: Routledge, 1996.

Murray, Arthur. *Arthur Murray's Dance Secrets.* New York: Arthur Murray, 1946.

———. *Dance Instructor, with Music for Every Type of Social Dancing.* New York: Robbins Music, 1946.

———. *How to Become a Good Dancer.* New York: Simon & Schuster, 1938.

———. *How to Become a Good Dancer.* New York: Simon & Schuster, 1942.

———. *How to Become a Good Dancer.* New York: Simon & Schuster, 1947.

———. *How to Become a Good Dancer.* New York: Simon & Schuster, 1954.

—————. *How to Become a Good Dancer: With Dance Secrets by Kathryn Murray.* New York: Simon & Schuster, 1959.

—————. *Let's Dance.* New York: Arthur Murray, 1953.

—————. *The Modern Dances.* New York: Arthur Murray School of Dancing, 1925.

—————. *The Modern Dances (Advanced Course): Parts I and II.* New York: Arthur Murray School of Dancing, 1924.

Murray, Kathryn, with Betty Hannah Hoffman. *My Husband, Arthur Murray.* New York: Simon & Schuster, 1960.

Murray, Kathryn, and Arthur Murray, eds. *Murray-Go-Round.* Arthur Murray International, 1954.

Myers, Edward A. "Ballroom Dance as a Commodity: An Anthropological Viewpoint." *Journal for the Anthropological Study of Human Movement* 3.2 (1984): 74–83.

National Dance Council of America. NDCA *Rules and Regulations.* January 2006.

Needham, Maureen, ed. *I See American Dancing: Selected Readings, 1685–2000.* Urbana: University of Illinois Press, 2002.

Nealon, Jeffrey. *Alterity Politics: Ethics and Performative Subjectivity.* Durham, NC: Duke University Press, 1998.

Ness, Sally Ann. *Body, Movement, and Culture: Kinesthetic and Visual Symbolism in a Philippine Community.* Philadelphia: University of Pennsylvania Press, 1992.

Novack, Cynthia J. *Sharing the Dance: Contact Improvisation and American Culture.* Madison: University of Wisconsin Press, 1990.

Omi, Michael, and Howard Winant. *Racial Formation in the United States from the 1960s to the 1990s.* New York: Routledge, 1994.

O'Neill, Rosetta. "The Dodworth Family and Ballroom Dancing in New York." *Chronicles of the American Dance.* Ed. Paul Magriel. New York: Henry Holt, 1948. 81–100.

Ortiz, Fernando. *Cuban Counterpoint: Tobacco and Sugar.* New York: A. A. Knopf, 1947.

Padura Fuentes, Leonardo. *Faces of Salsa: A Spoken History of the Music.* Trans. Stephen J. Clark. Washington, DC: Smithsonian Books, 2003.

Penny, Patricia. "Dancing at the Interface of the Social and the Theatrical: Focus on the Participatory Patterns of Contemporary Competition Ballroom Dancers in Britain." *Dance Research: The Journal of the Society for Dance Research* 17.1 (1999): 47–74.

Pierre. *Latin and American Dances for Students and Teachers.* London, 1948.

Postrel, Virginia. "A Golden World." *Glamour: Fashion, Industrial Design, Architecture.* Ed. Joseph Rosa. New Haven, CT: San Francisco Museum of Modern Art in association with Yale University Press, 2004. 24–35.

Project on Disney. *Inside the Mouse: Work and Play at Disney World.* Durham, NC: Duke University Press, 1995.

Quintero Herencia, Juan Carlos. "Notes Toward a Reading of Salsa." *Everynight Life: Culture and Dance in Latin/o America.* Ed. Celeste Frazer Delgado and Jose Esteban Muñoz. Durham, NC: Duke University Press, 1997. 189–222.

Rabinow, Paul, ed. *The Foucault Reader.* Harmondsworth: Penguin, 1984.

Riba, Brandis. "Differences in Latin Style Dancing: Authentic Latin vs. America Social Latin vs. International Competition Latin." *Dancing USA,* October–November 1998: 9.

Richardson, Philip J. S. *A History of English Ballroom Dancing, 1910–45: The Story of the Development of the Modern English Style.* London: Herbert Jenkins, 1946.

Roberts, John Storm. *The Latin Tinge: The Impact of Latin American Music on the United States.* 2nd ed. New York: Oxford University Press, 1999.

Robertson, Jennifer. *Takarazuka: Sexual Politics and Popular Culture in Modern Japan.* Berkeley: University of California Press, 1998.

Robinson, Danielle. "From the Turkey Trot to the One Step: The Cultural Politics of American Ragtime Dancing." Paper presented at the Society of Dance History Scholars Conference, Towson, MD, 24 June 2001.

——— "Qualifying Essay." Unpublished ms. Department of Dance, University of California, Riverside, 21 December 2000.

Robinson, Danielle Anne. "Race in Motion: Reconstructing the Practice, Profession, and Politics of Social Dancing, New York City, 1900–1930." Ph.D. diss., University of California, Riverside, 2004.

Roediger, David R. *The Wages of Whiteness: Race and the Making of the American Working Class.* New York: Verso, 1991.

Román-Velázquez, Patria. *The Making of Latin London: Salsa Music, Place, and Identity.* Aldershot, England: Ashgate, 1999.

Rosa, Joseph, ed. *Glamour: Fashion, Industrial Design, Architecture.* New Haven, CT: San Francisco Museum of Modern Art in association with Yale University Press, 2004.

Ross, Janice. *Moving Lessons: Margaret H'Doubler and the Beginning of Dance in American Education.* Madison: University of Wisconsin Press, 2000.

Ross, Stuart. "I Taught for Arthur Murray: High Pressure Ballyhoo Has Turned Ballroom Dancing into a Multi-million Dollar Business." *Dance Magazine,* August 1946.

Russo, Mary. *The Female Grotesque: Risk, Excess and Modernity.* New York: Routledge, 1995.

Said, Edward. *Orientalism.* New York: Vintage Books, 1978.

Salsation home page. http://www.salsationonline.com, accessed 16 September 2002.

Santos Febres, Mayra. "Salsa as Translocation." *Everynight Life: Culture and Dance in Latin/o America.* Ed. Celeste Frazer Delgado and Jose Esteban Muñoz. Durham, NC: Duke University Press, 1997. 175–188.

Savigliano, Marta. *Angora Matta: Fatal Acts of North-South Translation.* Middletown, CT: Wesleyan University Press, 2003

———. *Tango and the Political Economy of Passion.* Boulder, CO: Westview Press, 1994.

Schor, Juliet. *The Overspent American: Upscaling, Downshifting, and the New Consumer.* New York: Basic Books, 1998.

Scott, Anna Beatrice. "Spectacle and Dancing Bodies that Matter: Or If It Don't Fit, Don't Force It." *Meaning in Motion: New Cultural Studies of Dance.* Ed. Jane C. Desmond. Durham, NC: Duke University Press, 1997. 259–268.

Silvester, Victor. *Modern Ballroom Dancing.* London: Herbert Jenkins, 1927.

————. *Modern Ballroom Dancing.* London: Herbert Jenkins, [1942?].

————. *Modern Ballroom Dancing.* London: Herbert Jenkins, 1948.

————. *Modern Ballroom Dancing.* London: Herbert Jenkins, 1952.

————. *Modern Ballroom Dancing.* London: Herbert Jenkins, 1954.

————. *Modern Ballroom Dancing.* London: Herbert Jenkins, 1955.

————. *Modern Ballroom Dancing.* London: Herbert Jenkins, 1964.

————. *Modern Ballroom Dancing: History and Practice.* London: Stanley Paul, 1977.

————. *Modern Ballroom Dancing: History and Practice.* London: Stanley Paul, 1982.

————. *Modern Ballroom Dancing.* London: Stanley Paul, 1990.

————. *Modern Ballroom Dancing.* North Pomfret, VT: Trafalgar Square, 1993.

————. *Theory and Technique of Ballroom Dancing.* London: Herbert Jenkins, 1936.

Silvester, Victor, and Philip J. S. Richardson. *The Art of the Ballroom.* London: Herbert Jenkins, 1936.

Slater, Don. *Consumer Culture and Modernity.* Cambridge: Polity Press, 1997.

Solomon, Nancy. "Immigrant Dancers." National Public Radio, 27 June 2002.

Stallybrass, Peter, and Allon White. *The Politics and Poetics of Transgression.* Ithaca, NY: Cornell University Press, 1986.

Stearns, Marshall, and Jean Stearns. *Jazz Dance: The Story of American Vernacular Dance.* New York: Da Capo Press, 1994.

Stephenson, Richard M., and Joseph Iaccarino. *The Complete Book of Ballroom Dancing.* New York: Doubleday, 1980.

Stern, Carrie. "Shall We Dance? The Participant as Performer/Spectator in Ballroom Dancing." Ph.D. diss., New York University, 1999.

Studlar, Gaylyn. "Valentino, 'Optic Intoxication,' and Dance Madness." *Screening the Male: Exploring Masculinities in Hollywood Cinema.* Ed. Steven Cohan and Ina Rae Hark. London: Routledge, 1993. 23–45.

Taussig, Michel. *Mimesis and Alterity: A Particular History of the Senses.* New York: Routledge, 1993.

Thomas, Helen, and Nicola Miller. "Ballroom Blitz." *Dance in the City.* Ed. Helen Thomas. New York: St. Martin's Press, 1997. 89–110.

Thompson, Robert Farris. *African Art in Motion: Icon and Act in the Collection of Katherine Coryton White.* Los Angeles: University of California Press, 1974.

Thornton, Sarah. *Club Cultures: Music, Media, and Subcultural Capital.* Hanover, NH: Wesleyan University Press, 1996.

Tomko, Linda J. *Dancing Class: Gender, Ethnicity, and Social Divides in American Dance, 1890–1920.* Bloomington: Indiana University Press, 1997.

Trinh, Minh-ha T. *Woman, Native, Other.* Bloomington: Indiana University Press, 1989.

United States Amateur Ballroom Dancers Association Press Release. 12 August 1999.

Veloz [Frank], and Yolanda [Veloz], with Willard Hall. *Tango and Rumba: The Dances of Today and Tomorrow.* New York: Harper & Brothers, 1938.

Vermey, Ruud. *Latin: Thinking, Sensing and Doing in Latin American Dancing.* Munich: Kastell Verlag, 1994.

Vianna, Hermano. *The Mystery of Samba: Popular Music and National Identity in*

Brazil. Trans. and ed. John Charles Chasteen. Chapel Hill: University of North Carolina Press, 1999.

Wagner, Ann. *Adversaries of Dance: From the Puritans to the Present*. Urbana: University of Illinois Press, 1997.

Wallace, Michele. "Modernism, Postmodernism and the Problem of the Visual in Afro-American Culture." *Out There: Marginalization and Contemporary Cultures*. Ed. Russell Ferguson, Martha Gever, Trinh T. Minh-ha, and Cornel West. New York: New Museum of Contemporary Art; Cambridge, MA: MIT Press, 1990. 39–49.

Walters, Glenn D. *The Addiction Concept: Working Hypothesis or Self-fulfilling Prophesy?* Boston: Allyn & Bacon, 1999.

Watson, Sonny. *Sonny Watson's StreetSwing.com* http://www.streetswing.com/homepage.htm, accessed 8 February 2006.

Waxer, Lise. "Of Mambo Kings and Songs of Love: Dance Music in Havana and New York from the 1930s to the 1950s." *Latin American Music Review/Revista de música latinoamericana* 15.2 (1994): 139–176.

Waxer, Lise, ed. *Situating Salsa: Global Markets and Local Meanings in Latin Popular Music*. New York: Routledge, 2002.

Wiegman, Robyn. *American Anatomies: Theorizing Race and Gender*. Durham, NC: Duke University Press, 1995.

Williams, Raymond. *Problems in Materialism and Culture*. Trowbridge: Redwood Burn, 1980.

Wilson, G. Hepburn. "Danse moderne à la Parisienne." *Fellowship: The Spirit of the Dance* (March 1914), 2.

World Dance and Dance Sport Council Web Site. http://www.wddsc.com/dancesport/dscommittee/index032, accessed 3 March 2006.

FILMOGRAPHY

Arthur Murray Party. Film reel, New York Public Library. [1957?].

Bamboozled. Dir. Spike Lee. Dist. New Line Cinema, prod. 40 Acres & a Mule Filmworks, 2000.

Dance of a Dream. Dir. Andrew Lau. Mega Star/Media Asia, 2002.

Dance with Me. Dir. Ronda Haines. Columbia, 1998.

A Day at the Races. Dir. Sam Wood. Metro-Goldywyn Mayer, 1937.

Dirty Dancing. Dir. Emile Ardolino. Vestron, 1987.

Flying Down to Rio. Dir. Thornton Freeland. RKO, 1933.

Four Horsemen of the Apocalypse. Dir. Rex Ingram. Metro Pictures, 1921.

Palladium: Where Mambo was King. Prod. Kevin Kaufman and Bobby Sanabria. Dir. Kevin Kaufman. Bravo, 2002.

Saturday Night Fever. Dir. John Badham. Paramount, 1977.

Shall We Dance? Dir. Masayuki Suo. Altamira (Miramax), 1996 (1997).

The Story of Vernon and Irene Castle. Dir. H. C. Potter. RKO, 1939.

Strictly Ballroom. Dir. Baz Luhrmann. Miramax, 1992.

Swingtime. Dir. George Stevens. RKO, 1936.

PERFORMANCES

Against Line of Dance. Chor. Tsha Marie. 9 January 2000.

Ballati. Chor. Louis van Amstel. Van Dance Creations. Doubletree Hotel, Costa Mesa, CA, 13–14 February 1998.

Batty Moves. Chor. Jawole Willa Joe Zollar. Urban Bush Women, 1995.

Latin Fusion. Chor. Louis van Amstel. VanDance. City Center, New York, 22 and 23 June 2002.

Index

African: dance, 115, 118, 154; dance characteristics, 71, 83, 222n.86, 224n.108; dance heritage, 110, 119, 120, 127, 152–154, 159, 160, 162, 170; exoticism, 153; people, 132; rhythms, 121

African American: culture, 209n.11; dance, 71, 72, 76, 126

African Americans, 146, 147, 153, 155, 167, 195, 204n.6, 223n.101, 225n.110

Against Line of Dance, 187, 191

Aguilar, Amalia, 216n.20

Albright, Ann Cooper, 10–11, 43

Algoso, A., 208n.6

Ambroz, Natasa, 137

American Rumba Committee, 121

American: Style, 86–87, 91–92, 95, 106, 121, 128–130; Rhythm, 19, 26–27, 29, 220n.59; Smooth, 19, 220n.59; tango, 153

"animal dances," 66

Argyle, Michael, 172

Arkin, Lisa, 214n.2

Arrizón, Alicia, 220n.67

Arthur Murray Party, The, 77, 79

Arthur Murray Studios, 6, 79–80, 86, 87, 88, 91, 104

Asian Americans, 18, 223n.101

Asians, 19, 23, 31, 154, 160, 168, 204n.6, 223n.101

Astaire, Fred, 26, 46, 79, 85, 106, 125, 206n.19

authenticity, 114, 116, 122, 125, 127, 147, 150, 155–158, 160, 221n.73

Azpiazú, Don, 216n.18

Babineau, Michael, 183

Babitz, Eve, 103

Bailey, Peter, 2

Bakhtin, Mikhail, 43, 44, 184–185

Ballati, 180–182

ballet, 22, 27, 32, 46, 47, 72, 81, 86, 88, 92, 93, 120, 127, 133, 148, 150, 162, 174, 195–197, 199, 214n.2, 222n.83

Ballroom Bootcamp, 40, 199

Bamboozled, 225n.110

Banes, Sally, 10

Barber, Nancy, 193–195

Barrera, Margaret, 225n.4

Bartinieff, Irmgard, 171

Batty Moves, 222n.86

Baudrillard, Jean, 207n.37

Bauman, Rudolf, 137

beguine, 83, 215n.10

Benesh, Rudolph, 171

Benitez Rojo, Antonio, 201n.3

Bennati, Marge, 210n.23

Best, Amy, 42

blackface, 16, 110, 119, 146–148, 167. *See also* minstrelsy

blackness, 76, 126, 147, 151, 152; erasure of, 72, 153, 154, 159. *See also* African

Blair, Skippy, 87

Boekhoudt, Oslin, 163–168

bolero, 19, 121, 215n.10

Bordo, Susan, 41–42

Born, Georgina, 203n.22

Borrows, Frank, 123, 217n.26

bossa nova, 125

Bourdieu, Pierre, 4, 6, 220n.70

Bradley, Josephine, 217n.34

Brandis, Riba, 215n.10

Brigham Young University, 204n.27

British Dance Council, 81

British Official Board of Ballroom Dancing, 81, 85, 126

Brock, Vernon, 130

brownface, 16, 109–111, 133, 135, 146–148, 150–151, 167, 169–170, 221n.78

Buckland, Fiona, 208n.2

Buckman, Peter, 216n.21

Burns, Wilson, 225n.4

Butler, Judith, 17

239

About the Author

Juliet McMains is Assistant Professor in the Dance Program at the University of Washington. She is the co-author of "Swingin' Out: Southern California's Lindy Revival" (in *I See America Dancing,* University of Illinois Press, 2002) and the author of "Brownface: Representations of Latin-ness in Dancesport" (*Dance Research Journal,* Winter 2001), and has presented several papers and articles on topics relating to race, class, gender, and the American DanceSport industry. As a DanceSport competitor, she has twice been a U.S. National Rising Star finalist and has won professional competitions in the U.S. and Canada.